COMBAT MEDALS
OF THE
THIRD REICH

COMBAT MEDALS
OF THE
THIRD REICH

Christopher Ailsby

Foreword by Lieutenant-Colonel (Ret)
John R. Angolia

Patrick Stephens
Wellingborough, Northamptonshire

Dedication
To my mother and father, Mont
and Eve Ailsby, in grateful thanks
for all their help and support.

First published in 1987

*British Library Cataloguing in Publication
Data*

Ailsby, Christopher
    Combat Medals of the Third Reich
    1. Germany—Armed
    Forces—Medals,
    badges, decorations,
    etc.—Collectors
    and collecting
    I. Title
    737'.223'0943   UB435.G/
    ISBN 0-85059-822-2

*Patrick Stephens is part of the
Thorsons Publishing Group*

Printed and bound in Great Britain

Contents

Foreword   7
Author's Preface   9
Introduction   17
The Spanish Civil War   21
Second World War Decorations   35
Cuff Bands   87
Arm Shields   95
Naval War Badges   114
Army and Waffen SS War Badges   153
Luftwaffe War Badges   185
Ribbon Awards   226
Glossary   227
Index   237

SS-Obergruppenführer Friedrich Alpers wearing his unique uniform as General Forestmeister and General Jägermeister with his Knights Cross (D.018) at throat and Reconnaissance Operational Flying Clasp (L.043). On page 8 is the magnificent document which accompanied the presentation to him by Göring of his hunting Association Dagger (see index of personalities). The inscription reads: 'In unspeakable gratitude, Brunswick Chief Hunting Master Alpers, for supreme merit in the Reich National German Hunting association. National Hunting Day Harz. Spirit of 4 November 1936. In heartfelt comradeship, Reich Hunting Master, Hermann Göring.' Worthy of note are the Iron Crosses with Swastikas portrayed before their official introduction.

Foreword
by Lieutenant-Colonel (Ret) John R. Angolia

Normally, the production of a book is the conclusion of a great deal of research and writing effort. However, in this case, it serves merely as an introduction to a future work planned by the author, as well as an introduction to the author himself. Christopher Ailsby is not only an advanced collector in his own right, but a thorough research historian as well. He has not been satisfied to merely accept the work of others as the final word, but takes the questions that are posed, and pursues them to a rewarding conclusion.

Military awards and decorations of the Third Reich are nothing more than a visible mark of accomplishment and distinction, often in the face of uneven odds on the field of combat. More than fifteen million men served in the German Wehrmacht during the war years 1939 to 1945. They initially fought for conquest, only to see this dream fade, and then were faced with a fight for survival. During the early years, the cream of the German military earned awards at the head of the successful juggernaut. When the tides turned, survival conditions made unlikely heroes on the battlefield. The awards contained in this reference were those presented to the likely and not-so-likely participants on the field of combat, in the air, and on the sea.

The production quality of these awards directly reflected the success of the German armed forces —initially produced with excellent materials and very eye-appealing; during the mid-war years the materials deteriorated, but the manufacturing techniques remained high; from 1944 to the end of the war, both quality of material and production left much to be desired. The author has provided the reader with an excellent study of these combat awards. With your appetite whetted, be prepared for more to follow from this most qualified author.

LTC [Ret.] John R. Angolia

IN UNAUSLÖSCHLICHER DANKBARKEIT
BRAUNSCHWEIG OBERJÄGERMEISTER

ALPERS

FÜR HÖCHSTE VERDIENSTE DEM
REICHSBUND DEUTSCHE JÄGERSCHAFT
NATIONALJÄGERSTAG HARZ
GEIST ZUM 4-11-1936
IN HERZLICHER KAMERADSCHAFT

REICHJÄGERMEISTER, HERMANN GÖRING

Author's Preface

Collecting German medals and decorations has grown in popularity ever since the first encounter between British and later, American military personnel, and those of Germany, her puppets and allies. The tradition of cutting off the shoulder straps had really started in the First World War, and was to enable commanders to have a reliable record of what enemy units had been overrun and subsequently, where they had been deployed on the battlefield. This procedure continued in the Second World War but did not have the same importance as in the former one. One often finds an 'old sweat's' belt festooned with varying cap badges of his mates, intermingled with German badges that he had encountered along the way.

The real growth in purloining badges—I will not use the term 'collect' for this form of annexation—came with the international control of Germany and the subsequent de-Nazification of the country. The four powers that led the Allies had decided in their wisdom that the German people should surrender all things that were offensive in the form of arms and daggers, and these were to be surrendered to the appropriate authority. All badges and insignia showing the hated Swastika or SS emblems should also be destroyed. This led to either the total destruction of the item concerned, or as often is the case, the removal of just the Swastika. This in some cases, on the prized decorations which are described in this book, was most skilfully done by either the recipient himself, if his handiwork enabled him to be proficient in such a task, or by a competent jeweller. Badges that have been thus de-Nazified, considering the political climate that hung over Europe in the first ten years that followed the end of the war, show no mean love and pride in their award. Some recipients just buried the items and hoped that time would be a great healer and, subsequently, they would be allowed to wear their decorations again when the fuss and furor had died down. I was amazed on attending a conference and convention of the ODR, to find that many of the Knights Cross winners present were wearing their prized decorations back to front, only to find upon enquiry that, as one recipient showed me, the Swastika was being worn to the reverse of the medal. He said, 'What the eye does not see, the heart and Germany does not grieve over, and anyway this is the one I was presented with by my General, not Hitler'.

I think this statement summed up the feeling of a number of members who still retained their original award.

The second great flood of medals was obtained by swapping or trading them with the Allied troops who occupied Germany for chocolate, food or tobacco and all sorts of rare pieces, citations and documents were obtained for twenty Woodbines! This went for all forms of Nazi memorabilia. Art treasures were also treated in much the same way.

The last method and possibly the most repugnant, was the general looting of the homes and persons of the German people for their possessions. This happened in the case of many people, and can be summed up by three examples which illustrate the more common ways in which the Allied troops 'liberated' hundreds of items which are currently available through auctions and dealers' lists. The first example is that of Hans Rudel who was taken prisoner by the Americans and went into captivity with all his documents and diamond-beset decorations. While he was asleep, his personal belongings were gone through and his prize possessions stolen. Of course, this is contrary to all rules of war. Once a soldier goes into captivity after the capitulation of his country, then he and his belongings are subject to the laws of the protecting power. However, the American commanding general acted most correctly and had the items returned to him, and those responsi-

ble for the deed punished. Unfortunately, his Knights Cross document and flight log book were not among the items that were returned and they could not subsequently be found. The Knights Cross document has luckily come to light in England in 1984 but regrettably his widow was unable to afford to purchase it, as it made £20,000 at Phillips' auction in London. This story and the honourable outcome was not always the case for other officers.

The second story which I include concerns not just the stealing of medals as such, but the family silver and jewels as well. This story was told to me by Baroness Elke von Mearchen, whose father was an early Knights Cross winner and finally a fatal casualty on the Eastern Front in the last days of the war. She recalls that her grandparents, at their country estate at the end of the war, secretly went into the garden and dug a very deep hole into which they deposited the medals of the family, to include those of the fallen Baron, plus the family jewellery and silver wrapped in oilskins. They, equally surreptitiously, returned to the house. In the morning, on the return of the family retainers, they explained that the house had been looted, which deeply upset the remaining servants. A few nights later, the aged Baron and his lady were filled with horror when they heard the sounds of digging. Gingerly going to the window they saw the old family retainer digging up what was presumably the family fortune. As they were surrounded by Russians, the family felt betrayed and that the servants were going to obtain special privileges from the invaders, which had been the experience of other notable families.

To their horror, but personal pleasure, the servant started to place in the hole (which, not being as dexterous as the old Baron, he had not dug so deeply as to find the hoard) the wines and ports that had made up the excellent cellar of the house. Being afraid to disturb the double hoard, the Baron lived on tenterhooks and finally the inevitable happened, the Russian de-Nazifiers arrived. Due enquiry was made, Baron and servants told their own stories. The Russian Commissar, not being fully convinced, sent his troops to scour the grounds. Finding the place where the ground was freshly disturbed, two privates were instructed to dig up what might have been interred there. The Russian Commissar was well pleased to have something to get his teeth into, especially at the expense of a notable Baron, and must have been gloating at the thought of the possible chance to deport him at the best, or imprison him at the worst.

The two soldiers soon uncovered the store of wine, whereupon the Commissar asked the Baron whether he did not have something of greater importance to hide than Bourgeois wine? At this the faithful retainer honestly retorted that it was he who had hidden his master's favourite wines and everything else of value had been looted a few days earlier, not of course realizing that it was the Baron himself who had removed the valuables. The Commissar, most put out at only finding the wine, admonished the servant for such Bourgeois ways, and instructed the soldiers to drink their fill and destroy the remainder as a punishment to the Baron. Needless to say, none was destroyed and the Russian troops left later in the day very much the worse for wear. The hole was filled in by the old retainer during this orgy of drinking, as his punishment, to many jibes as to his unworthiness to become a communist.

Needless to say, this story had a happy ending in the fact that the Baroness' granddaughter's table is graced by that silver. I have had many happy meals at that table and this book has benefited as a result.

The third example concerns the method of payment of certain Russian volunteers. One case that was quoted in the court-martial of a Russian Cossack illustrates this. The bounty that they were paid was on the principle that one could take as many goods and chattels as one could put on the back of one's saddle. However, much to this young man's dismay, he was given a Dodge ten-ton truck and his horse was taken back to the stable. Drinking with his companions, he was told all about the things which they had been able to put on their horses. He was ridiculed by them because he would have to return home without the spoils of war that they were now enjoying. Then one bright Cossack came up with the idea that the ten-tonner was a surrogate horse and, therefore, he was entitled to fill it up and return home. The young Cossack was delighted and the next day, with his comrades, who no doubt were a little crestfallen, started to load the 'beast', only to be apprehended by the Allied military police, who duly charged him with looting.

The outcome of the trial was equally bizarre. The four Generals, one from each country, decided that a large horse should be brought and the young Cossack could load what he could on to its back, the rest he must return to the rightful owners. The 'wisdom of Solomon' had been administered, and some resemblance of justice, although rough justice, had been done.

It was from this pool of memorabilia that collections sprung. I started my collection, although it was not until 1971, from those items which had been originally given to me by my uncle Fred, who had been in the Control Commission after the war. The interest was stimulated by the publication in 1968 of *Orders, Decorations, Medals and Badges of the Third Reich* by David Littlejohn and Colonel C. M. Dodkins. David, an advanced collector and historian, has become a valued friend and advisor since that time. I never had the opportunity or pleasure of meeting the late Colonel Dodkins, who produced one of the best collections of artefacts and photographs and has since set provenance to a number of exciting items, and has started the pedigree and first name to items that will be passed through many, hopefully, notable future collections. The publication of the first good reference book brought more serious collectors into the net with these collectors pushing the quest for knowledge. This spawned a number of reproductions, at the best, and downright frauds at worst.

It was at this time, I came into collecting Third Reich items, after having seen the film *The Blue Max*. I saw in the local newspaper an article on a local collector in Peterborough holding a Pour le Mérite. My spririts ran high, I rang him and he informed me of the source of his seemingly fabulous collection. I contacted the dealer and he told me he could supply me with the items I required. Armed with David's book and good intentions, I started my collection. After about three months, I began to sense something wrong. Every item I required turned up. The crisis came when I asked for a silver and gold Gau Berlin, and a Coberg Badge (to be covered in a later book). All three are very difficult to find. Three days later by recorded delivery, not registered mail, came the badges. On further enquiry as to their authenticity, I was told by the dealer that they were from a really good supply on the Continent and fully original. These gems were from the Continent all right, but made the previous week by Rudolf Souval, an expert in reproduction items.

It was at this point that I decided to study the subject as thoroughly as possible, and I was pointed in the direction of Adrian Forman, now of Shepherds Market, London, who has helped me form my collection and guided me through some tortuous research projects. His help has been greatly appreciated both as a tutor and obtainer of specimens for illustrations in the book. The other helper, who emerged at an Arms Fair at Bedford, was Frederick J. Stephens, who also has been of invaluable assistance and given a great amount of his knowledge on spotting reproductions on edged weapons, which is also relevant to badges.

In 1973, the second volume of David Littlejohn's book was published and expanded the scope of collecting, by including the awards that were given by Nazi movements in other European countries, and it has become the standard work on the subject. During that time I was corresponding with Jack Angolia, who also was compiling a book on the subject and in 1976 *For Führer and Fatherland* was born. This work is most thorough and encouraged even more collectors into the hobby, but possibly the most important event to come out of the publication of this work was that collectors began to specialize in individual types of award, medal and badge and not, as a general rule, to collect across the board. Hence, collectors of Nazi memorabilia who had been split into uniform, dagger and medal collectors, became sub-divided in the medal collecting world. This in itself produced even greater knowledge about each item. In 1978 Volume 2 of Jack Angolia's work was produced, which covered the political and civil aspects of German awards. This again breathed new life into the hobby and introduced the collector into a hitherto little known part of the subject.

It was these firm research bases which prompted me to further try and expand the field of knowledge. Analysing the subject, I discovered that if it was split into four, the hobby could be brought into line with that of British coin and medal collectors and be made more understandable. Hence, I have tried to bring in a comprehensive numbering and reference system, that should make identi-

fication of medals between collectors and dealers easier. This first volume covers military awards and decorations. Later books will cover political and civil awards and foreign volunteer units and Nazi organisation awards, medals and badges of satellite and puppet states allied to Germany. The last volume is not a book in the true sense of the word, but is intended to be a complete listing of all known types, describing the rarity of each individual item, with a composite photograph of as many of the listed items as possible. In this will be space for collectors to write in themselves where the badge was obtained, how much it cost, and any further relevant information, such as maker. This is hoped to make collecting of series of medals easier, plus enabling a record of your collection to be portable when visiting arms fairs, gun shows or your favourite dealer. It will make it easier for your loved ones to buy you that 'super surprise present' by contacting the dealer of your choice, whose name conveniently is in the front of your records. It beats receiving socks and handkerchiefs for Christmas!

I have not tried to describe the types of reproductions or methods of determining the originals from fakes. This is a study in itself, and I am envisaging two more books on the subject of reproduction medals and fakes of the Third Reich. I would at this point like to point out that I am not opposed to good reproductions, if they are sold as such. Many items could only be collected in the form of reproductions, and many of the early reproductions are worthy of collecting for their own sake. In fact, a solicitor friend has one of the best collections of reproductions I have seen, and they are of the most use in determining whether or not the piece one has is original. This showed its worth at an arms fair in London, when a German dealer scrutinized a cased German Order, or Order of the Dead, an item of immaculate workmanship. It was shown around the various dealers at the show and he subsequently made an offer. By a strange quirk of fate, the piece was also shown to me, and we had the opportunity of comparing the item by placing it next to my original. If anything, the quality of the reproduction was superior to the original, being produced in real silver and gold-plated, while my original was produced in tombac and fire-gilded. The dealer withdrew his offer but needless to say, this item was auctioned at Wallis and Wallis and a client bought it for £1,500. Hence a reproduction can be better than the original and command a high price from the unsuspecting collector who has not done his homework, thus losing a considerable sum of money.

The whole point is that if an item is so rare and unobtainable, to have a representative item is worthwhile —but not, I would hasten to add, at this high price. The practice of passing these items, however, as originals is, thank goodness, illegal for such an act brings the whole collecting world into disrepute. But never fear, it is not just the Nazi world that is bedevilled with forgers. There is more Hepplewhite furniture available to the collector today than he produced in his factory in all the years of its production.

The last area of collecting that has been overlooked is that of miniatures, and I hope to produce a book on them in the near future as well. It is hoped that this will complete the circle of Third Reich medal collecting. It is intended that this first book will help both the collector and dealer, and the author invites readers to draw his attention to any variations which have not been included, so that he can make the listings as complete as possible in future revisions. Political items and information, especially on Gau Badges and Citations, would be most gratefully received for help in the production of the title on political and civil awards. Any information and all pictures will receive the usual acknowledgements.

To the new collector, may he or she be nine or ninety, I would like to pass on the advice I was given many years ago, by repeating the excellent tips given to me by a delightful young lady at Spink and Sons of St James, London, when I was about eleven years old. She advised me to be very selective and collect quality and rarity. She also suggested that I should be very firm in deciding the theme of my collection so that, having made my decision, I could obtain the specific reference books which all collectors require. Subsequent experience has shown that £10 or more, as is often the case now, spent on a good reference book can save you far more in the long run, witness the experience of the German Order.

In terms of quality and rarity your collection will be one of your best investments, particularly if you keep the above observations always in mind. Comments like 'combat worn', are usually nothing more than a salesman's way of saying, 'relic condition'. This, from the serious collectors' point of view, would indicate a medal which is really not worthy of including in your collection.

A question often put to me is, 'What badges are available?' The answer is all Third Reich badges are available, and many in their cloth form. It is hoped that this book will help you with your choice. I would also recommend you to build your library, starting with David Littlejohn's two books and Jack Angolia's two volumes.

I hope this book and the subsequent volumes will give you an idea of what there is to collect, and from that you should then decide what you would like to specialize in. Choose a small section and try to obtain a representative set. Find a reputable dealer, who gives a money back guarantee, who will look after you, and send him your 'wants' list. Make as much contact with other collectors and take every opportunity to interchange information and look at rare and interesting pieces. One can look at a hundred pictures, but holding a rare piece just once, makes you realize its originality. I can coin a phrase, 'It cries out to you, "I'm original"'.

I would lastly like to take this opportunity of thanking Lieutenant Colonel J. R. Angolia (Rtd) for writing the Foreword to this book. After spending an all too short holiday with us this summer, accompanied by his charming wife Joy, many excellent meals, followed by late evenings were spent discussing the hobby. He read the draft manuscript and agreed to do the Foreword plus, as is his way, said 'any photos or assistance, just ask'. The next great thank you is to Lynne, without whom I would not have been able to get the manuscript from my jotting pad to readable form. Last but not least, thanks to all the collectors who have helped in all sorts of ways and who have helped to obtain items for the collection for which the data has been produced to form this book: Mrs E. Ailsby, Mrs L. Hopcraft-Ailsby, J. R. Angolia, Stan Andrews, Lee Bambera, Malcolm Bowers, Colin Brown, Josef Charita, Alberts Flipts, Alan Fordham, Adrian Forman, Derek Gloster, Trevor Grice, Peter Groch, Eric Hitchcock, Dr Klietmann, David Littlejohn, Sue Marchant, Jan Munk, Howard Reynolds, Tim Stannard, Frederick Stephens, Keith Thompson, David Maitland-Titterton, Friedrich Trenz, Gordon Williamson and Michael Xilas.

My sincerest thanks are given to all and I hope they will continue to assist me in the future projects. To Bruce Quarrie a special vote of thanks, because it was he who persuaded me to actually submit the work after meeting him and giving him a little information for his book *Hitler's Samurai*, with the words, 'You helped many other authors, why not do one yourself?'

To you, the reader, I hope this book gives you great help and pleasure.

Christopher J. Ailsby
8–10 High Street
Whittlesey, Cambs,
England, 1986

Introduction

The period between the two Great Wars produced radical social changes, due in part to the return of men, and to an extent women, from the First World War who had never, in many cases, previously been away from their village or town, let alone outside the borders of their own country. They had experienced and learned from life's great university and wished on their return for better things, not only in the material sense but in the aesthetic and social field as well. There was the feeling that the class distinction of the Victorian and Edwardian periods had been swept away by the winds of war. A time of change had arrived in Europe, those winds of war had dashed the last great dynasties. They had fallen, leaving in their stead weak new embryo democracies which, having fears of the past, removed the trappings of the former emperors and kaisers, and forbade the wearing of their old awards. These democracies soon became the casualties of either 'The Far Left' or 'The Far Right', nowhere more so than Germany following the depriva-

Left *Göring as Minister of Police addressing the Prussian Parliament, well illustrating the Nazis' love of pageantry.*

tions suffered by the general populace in the closing year of the war, and the corruption and 'graft' that emerged in the 1920s. The country saw the birth of National Socialism in 1919, and to it was drawn a Corporal who would soon embrace its policies and find that this was the vehicle that would catapult him on to the world's stage, allowing him to live out his fantasies and to try and bring about a world order built on the myths which he had conjured up in his able and fertile imagination.

At this time, as has already been stated, all the awards of the old, former Second Reich empire were prohibited and only the civilian grade of the Pour Le Mérite was allowed. In the chaotic period leading up to the National Socialist takeover in January 1933, only this, certain approved Free Corps awards and some of the old Ducal States Orders were permitted to be worn. With the success of Hitler and the Nazis' grab for power, there emerged a need to reconstitute the various official orders, decorations and medals that applied to all aspects of German military, diplomatic, political and civil life. The rôle of medals and decorations combined with all the aspects of uniform and pageantry, fitted in well with Nazi ideology and the German love of theatrical splendour and dressing up for occasions of state. It presented an opportunity to redesign and restrike the official decorations of the new regime, modelled in part upon older awards but restyled and upgraded in keeping with the image of the new Germany.

The best designers, jewellers and artists now finding favour and patronage under the National Socialist yoke were commissioned to create the new orders for the new uniforms that abounded in the upsurge of military revival. It was a revival of some of the lost splendour and removed tradition of the old Germany, a harkening back to old standards and styles under the colours of the new regime. The Art Nouveau trend of the rest of Europe was virtually bypassed in the quest to restore the injured pride of a defeated Germany, a Germany however which had not been defeated on the battlefields of Flanders, but as Nazi ideology described, 'stabbed in the back' by its own far left politicians. The old styles and traditions were revived and esconced in the new image of the Third Reich. Hitler, an aspirant artist in his youth, took a keen interest in the design and implementation of these new decorations. He well understood the sense of importance that was engendered when a man was uniformed and bedecked with medals proclaiming his fine status, or the honour that he had bestowed upon himself with brave deeds in battle. Glittering decorations began to adorn the prestigious chests of the new statesmen of the Reich, pro-claiming beyond all doubt who worked for the benefit of the new regime, and who visibly benefitted from it.

Paradoxically, Hitler himself wore few decorations, only his Iron Cross and wound badge earned in the Great War which changed his life so completely. His Golden Party Badge and Blood Order were the only badges of his National Socialist Party that he wore. The plain effect of Hitler's uniform must have stood in sobering contrast alongside those of his medal-festooned cronies such as Göring or Ribbentrop, another example of his guile, the plain aspect of his uniform and the notable absence of decorations suggesting some identity with the common man.

Hitler's personal quirk in not awarding himself decorations did not preclude him from constantly reviewing and approving new designs and finding occasions to award them. Hitler's international aspirations, combined with diplomatic adventures in Spain, Czechoslovakia and Austria, the non-aggression pact with Stalinist Russia, the 'Pact of Steel' with Mussolini in Italy, the 'Peace with Honour' occasion with Chamberlain at Munich, were all opportunities for the honouring of statesmen and the giving of decorations. Palm-greasing and playing to the gallery though it was, it worked. Whatever the murmurings of the evils of Nazism uttered behind embassy doors or over diplomatic lunches or cocktail parties, Hitler succeeded in getting his own way and appeasing his international political opponents. More to the point, he also established firm political alliances with neighbouring European leaders in an Axis consolidation that was not to be separated without a fight. This fight started with the proving grounds of Spain in the Spanish Civil War for his fledgling Luftwaffe, army and highly mechanized and modernised navy, whose very personnel would become the recipients of the medals described in this book. It heightened with the invasion of Poland and Britain's Declaration of War on 3 September 1939, which instigated the Second World War, and it culminated on 8 May 1945 with the total destruction, both militarily and industrially, of Germany. This time, she had not been 'stabbed in the back' but betrayed by the leadership of the Führer Hitler, who had become a megalomaniac totally believing in his own invincibility and ideology, for whom his soldiers, sailors and airmen died heroically right up to the end well deserving, in most cases, the decorations explained in the following text.

The Spanish Civil War

The assassination of a politician, reminiscent of that of Archduke Ferdinand of Austria which fomented the First World War, was to be the catalyst which brought about the chain reaction of events that enabled Hitler to involve his embryo forces in the field of combat, without breaking the armistice agreement of 1919; and to show his future intentions in the 'Flower Wars' that were soon to evolve and the diplomatic wrangling that would enable him to annex certain countries. His desires were to reunite the old Germany and engulf and reorganize that which had formerly been the Austro-Hungarian Empire.

Spain provided the powder keg which ignited in the summer of 1936, blowing up into a bloody civil war, between the Nationalists and Republicans. The Nationalist General Franco, whose Moro battalians were stationed in Spanish Morocco, asked Hitler to supply him with Junkers transport aeroplanes in which to move those troops to Spain. Hitler did more than this by forming the HISMA Transport Company which, with aeroplanes crewed by the Luftwaffe, ferried the Moros, in the first large-scale air lift in history, from north Africa to Spain.

August 1936 saw the first members of the 'Condor Legion' arrive in Spain. The Legion was first led by General Hugo Sperrle and consisted of a bomber and fighter group, a reconnaissance Staffel which had been enlarged, three flak regiments, three air signals units and a marine gruppe. General Volkmann took command of the Legion in November 1937 and continued to command it for a year, and then the cousin of the famous (or infamous, depending upon which point of view you have) 'Red Baron' of World War One fame, Generalmajor Wolfram von Richthofen, assumed command in November 1938.

November 1936 witnessed three fighter squadrons become operational. These had the nicknames 'Marabu', 'Top Hat' and 'Mickey Mouse', and were commanded respectively by Oberleutnant Gunther Lutzow, Oberleutnant Joachim Schlichting and Oberleutnant Adolf Galland who was followed by Werner Mölders. The Legion's bomber and fighter squadrons were known as 'Franco's Fire Brigade', and participated in the heaviest fighting. 340 Republican aeroplanes fell foul of the Legion's guns and were confirmed as shot down. The experience gained in these dogfights and aerial combats and bombing missions served the pilots well and helped them to become aces in the Second World War.

It is perhaps relevant to enlarge on the term 'Condor Legion' now, for it referred to all personnel fighting in Spain, not just the air arm. They had been openly recruited from Wehrmacht training establishments throughout Germany. The bomber group consisted of four Staffels, each comprising 48 planes, four fighter Staffels a reconnaissance Staffel, a sea plane Staffel, four batteries of 20 mm anti-aircraft artillery which comprised sixteen guns in total and four batteries of 8.8 cm guns which comprised a further sixteen. There was a Panzer Korps attached to the Legion under the command of Oberst von Thoma and an army group, named Imke Gruppe, which was christened after its commander. By January 1937 it was estimated that there were 12,000 German personnel serving in the Legion.

The early months of 1939 saw the final rebel offensive and the war ended on 1 April 1939 with the complete and unconditional surrender of the Republicans to General Franco. The victorious Condor Legion returned to Germany and disembarked at Hamburg to receive the plaudits of the Führer and Göring, the award of medals described in this section and a memorial service for those who did not return, in Berlin's Lustgarten. Ironically the names of the fallen, mounted on plaques, were held above the heads of Hitler Youth members. How many of these boys would receive medals in the ensuing years, or in fact, see out the short life of Nazi Germany...

Index to Spanish Civil War Badges 1936-1939

S.001	Spanish Cross with Swords—Bronze	23
S.002	Spanish Cross with Swords—Silver	23
S.003	Spanish Cross with Swords—Gold	23
S.004	Spanish Cross without Swords—Bronze	24
S.005	Spanish Cross without Swords—Silver	24
S.006	Spanish Cross in Gold with Diamonds	25
S.007	Spanish Cross in Gold with Diamonds—Dress Copy	28
S.008	Cross of Honour for the Relatives of the Dead in Spain	29
S.009	Tank Badge of the Condor Legion—First Type	30
S.010	Tank Badge of the Condor Legion—Second Type	31
S.011	Tank Badge of the Condor Legion—Gold Type	32
S.012	Cuff Title 'Spain 1936-1939'	32
S.013	Cuff Title 'Spain 1936-1939'—Gothic Script	33
S.014	Spanish Wound Badge—Black Class	34
S.015	Spanish Wound Badge—Silver Class	34
S.016	Spanish Wound Badge—Gold Class	34

S.001 Spanish Cross with Swords—Bronze
S.002 Spanish Cross with Swords—Silver
S.003 Spanish Cross with Swords—Gold

On 14 April 1939 Hitler instituted an award for the bravery of members of the Condor Legion. It was on 10 August that conditions for the award were laid down. The basic design was the same for each version and took the form of a Maltese Cross. The arms of the Cross had a rim, while in the centre was a circle which was pebbled, as were the arms of the Cross. This circle had an inner circle, which had a Swastika with the arms touching the rim. The raised parts of the medal were polished, while the pebbled areas were matt. Between the arms of the Cross were flying Luftwaffe eagles clutching Swastikas in their talons. Beneath the eagles ran two crossed swords with their hilts at the bottom of the Cross. The Cross

was convex and on the reverse was a massive pin. It was made in either silver, which came in varying grades and was then bronzed, left silver or gilded, or it was made of bronze and then silverplated or gilded.

It would appear that there was no prerequesite for having a higher award and the grade of the Cross tended to be related to the rank of the person to whom it was awarded.

The Criteria for the award were:
1) To have been a volunteer in the Condor Legion and to have fought in Spain.
2) To have taken part in the naval actions:
   a) The air attack on 29 May 1937 on the German battleship *Deutschland* in the waters off

Spanish Cross with Swords — Bronze (S.001).

Spanish Cross with Swords — Silver (S.002).

Ibiza in which 32 Germans were killed and 73 wounded, the dead and wounded being attended to by the British at Gibraltar. This led to a number of awards to British medical personnel of the German Red Cross Decoration 1937–1939* in varying grades, but not the Spanish Cross of any grade.

b) The bombing on 31 May of Almerica in reprisal for the attack on the *Deutschland*.

3) To have served continuously for three months in Spanish waters.

4) For special acts of valour or merit, appertaining to a combat-oriented situation.

Numbers awarded of the Spanish Cross with Swords were: Bronze,

*Known British recipients of the German Red Cross Decoration 1937–1939: Captain John Primrose Douglas, RAMC, Cross of Merit 26 July 1937; Sister Catherine McShane, Frauenkreuz 26 July 1937; Mrs M. G. Burton, Frauenkreuz 26 July 1937; Mrs Margaret Paula Lewis, Frauenkreuz 26 July 1937; Miss Cargill Lockhead, Frauenkreuz 26 July 1937; and Commander H. J. Murphy, Cross of Merit 13 January 1938.

Spanish Cross with Swords — Gold (S.003).

8,462; Silver, 8,304; Gold, 1,126

The badge was awarded in a green box with a burgundy or sometimes dove grey lining, while the outer case has been encountered in blue, with a blue satin liner and blue velvet base. There are cases which have the LDO emblem or just the letters stencilled on to the lid in silver.

The Citation was plain with no facsimile of the medal printed on the top, just plain printing and Hitler's signature at the bottom and the Nazi seal in the bottom left-hand corner.

S.004 Spanish Cross without Swords—Bronze
S.005 Spanish Cross without Swords—Silver

Again this badge was introduced on 14 April 1939 and comprised a Maltese Cross as before with the Luftwaffe eagles in the quadrants, each clutching a segmented Swastika in its talons as before. The Cross was con-

cave with a massive pin on the reverse. It was made in either silver that was bronzed, or bronze that was silvered. There was no Spanish Cross without Swords in gold, although there seems to be evidence that an order authoriz-

Spanish Cross without Swords — Bronze (S.004).

Spanish Cross without Swords — Silver (S.005).

ing it to be instigated was issued. This award was rendered to military personnel serving in Spain or Spanish Morocco and could also be awarded to civilians and technicians who had taken part in assisting the forces in Spain from July 1936 to March 1939. This was to include members of Lufthansa who ferried materials and aeroplanes to Spain, and probably gives rise to the relative rarity of the bronze and silver crosses and the fact that no gold crosses were awarded.

The Criteria for the award were:
1) Three months' service in Spain.
2) An act that substantially assisted the war effort but not in a combat-oriented field.

Numbers awarded of the Spanish Cross without Swords were: Bronze, 7,869; Silver, 327.

The badge was awarded in a green box with burgundy lining, but blue boxes with blue liners and blue velvet bases and green boxes with dove grey liners have been encountered. Examples with the LDO symbol, or LDO stencilled in silver on the lid, have also been observed.

The Citation was a plain piece of paper again, with no facsimile of the medal at the top. The printing was in plain black type with Hitler's signature at the bottom and in the left-hand bottom corner the Nazi seal.

S.006 Spanish Cross in Gold with Diamonds

This badge again was instigated on 14 April 1939. The precise nature of the Criteria for the award of this badge are not known, but Hitler took it upon himself to award personally this decoration to all the recipients on their return from Spain, of whom there were 27. (However, David Littlejohn states in his book, as does Dr Klietman in his, that there were 28.)

The known recipients were: Oberleutnant Wilhelm Balthasar, Oberleutnant Otto Bertram, Leutnant Wilhelm Boddem, Oberleutnant Kraft Eberhard, Oberleutnant Wilhelm Ensslen, Leutnant Paul Fehihaber, Oberleutnant Adolf Galland, Hauptmann Harro Harder, Major Martin Harlinghausen, Leutnant Oskar Henrici, Oberleutnant Max Graf Hoyos, Oberleutnant Hans-Detlef von Kessel, Hauptmann Gunther Lutzow, Oberleutnant Karl Mehnert, Hauptmann Werner Mölders, Hauptmann Rudolf Frhr von Moreau, Hauptmann Wolfgang Neudorffer, Oberleutnant Walter Oesau, Generalleutnant Wolfram Frhr von Richthofen, Leutnant Heinz Runze, Hauptmann Wolfgang Schellmann, Hauptmann Joachim Schlichting, Oberleutnant Reinhard Seiler, Gen.d.fl Hugo Sperrle, Oberleutnant Berhard Starcke, Gen.d.fl Helmut Volkmann and Major Karl Heinz Wolff.

This badge was produced in genuine yellow gold and took the form of the preceding decorations, but in this case the cross was more convex than in the former and the reverse had a large pin and hinge construction which was fixed at the upper arm of the cross with a large hook attached to the middle of the bottom arm. It was produced with the pebbled parts matt, these pebbled marks being hand-raised with the raised portion highly polished. The centre, however, was quite different in the fact that it was a separately constructed plate, which was fixed to the body of the cross independently. The construction of this plate again was by hand and, in this case, the Swastika's arms were broader and the circle that surrounded it was also broader. Next to this circle were set fourteen rose-cut diamonds. There was no outer circle to the border of the diamonds, so that the actual cutting and claw setting of the diamonds formed the outer edge of the circle. This is an important distinguishing point to an original awarded example, as opposed to the silver gilt dress copy described in S.007. The setting for these diamonds has been described in other references as silver, but I would suggest that it is in fact platinum, as it was on the other awards constructed in this manner to mount this type of diamond. This is borne out by close scrutiny of the

Oberleutnant Walter Oseau wearing the Spanish Cross in Gold with Diamonds (S.006), Knights Cross with Oak Leaves, Swords and Diamonds (D.021), Iron Cross First Class (D.016) and Spanish Wound Badge (S.014).

Spanish Cross in Gold with Diamonds (S.006).

example illustrated, which is in the collection of Lynne Hopcraft-Ailsby, and which is produced in platinum. This central device was held on to the cross in two distinct ways. In the first type the central device was held on to the body of the cross by two ball rivets. That is to say, the rivet was one piece of wire which was tapped over to retain the plate to the cross and gave the impression of a round ball or mushroom-shaped head. The reverse was plain with only its silver quality or hallmark, giving rise to the assumption that some of the award-type crosses were produced in yellow gold and platinum, and some were produced in silver gilt and platinum, the latter taking this form. The second type of construction had a disc on the reverse which was slightly convex, which mirrored the front plate and had two open-type rivets protruding through it. That is to say, there was a small hole down the centre of the rivet which allowed the outer edge to be hammered over from the centre. On this plate is, hand-engraved in flowing script, 'J. Godet & Sohn. K,G.' and underneath, 'Unter den Linden', followed in the centre, in larger arabic numerals, '53'.

The overall size of the piece was larger than the others described in S.001—S.005, the height of the badge measured from point to point of the Maltese cross being 60 mm and the length of the swords 65 mm. The Swastikas that the Luftwaffe eagles were clutching in their talons were segmented. The central plate, with the diamonds, measured 18 mm as did the name disc on the reverse.

The box for this award has been described as a white case which was covered with calf skin, with a gold line round the lid. This box was square with rounded corners and was produced with a white flock base and lid liner. It has also been concluded by authoritative sources that some were produced to be similar to the previously described blue box in which the crosses in the series S.001—S.005 were awarded.

The Criteria for the award of this medal are a little obscure, but it would seem they were rendered to the commanders and particularly successful pilots of the Condor Legion, but any hard and fast information as to their award, or conditions of award, would be gratefully received by the author.

The Citation to this award was just a simple piece of printed paper with Hitler's signature at its base and the Nazi seal at the bottom left-hand corner.

S.007 Spanish Cross in Gold with Diamonds—Dress Copy

Spanish Cross in Gold with Diamonds — Dress Copy (S.007). The Swastikas clutched in the eagles' talons are unsegmented.

This cross was similar to that of the awarded type, S.006, save for the central ring which was formed in two parallel circles. The Swastika in this version, as opposed to that found in the awarded type which was below the level of the circle that surrounded it, was at the same height as the two circles and the points of the Swastika touched the inside of the smaller circle. The field produced between the circle's edge and the arms of the Swastika were pebbled, as was the field between the two lines and into this were directly set twelve white sapphires. These were smaller in size and number to the diamonds in the awarded type, S.006. They also fitted directly between those two lines which gave a completely different appearance to the centre of this award. The plate that the Swastika and sapphires are set on to was fixed to the body of the cross by two ball rivets.

The cross and the plate were made of silver and the reverse sometimes had the hallmark applied between two rivets. It had a large pin with a hinge fixed to the upper arm. The lower one had a large retaining hook. The whole of the badge was gilded and produced in a very high quality.

There was no Citation for this item as it was a private purchase piece and variations do occur in the construction of the badge. It is not known if every recipient purchased an example of this type for general wear, or if these private purchase examples were issued on certain occasions to the original recipient.

The form of box is also unknown but it is assumed that it was just the manufacturer's or jeweller's protective case.

S.008 Cross of Honour for the Relatives of the Dead in Spain

Again on 14 April 1939 this medal was announced to honour those volunteers who had fallen in combat, or who had died as a consequence of wounds received in combat, died as a result of illness or disease directly attributable to those wounds or had died due to that illness or accident being sustained while serving in Spain or Spanish Morocco. It was also awarded for those listed missing in action in that conflict.

The Cross was constructed of silver which was bronzed and took the same form as the breast cross but was smaller. At the top was a ring for the suspension ribbon, which was 30 mm wide and consisted of the German and Spanish national colours, with thin outer vertical stripes of red, yellow, red, yellow, red, white and a wide central stripe of black to represent mourning.

The reverse was concave and had

Cross of Honour for the Relatives of the Dead in Spain (S.008).

Reverse of the Cross of Honour for the Relatives of the Dead in Spain showing the maker's mark, name and silver content.

the maker's mark which was J. GODET u SOHN BERLIN and the .938 silver content mark. One point of interest on an example in my own collection are marks on the ring of a stamped 21, which was the Godet trade mark.

The Criteria for the award were:

1) If the fallen was married, the wife of the fallen, the eldest son of the fallen and the daughter of the fallen.

2) In the case of the fallen not being married, the father of the fallen, mother of the fallen, brother of the fallen and sister of the fallen. Should a recipient die, then the award was rendered to the next of kin in line of succession.

The award was to be worn at all times and in the case of men, it was fixed over the left breast pocket and was usually found on a court-mounted ribbon, that is to say the ribbon was furled below the medal and the reverse of the ribbon was padded, the whole item being formed on a metal plate with its own individual pin mounting at the top. The medal was again usually found clipped on to a hook which enabled the ring of the medal to be easily removed. In the case of women, the ribbon was formed into a bow.

Numbers awarded of the Cross of Honour for the Relatives of the Dead in Spain: 315. The known recipients were: Friedrich Beuche, Ulrich Bonisch, Wilhelm Boddem, Willi Deriesch, Albert Echart and Werner Fischer.

The box to this award again is not known to the author but it has been suggested it is a green case with an off-white liner.

The Citation again was a plain piece of paper with black printing with Hitler's signature at the bottom, no medal facsimile at the top, and in the bottom left-hand corner, the Nazi seal.

S.009 Tank Badge of the Condor Legion—First Type

In the autumn of 1936, to reward the armoured personnel of the Condor Legion their commander Oberst von Thoma instituted a silver-coloured badge which took the form of an oak leaf wreath which broadened from the base as it rose to its apex. In the First Type badge the apex was fretted out. The base of the wreath was formed by a pair of crossed twigs tied together with a ribbon. The outside edges of the wreath took the outline of the oak leaves and gave the impression of a rough appearance. The central design of the badge comprised a skull surmounting crossed bones. This emblem was over an early tank. The teeth that comprised the lower jaw of the skull on this version were quite pronounced, as were the eye sockets and the joints of the skull.

The reverse of the badge took the form of the obverse due to the fact that the badge was die-struck. The pin was of a needle type with the hinge being applied to the apex of the

Tank Badge of the Condor Legion — First Type (S.009).

one had to be produced, giving rise to the badge S.009. The fact that production was in two locations makes one speculate as to whether this is entirely true. A theory exists that the badge was redesigned to have a more appealing appearance.

Von Thoma authorized the award of 415 of these badges. General Oberst von Brauchitsch, the commander-in-chief of the army, on 10 July 1939 granted official recognition of this badge for appreciation of services rendered in the Spanish Civil War. The badge could be worn by discharged Condor Legion veterans on any other uniform of any organization which they may have subsequently joined, or have previously been a member.

The badge was awarded with a Citation personally signed by von Thoma. The box or presentation packet is unknown to this author, as are the Criteria for the award of this badge.

Known recipients were Sanitäts-Unteroffizier Werner Graf, Unteroffizier Boche and Oberfeldwebel Rudolf Vogt.

badge. The catch at the base was also applied. The badge can be found in silver, silver-plate or white metal and the first version is considered to have been produced both in Berlin and Lisbon. It is, in this form, considered rare due to the fact that the matrix from which the badge was produced was damaged in an air raid and a new

S.010 Tank Badge of the Condor Legion—Second Type

This badge was constructed from the second matrix and varied quite considerably from S.009, the main differences being as follows. The oak leaves in the wreath were not so nicely executed and gave a flat appearance to the wreath. The apex of the badge was not fretted out, thus having a solid appearance. The edges of the leaves, on both the inner and outer edges of the wreath, were not cut out, giving a totally different appearance to the silhouette to the wreath. The twigs at the base of the wreath were shorter and at a slightly different angle to those in the former badge. The ribbon ties at the base were quite different in construction, being part

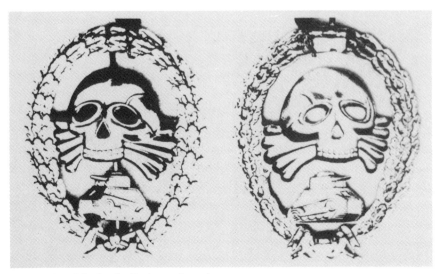

Tank Badge of the Condor Legion — Second Type, showing obverse and reverse (S.010). (J.R. Angolia Collection).

of the base of the badge instead of apart from below the oak leaves, as in S.009. The teeth in the jaws of this badge were represented by squares, as opposed to the stylized teeth in the jaws of the former badge. The eye sockets and joints of the skull were not as pronounced in this badge.

The badge was produced from thin pressed metal, which in this case was silver-plated, and this version of the badge was only produced in Germany.

S.011 Tank Badge of the Condor Legion—Gold Type

Colonel von Thoma received, after the successful conclusion of the Spanish Civil War, a special gold version of the badge at the time of the Madrid Victory Parade from the personnel of his armoured group of the Condor Legion. This badge was produced from genuine gold. Further details of this unique badge and its present whereabouts are unknown to this author.

S.012 Cuff Title—'Spain 1936–1939'

To reward the members of the Imke Group who were in either the signals demonstration detachment or armoured demonstration regiment, a

Cuff Title — 'Spain 1936-1939' (S.012)
(David Littlejohn Collection).

cuff title was introduced on 21 June 1939, by order of the army high command. This took the form of a red band with yellow cotton edge. The material of the band could either be felt or cotton, on which was embroidered the words '1936 —SPANIEN—1939' in yellow cotton. However, examples are encountered with this legend being produced in gold wire. This gives rise to the possibility of there being two varieties of the cuff band, namely NCOs' and officers' patterns. As the award was only in existence for a short time, however, being cancelled by order of the high command, this observation is pure speculation.

The Criteria for the award are unknown as are details of the Citation which accompanied the cuff title.

S.013 Cuff Title—'Spain 1936-1939'—Gothic Script

This type of cuff band was awarded under exactly the same conditions as S.012, and is merely a maker's variant. The main difference in this cuff title is

The only known authentic example of the Cuff Title — 'Spain 1936-1939' — Gothic Script (S.013) (Forman Collection, Piccadilly).

that it was produced in Gothic Script, with the dates larger than the word SPANIEN and the title being woven in BEVO style in gold wire. The backing was of ridged rayon, similar to that found in SS officers' cuff titles, which gave the impression of silk. The colour of this band was a deep red.

S.014 Spanish Wound Badge—Black Class
S.015 Spanish Wound Badge—Silver Class
S.016 Spanish Wound Badge—Gold Class

To reward military personnel involved in the Spanish Civil War who were wounded, this badge was introduced on 22 May 1939. It took the form of its First World War counterpart, but with the difference that it had a Swastika stamped into the helmet. At this point it is important to dispel some of the misconceptions surrounding the award of this badge. The actual number of badges awarded for participation in the Spanish Civil War were: Black, 182; Silver, 1; Gold, 0. However, this design of badge continued to be awarded at least until 1942. Also, it is possible that original recipients of the badges which were actually awarded for the Civil War could, for subsequent wounds sustained in the Second World War, receive the higher grade in this form. This theory has been denied in other reference books, but due to the limited number of awards, it is highly possible that this practice was applied.

The badge consisted of a wreath of laurel leaves with a bow at its base and five berries, or dots, at its apex. The central device of the badge comprised a First World War steel helmet surmounting crossed swords, with a Swastika stamped into the helmet from the reverse. The field was pebbled but some examples of the badge have this field cut out, leaving the swords and helmet in silhouette.

The reverse of the badge followed the design of the obverse, as the badge was stamped out. However, one example I have examined of the silver grade is stamped out as previously described but has then been attached to a backing plate. This gives the impression of the badge being formed in a solid manner. This badge is constructed in real silver. The pin to all the badges encountered is usually of a needle pin design.

The criteria for the award were:
1) Up to two wounds—Black award.
2) Three to four wounds—Silver award.
3) Five or more wounds—Gold award.

It is assumed that they were awarded with a Citation, but so far none of these have turned up. The badge came in a black box with a cream flock lining.

Spanish Wound Badge — Black Class (S.014).

Second World War Decorations

The new Germany that emerged in 1933 saw the need for a total reorganization of the orders and qualification badges that were required for all branches of military and civilian life. The qualification badges of a military nature are covered separately in the relevant sections of the book. Here I just wish to briefly describe the decorations awarded for bravery from 1 September 1939 through to 8 May 1945. Hitler and his advisors saw the necessity to revamp and reclassify the decorations so that they came up to the conditions of a modern mechanized war. This gave Hitler the opportunity of setting his stamp and that of his fascist government on to all aspects of military life, by including the Swastika on all these new creations. This tends to make the series of medals and badges particularly collectable, by virtue of the fact that the new designs were introduced gradually from 1933 and speeded with the approach of the war ending with the fall of the Third Reich on 8 May 1945. No other series of medals has been so complete in all their transitions from Imperial to Republic and finally despotic dictatorship, or redesigned with such precision and style as those encountered in the twelve-year life of the Third Reich.

Their popularity has captured the imagination of the world's collectors, coupled with the sinister appeal of the regime and the courage of the men who won the awards that are described in this section. One Belgian volunteer who was a gunner/pioneer in the Waffen SS witnessed his friends being crushed in their foxholes by the tracks of Russian tanks which drove up on to the foxhole and then pirouetted from side to side, accompanied by the horrific screams of the victims being crushed lifeless beneath the grinding track. He was incensed to find that the Panzerfaust which he picked up in hope of destroying the enemy, had been sabotaged and on successive loadings the projectiles were repeatedly faulty. Again his feelings were of immense rage that the tools of his trade had been rendered ineffective. Remy Schrÿnen of the SS Sturmbrigade *Langemarck* picked up a demolition charge, known as a satchel charge, and ran forward and attacked the first of the Russian tanks, then returned for more and in all destroyed seven tanks in this manner, although he had been gravely wounded by machine-gun fire from the tanks during his attacks. For this

Hans Rudel's complete collection of medals. **Top Left** *one of the two sets of Golden Oak Leaves, Swords and Diamonds with which he was awarded (D.022).* **Centre top** *Knights Cross of the Iron Cross with Golden Oak Leaves, Swords and Diamonds.* **Top right** *Oak Leaves, Swords and Diamonds (D.021).* **Centre left** *Oak Leaves (D.019).* **Centre right** *Oak Leaves and Swords (D.020).* **Bottom left** *Combined Pilots and Observers Badge in Gold with Diamonds (L.004).* **Bottom centre** *Air-to-Ground Support Operational Flying Clasp — Diamond Class (L.060).* **Bottom right** *German Cross in Gold (D.025).*

heroism he received the Knights Cross of the Iron Cross, D.018.

The bravery awards that are covered in this section are still worn with great pride by their recipients but they have to be worn in the new permitted designs, which were authorized by order of the German Federal Government in 1957. These have been, incidentally, redesigned to remove the hated Swastika and the vestiges of Hitlerism. In the case of the Knights Cross of the Iron Cross, D.018, the Swastika has been replaced by the three Oak Leaves of the original design which was instigated in 1813 but retaining the date of instigation 1939 in the lower arm of the cross on the obverse. One point of interest is that, for those winners of the Knights Cross who were Austrians, of whom there were a number, the Oak Leaves on the obverse have been changed for the Eidelweiss, the emblem of Austria. This illustrates the high regard that even the Austrian government has for the bravery of the winners of this prestigious award, to allow the wearing of what is basically a foreign award in this manner.

Index to Decorations common to all Services 1939-1945

D.001 Wound Badge 1939—Black Class   38
D.002 Wound Badge 1939—Silver Class   38
D.003 Wound Badge 1939—Gold Class   38
D.004 Wound Badge '20 July 1944'—Black Class—First Type   40
D.005 Wound Badge '20 July 1944'—Silver Class—First Type   40
D.006 Wound Badge '20 July 1944'—Gold Class—First Type   40
D.007 Wound Badge '20 July 1944'—Black Class—Second Type   43
D.008 Wound Badge '20 July 1944'—Silver Class—Second Type   43
D.009 Wound Badge '20 July 1944'—Gold Class—Second Type   43
D.010 Wound Badge '20 July 1944'—Black Class—Third Type   45
D.011 Wound Badge '20 July 1944'—Silver Class—Third Type   45
D.012 Wound Badge '20 July 1944'—Gold Class—Third Type   45
D.013 Iron Cross—Second Class   45
D.014 Iron Cross—Second Class 1939 Bar—First Type   48
D.015 Iron Cross—Second Class 1939 Bar—Second Type   49
D.016 Iron Cross—First Class   50
D.016a, b and c Iron Cross—First Class—Variations   50
D.017 Iron Cross—First Class 1939 Bar   51
DV.017 Iron Cross—First Class 1939 Bar—Variation   51
D.018 Knights Cross of the Iron Cross   52
D.019 Knights Cross of the Iron Cross with Oak Leaves   58
D.020 Knights Cross of the Iron Cross with Oak Leaves and Swords 59
D.021 Knights Cross of the Iron Cross with Oak Leaves,
       Swords and Diamonds   61
D.022 Knights Cross of the Iron Cross with Golden Oak Leaves,
       Swords and Diamonds   63
D.023 Star of the Grand Cross   64
D.024 Grand Cross of the Iron Cross   69
D.025 German Cross in Gold   70
D.026 German Cross in Gold with Diamonds   72
D.027 German Cross in Gold—Cloth Version—Air Force Blue   73
D.028 German Cross in Gold—Cloth Version—Navy Blue   73
D.029 German Cross in Gold—Cloth Version—Field Grey   73
D.030 German Cross in Silver   73
D.031 German Cross in Silver— Cloth Version—Air Force Blue   74
D.032 German Cross in Silver—Cloth Version—Navy Blue   74
D.033 German Cross in Silver—Cloth Version—Field Grey   74
D.034 War Merit Medal   74
D.035 War Merit Cross—Second Class—Bronze without Swords   75
D.036 War Merit Cross—First Class—Silver without Swords   77

D.037	War Merit Cross—Knights Cross—Silver without Swords	78
D.038	War Merit Cross—Knights Cross—Gold without Swords	79
D.039	War Merit Cross—Second Class—Bronze with Swords	79
D.040	War Merit Cross—First Class—Silver with Swords	80
D.041	War Merit Cross—Knights Cross—Silver with Swords	81
D.042	War Merit Cross—Knights Cross—Gold with Swords	82
D.043	Roll of Honour Clasp—Army	82
D.044	Roll of Honour Clasp—Navy	83
D.045	Roll of Honour Clasp—Air Force	84
D.046	Medal of the Winter Campaign in Russia 1941–1942	84
D.047	Führer Commendation Certificate	86

D.001 Wound Badge 1939—Black Class
D.002 Wound Badge 1939—Silver Class
D.003 Wound Badge 1939—Gold Class

Hitler's concern for the combat-wounded, due to his experiences in the First World War, prompted him to reintroduce yet another badge to reward those honourably wounded. It came into being on 1 September 1939.

It varied from the Spanish form S.013, in that the laurel leaf wreath was smooth round the outer rim. The swords were of a broader blade design and the helmet that surmounted them was of the new pattern used by the German armed forces, again with the Swastika surmounting it. This was more prominent than in the Spanish type. The field had dots but these were in horizontal lines, resembling the effect by which newspaper pictures are produced. The base of the wreath had a bow and the apex had three dots or laurel berries.

The Black Class is usually found hollow, while the Silver and Gold Classes are normally sold. There were numerous makers and pin construc-tions. The material also varied, embracing bakelite through to genuine silver.

As the air war progressed, numerous civilian personnel became injured and Dr Goebbels considered it fitting

Wound Badge 1938 — Gold Class (D.003).

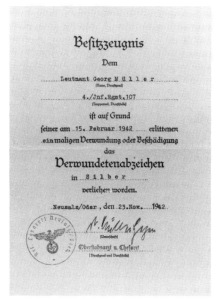

Wound Badge Citations to Leutnant Georg Müller of the 4th Battalion, Infantry Regiment 107, dated 15 June and 23 November 1942 for a leg wound he received on 15 February that year. The earlier award is for the Black Class, the subsequent one for the Silver because his leg had to be amputated.

that they should be rewarded, so from March 1943, at his suggestion, all civilians became eligible for the award. One particularly interesting award was to a Sergeant Thomas Hellor Cooper, a member of the *Britische Freikorps* who, while serving with the SS division *Das Reich*, was awarded the black wound badge. He is the only known British recipient of a German combat award.

The Criteria for the award were:
1) Up to two wounds—Black award.
2) Three to five wounds—Silver award.
3) One wound resulting in the loss of hand, foot, eye or causing deafness—Silver award.
4) Five or more wounds—Gold award.
5) One wound resulting in total disability, permanent blindness or loss of manhood—Gold award.

The only illness or disease the badge could be awarded for was that of cases of frostbite.

The black badge was awarded in a paper packet. The silver and gold badges were usually awarded in black or burgundy boxes, with respective black or burgundy flock bases. However, as the war progressed they were also issued in paper packets. There was a cloth version in black printed on to green cotton. It is possible that there were examples of this packet in silver and gold.

The Citations were extremely varied and even came printed in foreign languages, including Russian.

D.004 Wound Badge '20 July 1944'—Black Class—First Type
D.005 Wound Badge '20 July 1944'—Silver Class—First Type
D.006 Wound Badge '20 July 1944'—Gold Class—First Type

On 20 July 1944 an attempt was made to assassinate Hitler by Colonel Count Claus Schenk von Stauffenberg at the Wolf's Lair in Rastenburg, Hitler's HQ in the east. This was unsuccessful but killed or wounded 24 occupants of the room. The most serious casualties were Colonel Brant and Herr Berger, who died immediately, and Generalleutnant Schmundt and General Korten who subsequently died from wounds received. The remaining twenty suffered superficial wounds and shock, save for General Buhle and Generalmajor Scherff, who were more seriously injured.

Hitler, to commemorate this attempt on his life and his escape, introduced a special Wound Badge which he awarded to the 24 occupants, or dependants in the case of the dead. He declined to give himself one of these medals. The first awards of this medal were made on 20 August 1944.

The recipients of the medal were: Generalfeldmarshcall Wilhelm Keitel—Black Class; Generaloberst Alfred Jodl—Black Class; General der Artillerie Walter Warlimont—Black Class; Konteradmiral Jesko von Puttkamer—Black Class; Kapitän z.See Heinz Assmann—Black Class; Oberst Nicolaus von Below—Black Class; Konteradmiral Hans-Erich Voss, Black Class; SS-Hauptsturmführer Otto Gunsche, Black Class; SS-Gruppenführer Hermann Fegelein, Silver Class; Generalleutnant Adolf Heusinger—Silver Class; Oberstleutnant G. Borgman—Silver Class; General der Flieger—Karl Bodenschatz—Gold Class; General der Infanterie Walter

Wound Badge '20 July 1944' — Black Class — First Type (D.004). This was Generaloberst Alfred Jodl's medal.

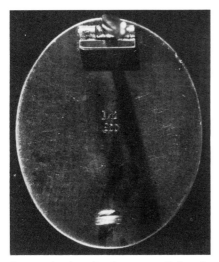

Reverse showing the pin open to disclose the maker's mark, L/12, and the silver content, .800.

Buhle—Gold Class; Generalmajor Walter Scherff—Gold Class; General der Flieger Gunter Korten—Gold Class, posthumous; Oberst Heinz Brant—Gold Class, posthumous; (Civilian) Berger—Gold Class, posthumous; Generalleutnant Rudolf Schmundt—Gold Class, posthumous; Obersteleutnant von John—not known but presumed Black; Oberstleutnant Weizenegger—not known but presumed Black; (Civilian) Walter Hewell—not known but presumed Black; Hauptmann von Schimanski—not known but presumed Black; Buchs—not known but presumed Black; and Hagan—not known but presumed Black

The quality of these badges was very high and each example was hand finished. This is illustrated by very fine file marks round the edges of the badges. They were produced by the firm of C.E. Juncker of Berlin and it is

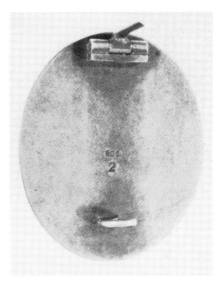

Reverse of Wound Badge '20 July 1944' — Black Class — First Type without a maker's mark but with silver content .800 and 2 to denote wear copy (D.004) (Forman Collection, Piccadilly).

estimated that 100 were made. The badge took the form of the ordinary wound decoration with a very finely formed wreath with a bow at the base and three laurel berries or dots at the apex. The helmet was nearer the apex than on an ordinary badge and the sword hilts were two bundles of laurel leaves up the wreath from the base, while the upper edge of the hilt of each sword touched the front and back of the helmet respectively. Beneath the helmet was the date and Hitler's signature. The date and signature were raised and polished. The field was hand pebbled and matt finished. The reverse was flat and bore minute scratches, which epitomize hand finishing.

The hinge was of the 'on its edge' type with a hook at the bottom. The

Left *Hitler presenting the Wound Badge '20 July 1944' to General der Artillerie Walter Warlimont. In the foreground are Generaloberst Alfred Jodl and Generalfeldmarschall Wilhelm Keitel.*

Middle left *Hitler shows Mussolini the damage after the bomb plot.*

Bottom left *Speer, Jodl and Keitel with Hitler in February 1945, Jodl and Keitel wearing the Wound Badge '20 July 1944'.*

pin was hand drawn and slightly curled up at the bottom where it fastened into the hook. On the reverse beneath the pin was the maker's mark L/12 and the silver content .800. At this point it is interesting to note that each recipient received two badges, the award one as described and a Dress Copy which had .800 and a small 2 to denote that this was the wear copy or second version. No other difference existed between the two types save for this small number.

The Black version had the wreath,

helmet and swords artificially blackened. The Swastika was less darkened while the date and signature were highly polished and the field was matt silver. The reverse, including the pin, hook and hinge, was also artificially blackened. The silver version was silver all over, with the signature and date highly polished as before, while the field was again a matt silver. The gold version had a gold or gilt wreath helmet and swords, with again the Swastika slightly lightened; the date and signature were highly polished silver, while the reverse and pin, etc, were matt gold. It has recently been discovered that a miniature version of the Silver grade also exists. It is

therefore possible that miniatures for the other grades were produced as well.

The Criteria for the award were as for D.001, D.002 and D.003. It is assumed that if the recipient was wounded again he received the higher grade of the badge in this form.

The badge was awarded with a Citation that was produced on Vellum paper with a large gilt eagle at its top. The name and grade was individually entered on to the Citation. At the base was Hitler's signature in ink plus an official seal. The badge came in a black box with black velvet base and silk lid lining.

D.007 Wound Badge '20 July 1944'—Black Class—Second Type
D.008 Wound Badge '20 July 1944'—Silver Class—Second Type
D.009 Wound Badge '20 July 1944'—Gold Class—Second Type

The author knows of only one badge of this type, and it is in the gold grade, but it is reasonable to suppose that it exists in black and silver also. It consists, as in the former badge, of a wreath of laurel leaves, but this example has a rough edge following the line of the laurel bunches. The ribbon tie at the base is tied tighter and formed of a thicker ribbon. The apex has five berries or dots as in the Spanish Wound Badge type (S.014—016). The date fills the gap between the hilts of the swords. It is

also interesting to note that the binding on the hilts on the right-hand sword runs in opposite directions on each of these types, and that there is a ferrel on this badge adjacent to the top of the hilt but no ferrel on the former kind. The centre of the hilt on this medal is square, with a plain box, whereas the former badge has a square box in the hilt with a bar in it. The signature is larger and is exercised in a flowing hand. It is possible that this badge was intended for further awards when the recipient was further

Wound Badge '20 July 1944' — Gold Class — Second Type (D.009) (David Littlejohn).

wounded, and was produced by a different maker, but this is pure conjecture. The reverse was stamped with the silver grade .935.

The original collector who owned this badge, Mr B. A. Beyerstedt, contacted Dr K. G. Klietmann of Berlin whose observations were recorded in a letter dated 10 September 1964, and I quote him verbatim:

'Many thanks for your letter of 3rd this month and for sending the wound badge of the 20th July on to me which I received yesterday and I will return it today by air-mail registered.

'The personal inspection of a badge—I must emphasize it again—is the most important point for telling what it is. This inspection shows me that

a) It is doubtless made in 1944.
b) And made in Germany
c) This item was made by hand from a jeweller
d) It is put together of the following parts:
1. Wreath
2. The grained ground
3. The steel helmet
4. The swords
5. Inscription

'All these parts are hollow made and were cut off from other badges except the inscription which was made in addition by hand and then all parts were put together and the silver gilt back was finally put on it. Until now I was not able to identify the hallmark. After this inspection I do not at all doubt that it is a genuine pattern for that time. But after the photographs I could never have told this. From the photographs alone it was not to recognize that it is a genuine item. The later on awarded items looked different and were made of solid silver.'

The good doctor gives two very important lessons in this text: firstly that personal inspection is all-important when deciding if an item is genuine or not; and secondly that for even the rarest of badges there can be many variations due to the innovation of varying manufacturers.

D.010 Wound Badge '20 July 1944'—Black Class—Third Type
D.011 Wound Badge '20 July 1944'—Silver Class—Third Type
D.012 Wound Badge '20 July 1944'—Gold Class—Third Type

This badge was identical in every respect to D.004, D.005 and D.006 except that it did not have the signature beneath the date. The date was larger and situated at the top of the sword hilts. These hilts were also not so spread, coming mid-way of the second laurel bunch forming the outer wreath of the badge. The reverse contained no differences. This badge is known in Silver and it is assumed to have been made in the other classes, Black and Gold. Being produced by C. E. Juncker of Berlin, it may be the second award type for subsequent awards for further wounds which the recipient may have received. Considering the date of the award and the number awarded, however, the rank and occupation (that is to say, civilian or non-active military) of the recipients, this is just a guesstimate as to its purpose. If it *is* the case, the badge would be found only in silver and gold, but probably it was an

Wound Badge '20 July 1944' — Black Class — Third Type (D.010). The reverse is marked with .800 silver content and L/12 manufacturer's mark (J.R. Angolia/Russ Hamilton Collection).

alternative design or pattern that was rejected and in that case, it would be found in all three types.

D.013 Iron Cross—Second Class

The medal was originally introduced in 1813 to reward the fighting forces of Prussia whose Kaiser had declared war on France and Napoleon on 13 March 1813. Details of the medal were announced on 20 March 1813.

It was originally intended to be a pure campaign award and was to replace the other state awards such as the Order of the Red Eagle and the Pour le Mérite.

The original design submitted by its instigator Kaiser Fredric Wilhelm was that of a cross 'Platte' with a square box centre with chamfered corners. In this box was the Royal Cipher surmounted by the Crown of Prussia. The arms had superimposed upon them a sprig of oak leaves. The quarters of the cross were semi-filled and the date of instigation superimposed one numeral in each quadrant. The medal was to be suspended from a ribbon which was comprised of stripes of black, white, broad black, white and black, these being the colours of Prussia. However, this design was not taken up but another submitted by the architect Karl Friedrich Schinkel was adopted. This was welcomed by the Kaiser who preferred it to his own submission. It comprised a cross 'Platte' of blackened iron. This time the centre had a sprig of three oak leaves. The upper arm had the cipher FW, the initials of the Kaiser, surmounted by the Crown of Prussia, while the lower arm had the date of introduction, 1813. The reverse was plain. Originally the plain side was supposed to have been worn to the front; however, it was decided later to wear the medal the other way round. The blackened iron core was surrounded by a silver frame which was in two parts and soldered together. At the apex was an eyelet through which was put a ring to hold the ribbon. The ribbon was, in this case, the same as for that of the former design.

The medal was reintroduced for the subsequent campaigns of 1870–1871 (the Franco-Prussian War) and 1914–1918 (the First World War). In each case the only change in the basic design was that the ciphers were altered. That is to say, in the former instance the centre had a W, the top arm the crown and the lower arm 1870, while the reverse was the same as the obverse of the 1813 type; and in the latter the only alteration was the date, 1914, on the lower arm of the cross.

The ribbon was the same for each period save that there was a non-combatants' version which had the colours reversed, in other words in white, black, broad white, black and white stripes. The order had origi-

Iron Cross — Second Class (D.013).

Citation dated 9 July 1941 for the award of the Iron Cross — Second Class to Leutnant Georg Müller who was then with Jäger Regiment 253.

nated from a purely Prussian award to become the highest award of the German empire in all its grades, and an internationally acclaimed decoration.

Hitler introduced on 1 September 1939 the last version of the Iron Cross which to all intents and purposes took the same form as all the former types, except he recognized the 'all-German' nature of the award and substituted for the oak leaves which formed the central design of the medal the Party or Third Reich emblem of the Swastika. The lower arm had the date 1939 while all the other arms were plain. The reverse was plain also, save for the lower arm

which had the year of instigation, 1813. The ribbon in this type also changed to stripes of black, white, broad brick red, white and black. This change has been attributed to recognition of the blood shed in the First World War, which was to be represented by the broad red stripe.

The Criteria for the award were:
1) For outstanding service to Service personnel and for bravery in the face of the enemy.
2) The Cross for a higher grade must be preceded by the award of this grade.

Hitler did not reintroduce the non-combatants' version of the award, but introduced instead the War Merit Cross series which is covered later in D.031–D.039.

The Citation to the award was found in many different varieties but can be condensed into two main types, which were Gothic Script or plain capitals. The wording of the Citation also changed as Hitler took over greater control of the military machine. The top had a facsimile of the medal, while the bottom had the signature of the commanding officer and the name of the unit to which the recipient was attached, with the official stamp of that unit in the lower left-hand corner. The medal was usually awarded in a blue paper packet, with the name printed on it. It is also found in a black presentation box, which sometimes has a see-through lid, with a white flock lining and recess for the medal and a recessed area for the ribbon. The lid is lined with white satin. The overall appearance is that of a miniature Knights Cross box, and this type of box is considered very rare. During the period of 1939-1945 it is estimated that nearly five million awards were bestowed and these covered all the nationals fighting with the Germans, even to a unit in which Eddy Chapman, the triple spy, was attached, although if he received the award personally is in some doubt.

D.014 Iron Cross—Second Class 1939 Bar—First Type

This Bar was introduced on 1 September 1939 to reward recipients of the Iron Cross Second Class of 1914 who had distinguished themselves again in the Second World War. It comprised an eagle with outstretched wings with spread legs which clutched in its talons an oak leaf wreath with a Swastika inside it. The field around the Swastika was pebbled. Beneath the wreath was a rhomboid box (ie, with diagonal sides at each end). Round the edge of the box was a lip and in the centre the date 1939. The overall colour of the badge was matt silver with the raised parts polished. The overall size of the badge was 30 × 39 mm, and it was worn on a piece of 1914 ribbon, which was placed through the second buttonhole of the uniform jacket. The reverse was flat save for four lugs which were pushed through the fabric of the ribbon to secure it.

The Criteria for the award were:
1) For outstanding service to Service personnel and for bravery in the face of the enemy.
2) The Cross for a higher class must be preceded by that of a lower class.

The Citation was a plain piece of paper with a facsimile of the Iron Cross at the top. The printing was again in the two forms, the signature of the commander at the bottom with the unit to which the recipient was attached and in the left-hand corner the official unit stamp. The badge usually came in a brown or blue paper packet, but it was occasionally found in a small square box which could either be in black, green or burgundy. These boxes were usually unlined and sometimes had the LDO logo or just those letters stamped into the inner lid. Another rarer version was an oblong box which was quite plain

Iron Cross — Second Class 1939 Bar — First Type (D.014).

and black in colour. The badge was fastened by the method described above to a full length of First World War pattern ribbon which was secured at top and bottom of the lower portion of the box. That is to say, the lid section and the lower section of the box were in two separate halves. With this was the ribbon Bar with a miniature emblem attached.

For very high ranking officers an example has been encountered which contains both the Second Class Bar with a First Class Bar (D.017), the

Case containing both the First Class (left) and Second Class 1939 Bars to the Iron Cross (D.017 and D.014) (Forman Collection, Piccadilly).

latter on the left and the former on the right, with a piece of ribbon at the top positioned horizontally across the case. The badges are on a black velvet base. The case is red, pebbled simulated leather with a gold political eagle stamped on to it. The whole case is finely made with a hinge and press-stud opener. The upper, inner lining is of white satin.

D.015 Iron Cross—Second Class 1939 Bar—Second Type

This medal was in all respects identical in style to the former medal, D.014, except for its size, which was

25 × 25 mm. The reverse had only two prongs for attachment and the gauge for the material from which

Iron Cross — Second Class 1939 Bar —
Second Type (D.015). (Tim Stannard
Collection).

the badge was made, was correspondingly thinner. This type was known as the 'Prinzen' version, and was obtained by private purchase. The purpose of its size was to allow it to be attached to the ribbon of the Second Class 1914 Iron Cross, when it was worn on formal occasions. This type is usually of a much finer quality than that found on the awarded Bar.

Being private purchase, the form of containers for the medal were numerous and their quality, therefore, also depended greatly on the store from which the badge was obtained.

D.016 Iron Cross—First Class
DV.016a, DV.016b and DV.016c—Iron
Cross—First Class—Variations

This medal was also introduced on 1 September 1939 and took the form of its predecessor, but having the Swastika at its centre and the date at the bottom of the lower arm. The centre was blackened iron which could be either painted or chemically blued. The reverse was flat and silvered with a straight-bladed pin. Usually this pin had the maker's mark on it, either on the top or bottom face. In rarer cases the pin was omitted and replaced by a screw post with a large screw cap, which might be plain or have a raised line to help fasten or unscrew it.

Three variations in construction are encountered and have been separately catalogued: DV.016a—A standard First Class Cross as described but with slightly convex arms.

DV.016b—The firm of Godet and Son of Berlin produced for General Officers a smaller version which measured approximately 41 × 41 mm.

Iron Cross — First Class (D.016).

Citation to Leutnant Georg Müller, now with Jäger Regiment 107, for the award of the Iron Cross — First Class (D.016) on 13 June 1942.

This was usually manufactured in silver of .800 standard and occasionally the metal centre was black enamelled. DV.016c—For use by members of the German Navy, the iron centre was replaced by a brass core which was chemically blackened. The reason was that salt water rusted the iron centre.

A cloth version of the badge was produced and a few variations are encountered. On the whole they seem to be a little crude in their manufacture. These items were private purchase, and the reason for them is uncertain, but a theory has been put forward that they were intended for use in situations that required no magnetic sparks, as in the case of the new jet fighters; or silence, as in the case of submarine personnel, since in the later days of the war British sound locators had greatly improved and could hear the smallest of metallic noise. This theory has been included to prompt comment from the reader.

The Criteria for the award were:
1) To have distinguished oneself three or more times than required for the Second Class award.

The badge was awarded with a Citation which can again be described in two types, plain capitals and Gothic lettering. It had a facsimile of the badge at the top and the commanding officer's signature and unit at the bottom, with the unit stamp in the left-hand corner. The wording again changed with Hitler's control over the armed forces. The badge was awarded in a black box with a white flock base and silk lid liner, while on the outer lid was stencilled the outline of the award. An estimated 300,000–750,000 awards were made.

D.017 Iron Cross—First Class 1939 Bar
DV.017—First Class 1939 Bar—Variation

Another badge introduced on 1 September 1939, this was identical to the Second Class Bar D.014. There were two slight variations in the style of the eagle's chest and the fletching thereon but this did not warrant an

Iron Cross — First Class 1939 Bar (D.017).

introduction of a second type. The reverse was flat and had a pin of the broad blade type. Occasionally it is found with a thin needle pin. This type is usually encountered with the trade mark L/11 stamped on to the reverse and is generally of a poor quality of manufacture.

One variation is DV.017 which also

has the Bar which is attached to a 1914 Iron Cross First Class at the top of the upper arm. The reverse has the standard pin to the Iron Cross with the reverse of the bar completely plain. This variation is also encountered with a screw post instead of the pin. It was again a private purchase item and one must suppose it was to facilitate easy removal from one tunic to another.

The Criteria for the award were:
1) To have been awarded the Iron Cross First Class (D.016) again in the Second World War.

The Citation had an Iron Cross at its top and the signature of the commanding officer and the unit at the bottom with the official stamp in the lower left-hand corner. The box was black and pebbled with an exact facsimile of the badge in silver stencilled on to the outer lid. The base on which the badge rested was black velvet or flocking, and the lid liner was white silk.

D.018 Knights Cross of the Iron Cross

This medal was introduced on 1 September 1939, but unlike the former grades which had existed from the award's instigation in the year of 1813, was a new class to bridge the gap between the First Class and the Grand Cross. This award went on to capture the imagination of the German people and was used to great propaganda advantage by Dr Goebbels. In fact, there was a whole series of postcards depicting the recipients of the medal, not unlike cigarette cards but much larger,

which German children and serious postcard collectors collected avidly. The cross was identical to the Second Class award, D.013, with the exception of the size which was 48 × 48 mm, excluding the eyelet which in this case was flat to the cross and at the top of the upper arm. The eyelet allowed an unusual hanger to be put through it, which had the appearance of a 'paper clip'. Through this was worn a neck ribbon of the same colours as those attached to the Second Class award, D.013, but with the difference that this ribbon measured 45 mm in width.

The silver frame that surrounded the iron core in this case was of real silver, which varied in grade from .800 through to .950. This mark is usually found stamped beneath the eyelet on the reverse of the cross. This position sometimes has the maker's mark as well, but this seems to be a more unusual occurrence.

The number of Knights Crosses awarded was approximately 7,318.

Below *Freiherr von Mercken, one of the earliest recipients of the Knights Cross (D.018), photographed in September 1940. On his left breast are the Iron Cross Second Class Bar (D.013), eight-year long service (S.001), Austrian Anschluss (OC.002) and Czech (OC.004) ribbons; on his pocket the Iron Cross First Class (D.016) and below it the Silver Tank Battle Badge (A.004).*

Above *Knights Cross of the Iron Cross (D.018).*
Below *Unterscharführer Remiu Schrynen, a Flemish volunteer in the Waffen SS, wearing his Knights Cross of the Iron Cross (D.018).*

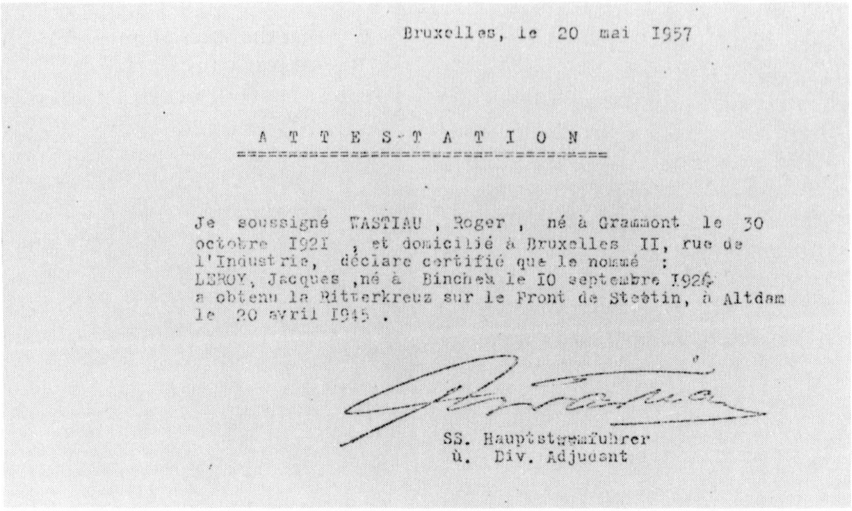

Bruxelles, le 20 mai 1957

A T T E S T A T I O N

Je soussigné WASTIAU , Roger , né à Grammont le 30
octobre 1921 , et domicilié à Bruxelles II, rue de
l'Industrie, déclare certifié que le nommé :
LEROY, Jacques ,né à Binche le 10 septembre 1926,
a obtenu la Ritterkreuz sur le Front de Stettin, à Altdam
le 20 avril 1945 .

SS. Hauptsturmfuhrer
ù. Div. Adjuesnt

Above *Attestation, dated 20 May 1957, from Roger Wastiau, affirming Jacques Leroy's entitlement to the Knights Cross.*

Below *The confirmatory attestation from Leon Degrelle, commander of the SS Wallonien Division, relating to Jacques Leroy's Knights Cross.*

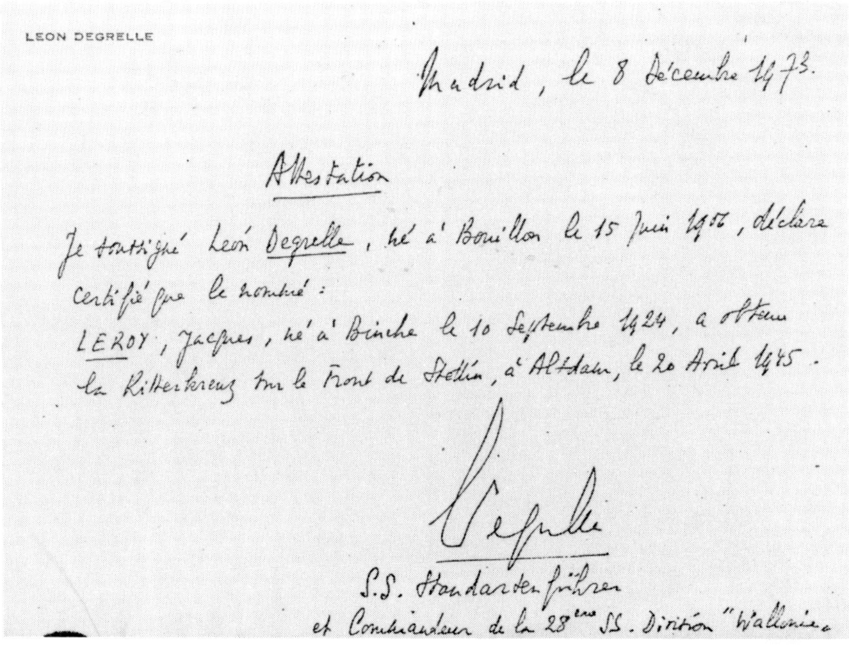

LEON DEGRELLE

Madrid , le 8 Décembre 1973.

Attestation

Je soussigné Leon Degrelle , né à Bouillon le 15 Juin 1906 , déclare
certifié que le nommé :
LEROY, Jacques , né à Binche le 10 Septembre 1924, a obtenu
la Ritterkreuz sur le Front de Stettin, à Altdam, le 20 Avril 1945 .

S.S. Standartenführer
et Commandeur de la 28eme SS. Division "Wallonie"

Again the actual figure is slightly obscure, because of the chaotic conditions prevailing at the end of the war. One good example of this is that of the award to Jacques Leroy, a Belgian SS man who was in the *Wallonien* Division. He had lost his eye and arm and was recovering in hospital when the award of his Knights Cross was made on 20 April 1945. He remustered with his unit, terribly wounded, to continue the fight, but the prestigious award had not been bestowed upon him, nor had he received the preliminary Citation, and worst of all, his name had not been entered on the role of

winners. It was not until 20 May 1957 that the ascertainment was produced to prove his entitlement to the award by the divisional adjutant Roger Wastiau and it was reaffirmed on 8 December 1973 by the famous SS leader and Leroy's commander Leon Degrelle.

The Citation to the award came in two parts. The first part, or preliminary award document, was itself produced in two varieties, either Gothic print and plain print. The actual wording also changed with the rise of the control of the armed forces by Hitler. The first type was printed as 'DER FÜHRER' and the high command of the fighting forces award ..., the second as simply 'DER FÜHRER' award ... At the top of both these types was a facsimile of the Iron Cross, then the title of the medal

Preliminary and full Citations for the award of the Knights Cross to Hauptmann Ferdinand Schneider-Kostalski of Panzer Regiment 6.

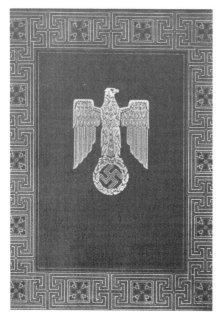

The ornate Citation folder for the award of the Knights Cross to Feldmarschalls.

cross. Beneath this was 'FÜHRER HAUPT QUARTIER', and the date of the award, followed by Hitler's full title. He then signed the award. It is considered that not all the award documents were personally signed by Hitler, but in some cases a facsimile of his signature was employed.

The whole of the Citation was then encased in a red leather folder which was padded on the front binding. On the red leather was a gold embossed eagle. The inside of the cover was white, and on the rear inner edge the gold inlaid name of the artist, Frieda Thiersch, who had produced the leather work. Professor Gerdy Troost had been appointed by Hitler to

Hauptmann Ferdinand Schneider-Kostalski after the award of his Knights Cross. Note he is holding the presentation case in his left hand.

'DAS RITTERKREUZ' and at the bottom the commanding officer's signature with the unit to which he was attached and in the lower left hand corner the stamp of the commander. At this point it is important to point out that Leroy did not receive either of these, nor did every recipient of these Citations receive the full Citation as I now describe.

The full Citation was a beautifully produced document that consisted of a vellum sheet on which was hand worked at the top a golden eagle, then the award wording in black ink and the rank of the recipient. The recipient's name followed in large letters that were executed in fire gilt. Beneath this was the grade of the Iron Cross followed by a facsimile of the

Right *Special presentation case for the Knights Cross of General der Infanterie Bohme, commander of the 7th Gebirgsjäger Division* (D. Plettinick Collection).

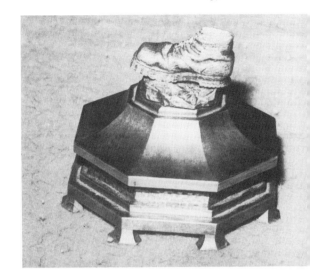

commission the work of the production of this type of document through all the upper grades which will be described in more detail later on in the book, as well as the promotion document covers for all branches of the armed forces. She employed Frieda Thiersch and Franz and Hermann Wandinger to execute the gold inlay work.

Another design of case was produced which was intended for the presentation of the Knights Cross Citation to Generalfeldmarschalls. This consisted of a red leather folder with a similar gold eagle, but in this case it was larger, and surrounded by a broad border, consisting of fourteen boxes containing facsimiles of the cross. These were surrounded by a maze design, which butted up to one another, giving a continuous appearance to the border. If indeed this design was ever presented is unknown, but considering the small number of Generalfeldmarschalls and the opportunity to inspect their personal files, it is probable that it was. So far none have come to light, however. The case that this cross was presented in was a plain black oblong box with a black velvet base which had a recess for the cross to lie in, also a small slit at the top into which the 'paper clip' hanger snugly fit. The portion above this was recessed to allow the neck ribbon to be accommodated lying horizontally across the box. The lid liner was of white satin.

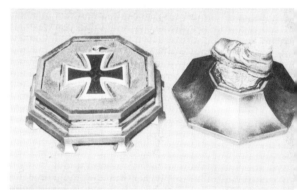

An alternative box was produced at the beginning of the war, which comprised a large red leather box with a large gold hand-embossed eagle on its lid. Round the edge of the lid was a thin gold border. Very few of these were presented; a possible theory is that this type of box was awarded to Generalobersts and above and could have been awarded with the ornate citation case previously described. Generaloberst von Brauchitsch received his Knights Cross on 27 October 1939 in just such a box. He had become on the overthrow of Fritsch, following fabrication of evidence of his improper conduct in 1939, at Rundstedt's suggestion, and the invitation of Hitler, the head of OKH and Commander in Chief of the German army. Hitler would have preferred the avowed pro-Nazi Reichenau, but Rundstedt suggested that 'that appointment would alienate the senior officer corps'. Hitler, not wishing to do this, appointed, reluctantly, Brauchitsch. Hitler had his way by placing the blame on him for the failure to capture Moscow in 1941, dismissed him and assumed the post himself, thus becoming the first civilian to lead the German army. It is at this point that the wording on the citations changed as has already been described.

D.019 Knights Cross of the Iron Cross with Oak Leaves

On 3 June 1940, to reward further acts of bravery, a small cluster of oak leaves was introduced. These were placed through the eyelet of the cross where the 'paper clip' hanger had been. These oak leaves were produced from real silver in grades from .800 to .950, whose hallmarks were stamped on the reverse of the cluster. The reverse could be slightly dished or concave with a piece of silver wire running around, similar to that of the 'paper clip' hanger. This was neatly secured to the reverse, a good guide in distinguishing a reproduction. The ends of the wire were also neatly rounded on the original award pieces. The silver content mark is usually stamped on the left-hand side of the reverse, and sometimes the maker's mark is stamped on the right. But

Knights Cross of the Iron Cross with Oak Leaves (D.019).

Reverse of a rare flat-backed Oak Leaf cluster bearing the silver mark .900.

polished vein in the centre; the outer edges of the leaves were raised and polished also, while the tissue that comprised the inner parts of the veins of the leaves were recessed and pebbled and finished in matt silver. It measured 20 mm × 20 mm. There were 890 awards made and this, unlike the other figures for the Iron Cross series, is an exact one.

The Citation was produced, like the former one, in vellum. This version did not have the Iron Cross drawn upon it, but just had the designation 'DAS EICHENLAUB'. The outer cover in this form was of white calfskin, again padded but instead of the gold stencilled eagle, it had a gilded metal eagle fixed on to it. The box in which the oak leaves were presented was either a small black box with velvet base, with a slit in which to hold the award clip, or a similar box, slightly longer, with a small compartment recessed above the badge to hold a piece of Knights Cross ribbon.

this, again, is more unusual. Very rarely one encounters oak leaves with flat backs and just the silver content stamped .900. These are very rare and desirable.

The obverse comprised three oak leaves in a fan or cluster, one surmounting the other with a broad

D.020 Knights Cross of the Iron Cross with Oak Leaves and Swords

On 15 July 1941 this decoration was introduced to reward continued acts of valour by Knights Cross recipients. The design was basically the same as that of the oak leaves but with a pair of crossed swords attached to the bottom of the cluster. The swords were at a forty degree angle and it was this angle and the finish to the hilts and blades of the swords, that distinguished what are called or known as

tne awarded type, from the jewellers' or private purchase versions.

It is important at this point to dispel some previous misunderstandings regarding the terms 'jeweller's' or 'private purchase' versions. As confirmed in correspondence between the author and Dr Hostert in Ludensheid, the official award requirements stated that the swords should be unfinished on their reverse.

Above *Knights Cross of the Iron Cross with Oak Leaves and Swords (D.020).*

The finished version, known as the 'award type', was both awarded and purchased. An award type was thus peculiar to a specific manufacturer and not produced to government order.

The first type had the sword hilts not touching the blades of the swords. The reverse of the blades and the hilts of the swords were finished in the same way as that which is found on the obverse. The jewellers' type had the balls at the tips of the hilts touching the blades of the respective opposite sword. The reverse was unfinished. The badges were produced from real silver and can be encountered with silver grades ranging from .800 to .950. This, again, is stamped usually in the left-hand upper corner of the badge when viewing it from the reverse, with the

Top *Reverse of the Oak Leaves and Swords cluster with .800 silver mark.*

Above *Cover of the Citation for the award of the Oak Leaves and Swords to Hans Rudel.*

maker's mark on the right. The jewellers' copy usually is found in .800 which is stamped in the position already described and very rarely has the maker's mark. There were a total of 159 awards of this cluster.

The Citation for this award became more exotic in that it was similar to the previous one, again with no Iron Cross motif, but had a metal gilded border which was patterned. The cover was white with a gilded metal eagle and had a gilded patterned border running round its edge. The box for the award was similar to the previous ones described.

D.021 Knights Cross of the Iron Cross with Oak Leaves, Swords and Diamonds

This grade was introduced on 15 July 1941. The basic design was as the oak leaves and swords, but it was produced hollow so that each stone fitted into a hole. This enabled the light to shine through and enhance the fire of the diamonds. The oak leaves had a more pear-shaped appearance with the swords below them, as in the former design. The sword hilts and handles were beset with diamond chippings. The first awards were produced in platinum but this was later changed to silver. The weight of the stones was, on average, 2.7 carats. However, as each of these awards was

Knights Cross of the Iron Cross with Oak Leaves, Swords and Diamonds (D.021). Notice that in this example the cluster is rather pear-shaped and that the blades of the crossed swords do not touch the hilts.

In this example of the Oak Leaves, Swords and Diamonds the cluster is broader and the sword blades do touch the hilts. It is possible that the first example is an early cluster and this a later pattern, or it may be a jeweller dress copy.

individually made, and not all by the same jeweller, that is to say the same craftsman each time let alone the same firm, the appearance of the individual clusters varied quite considerably. The jewellers' copies of this award were also varied, again for the same reasons. The example I examined was produced in .800 silver, the stones being recessed into the oak leaves, the sword hilts did not meet the blades and the hilts were set with chippings. The back was flat and was, in fact, a plate fixed exactly to the edges of the reverse of the oak leaves. This was very neatly done and it requires a good jeweller's glass to notice the join.

There were 27 known recipients: Oberst Werner Mölders, 16 July 1941; Generalleutnant Adolf Galland, 28 January 1942; Major Gordon Golob, 30 August 1942; Hauptmann Hans-Joachim Marseilles, 2 September 1942; Oberst Hermann Graf, 16 September 1942; Generalfeldmarschall Erwin Rommel, 11 March 1943; Kapitän zur See Wolfgang Luth, 9 August 1943; Major Walter Nowotny, 19 October 1943; Generalmajor Adalbert Schulz, 14 November 1943; Oberst Hans-Ulrich Rudel, 1 March 1944; Generalleutnant Hyazinth Graf Strachwitz, 15 April 1944; SS-Obergruppenführer und General der Waffen-SS Herbert Otto Gille, 19 April 1944; Generaloberst Hans Hube, 20 April 1944; Generalfeldmarschall Albert Kesselring, 19 July 1944; Oberstleutnant Helmut Lent, 31 July 1944; SS-Oberstgruppenführer und General Oberst der Waffen-SS Joseph Dietrich, 6

Citation for the Oak Leaves with Swords and Diamonds for Hans Ulrich Rudel.

Cover for the Citation to the Oak Leaves with Swords and Diamonds. The Swastika is studded with diamonds.

August 1944; Generalfeldmarschall
Walter Model, 17 August 1944;
Major Erich Hartmann, 25 August
1944; General der Panzertruppe
Hermann Balck, 31 August 1944;
General der Fallschirmtruppe
Bernard-Herman Ramcke, 20 Sep-
tember 1944; Major Heinz-
Wolfgang Schnaufer, 16 October
1944; Fregattenkapitän Albrecht
Brandi, 24 November 1944; General-
feldmarschall Ferdinand Schörner, 1
January 1945; General der Panzer-
truppe Hasso Eccard von Manteuf-
fel, 18 February 1945; Generalmajor
Theodor Tolsdorff, 18 March 1945;
Generalleutnant Dr Karl Maus, 15
April 1945; and General der Panzer-
truppe Dietrich von Saucken, 9 May
1945.

The Citation in this case has all the
lettering produced in fire gilt and is

superbly finished throughout. It,
again, has a border of stamped gilded
metal, but in this instance the design
is more ornate. The outer case comes
in three colours, blue for the Luftwaffe, a darker blue for the Kriegsmarine and morocco for the Heer and
SS. The eagle again is made of gilded
metal, but in this case the Swastika is
studded with small diamonds. The
outer metal frame is once more
gilded and the design was fretted out
to allow the colour of the leather to
show through the holes. This document was, in my opinion, one of the
most attractively designed of any produced for any grade of medal during
the period of the Third Reich. The
presentation box was the same as the
one for the former types of 'add-on'
awards to the Knights Cross.

D.022 Knights Cross of the Iron Cross with Golden Oak Leaves, Swords and Diamonds

On 1 January 1945, to reward probably the most unusual flying personality of any country, Hitler introduced
the highest grade of 'add-ons'. The
original idea was that it should be
limited to twelve recipients, but at
this late time in the war events over-
took actions, and only one award was
rendered. That was to Oberst Hans
Ulrich Rudel. His score of kills was
incredibly impressive, as was the
number of missions that he flew,
which amounted to 2,530 (although
it is estimated that he flew a few more
even than this). On later missions he
flew with only one leg, as his other leg

had been amputated after a crash.

The badge was identical to the
diamond award, D.021, except that it
was produced in 18-carat gold. The
firm that produced them was Godet
and Son of Berlin, and it is reported
that they manufactured six examples.
More than two were definitely made,
as Rudel had two examples in his
possession at the end of the war. In
correspondence with him, he did not
make it clear why he had two examples. One story is that Hitler gave him
one set and Göring gave him the
other, feeling that Rudel was his
greatest ace and it was his preroga-

Golden Oak Leaves, Swords and Diamonds to the Knights Cross of the Iron Cross awarded to Hans Rudel (D.022).

tive, as Reischmarschall of the Third Reich and Commander in Chief of the Luftwaffe, to present Rudel with this decoration. Göring had personally decorated Rudel with the Air-to-Ground Operational Flying Clasp with Diamonds, L.060, in April 1944 when he had completed his 2,000th mission.

Rudel also stated that he did not receive a Citation for the award, but that it was promised to be awarded to him when it was finished and in the fullness of time.

The badge was presented again in the same small black box in which the other 'add-ons' were awarded.

D.023 Star of the Grand Cross of the Iron Cross

Little is known of this award and it is considered to be but a prototype. An

Star of the Grand Cross of the Iron Cross (D.023).

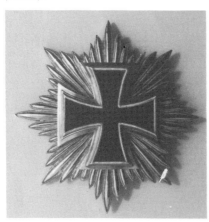

example of this star was found at the end of the war in Austria. The star consisted of an eight-pointed breast order, with an Iron Cross First Class surmounting the star. Each arm, or ray, was formed on the outer edge by a row of dots, with the centre portion of the rays rising at the middle. The rays widened from th ᵓcentre where the Iron Cross was positioned, then slimmed to points where they radiated from that centre. The reverse was plain, save for four rivets that held the cross to the star. The hinge was raised and was of the same type that is found on the reverse of Breast Stars of the Eagle Order. The pin was of a hand-drawn type, underneath which is found the maker's name, hand-engraved, which was Rath of Munich. The star was gold-plated

Above *Spanish Cross With Swords — Bronze (S.001).*

Above right *Spanish Cross without Swords — Silver (S.005).*

Right *Spanish Cross in Gold with Diamonds (S.006). L. Hopcraft Ailsby collection.*

Below *Cross of Honour for the Relatives of the Dead in Spain (S.008).*

Below right *Spanish Wound Badge — Black Class (S.014).*

Above *Iron Cross — Second Class (D.013).
Makers mark on ring — 65.*

Above *Iron Cross — Second Class 1939 Bar
— First Type (D.014).*

Below *Hans Rudel's complete collection of
medals.* **Top left** *One of the two sets of
Golden Oak Leaves, Swords and Diamonds
with which he was awarded.* **Centre top**
*Knights Cross of the Iron Cross with Golden
Oak Leaves, Swords and Diamonds
(D.022).* **Top right** *Oak Leaves, Swords
and Diamonds (D.021).*

Centre left *Oak leaves (D.019).* **Centre
right** *Oak Leaves and Swords (D.020).*
Bottom left *Combined Pilots and Obser-
vers Badge in Gold with Diamonds (L.004).*
Bottom centre *Air-to-Ground Support
Operational Flying Clasp — Diamonds
Class (L.060).* **Bottom right** *German
Cross in Gold (D.025).*

Above *Knights Cross of the Iron Cross (D.018).*

Above right *Knights Cross of the Iron Cross with Oak Leaves (D.019).*

Right *Wound Badge 1939 — Gold Class (D.003).*

Below *Iron Cross — First Class (D.016).*

Below right *Iron Cross — First Class 1939 Bar (D.017).*

Above left *Citation for the Oak Leaves with Swords and Diamonds for Hans Ulrich Rudel.*

Above *Cover for the Citation to the Oak Leaves with Swords and Diamonds. The Swastika is studded with diamonds.*

Left *Golden Oak Leaves, Swords and Diamonds to the Knights Cross of the Iron Cross awarded to Hans Rudel (D.022).*

Below left *Star of the Grand Cross of the Iron Cross (D.023).*

Below *German Cross in Gold (D.025).*

and highly polished. It has been stated that only one example has been encountered, and the description of this star is from that example, which now resides in the West Point Museum in America. However, the author knows of two other examples, but unfortunately at the time of writing has not been able to examine these to find out if they are similar to the one described, or of any notable difference.

The case in which the badge was awarded was a large red leather box with a gold eagle embossed on its lid. There was also an embroidered wire version of this star, but little is known of this particular piece although it is reported that there are other examples in existence in other collections. The originality and reason for it are unknown to this author.

D.024 Grand Cross of the Iron Cross

This cross was instituted on 1 September 1939 and was identical in every respect to the Iron Cross Second Class, D.013, save for its size which was 63 mm × 63 mm. It was suspended from a neck ribbon which was correspondingly larger than that of the Knights Cross ribbon, and was 57 mm wide. Originally the silver rim that surrounded the iron core was to have been changed to one of gold, but this idea was stillborn, and the medal was produced with a silver one, as had been the case of the Grand Crosses of 1813, 1870 and 1914. The only recipient of the Grand Cross was Hermann Göring who received it for the Luftwaffe's success in the Battle of France and that of the Low Countries in 1940. The award was thus rendered for those services on 19 July 1940.

The original award was lost when Göring's house was destroyed in a bombing raid on Berlin, but he had a number of copies, most of these being made by the firm of Godet and Son of Berlin. It is also reported that he had one copy made with a platinum rim. The truth of this story is unknown but his love of medals and regalia would not bring one to disbelieve it. Another story was that he had one made with an onyx core. All the stories that surround the Reichmarschall's eccentricities are possible, being borne out by the fact that he had an exact copy of his wedding sword, which had been presented to him by the Luftwaffe as a recognition

Grand Cross of the Iron Cross (D.024) (Forman Collection, Picadilly)

Citation for the Grand Cross of the Iron Cross for Hermann Goring. The photo was taken before it was signed by Hitler.

Cover to the Citation of the Grand Cross of the Iron Cross. The Swastika is set with diamonds.

of the esteem in which they held him, but had changed the contours of the grips and had made it in light weight, so that he could identify one example from the other.

The Citation was similar to that of the one with diamonds, but in this case his title and name were much larger, possibly to match the stature of his figure!

The outer case was a magnificent work of art. The eagle was again holding a Swastika which was set with diamonds. The frame that went around the case was again similar to that found on the diamond case, but was set with thirty red stones. Whether these were rubies or garnets is not known. Round each red stone were set eight diamond chips, giving in total 240 diamond chips. The presentation box was of red leather, with a black velvet base with a recess in which the cross was held. The inner liner was of white satin.

D.025 German Cross in Gold

This breast star was introduced on 28 September 1941 and was to recognize bravery of the fighting forces above that which was required for the bestowal of the Iron Cross First Class (D.016), but not up to that required for the award of the Knights Cross (D.018). It was a useful award in the fact that it could be bestowed upon a Knights Cross winner, if he had not already won it, to show further appreciation of his valour. This is borne out by the example of the award of this cross to Max Simon, who had received the Knights Cross in October 1941 and was awarded this medal at the end of 1943. Equally, it could be awarded from the Iron Cross First Class (D.016) if it had not been enough to warrant the Knights Cross (D.018). The idea that this was an intermediate award of the Iron Cross grading is erroneous, though. In fact it was really a half-way house, running in tandem to the Iron Cross.

The star was designed by Professor Klein and consisted of a large enamelled Swastika in black, which was outlined in gold. This was on a silver field around the edge of which ran a thin red line. Adjacent to this line was a wreath in gold which was made up of laurel leaves wound round with silk ties. At the base was a box with the year of instigation, 1941, impressed into it. From this wreath

emanated rays which covered the eight points of the star. These rays were chemically oxidized black. Beneath this was the gold back plate, which took the outline of the edge of the badge and the rays which have already been described, but the back plate slightly protruded from the rays, which gives to the badge an overall three-dimensional effect.

The reverse was normally slightly convex with four ball rivets, but it is also known in another variety which had six smaller ball rivets and is known as the Austrian type. It had a massive hinge, pin and hook which in some cases have the maker's mark on them, and the better examples are found with the maker's number 1, 4 or 21. The number of badges awarded was approximately 30,000, of which the army and Waffen-SS received approximately 17,000, the Luftwaffe and navy receiving approximately 13,000.

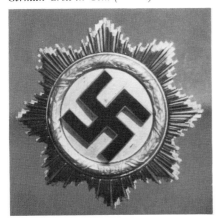

German Cross in Gold (D.025).

Reverse of the German Cross in Gold awarded to Major Walter Pössl; this is of the six-riveted Austrian type.

The badge came with a Citation. Like the Knights Cross citation it was first issued in a preliminary version. This was a small piece of paper and had a facsimile of the badge printed in black at the top, with the grade of the badge in the centre and the commander of the high command facsimile signature at the bottom, with the stamp in the lower left-hand corner.

The formal Citation was a much grander affair, being larger with a finely printed facsimile of the badge at its top in three colours, the grade of the award in the centre and the commanding officer's signature and unit at the bottom. The box in which the medal was awarded was a square black one, with a black velvet base and white silk lining.

D.026 German Cross in Gold with Diamonds

This was produced by the firm of Rath of Munich and approximately twenty examples were manufactured. The only difference compared with the former badge was that the wreath was set with a great number of small diamonds. The reverse was similar and was of the six-rivet Austrian-type construction. The pin had the maker's name engraved on the top of it, so

that it can be seen, or read, when the badge is looked at from the reverse. The box was a red square one with a black velvet base, with white silk lid lining. On this lining, at the bottom in gold, is the maker's name, Rath-Munchen. The lid had a gold eagle stencilled into it. As this was a prototype or unawarded order, there is no Citation to accompany it.

German Cross in Gold with Diamonds (D.026) (J.R. Angolia).

Reverse of the German Cross in Gold with Diamonds showing the maker's name, RATH MÜNCHEN, on the pin.

Presentation case for the German Cross in Gold with Diamonds (Philip C. Faber).

German Cross in Gold — Cloth Version — Air Force Blue (D.027).

D.027 German Cross in Gold—Cloth Version—Air Force Blue
D.028 German Cross in Gold—Cloth Version—Navy Blue
D.029 German Cross in Gold—Cloth Version—Field Grey

This badge was produced purely for 'in the field' use and comprised a black silk embroidered Swastika, outlined in gold wire cord. This had the metal wreath that had been used in the construction of the metal badge, fixed to the backing. Round the outer edge of the wreath was another circle of gold wire, from which emanated embroidered rays with white tips. The backing of the badge on to which the embroidery and metal wreath were applied was in the corresponding colours of the various branches of the Services referred to in the numbering of this section.

D.030 German Cross in Silver

This medal was exactly the same as the German Cross in Gold, D.025, save for the wreath which in this case was silver, and it was instigated on the same date as the former medal, 28 September 1941. This badge was rendered for the conduct of the war and for significant acts of leadership

German Cross in Silver (D.030).

that furthered the war effort, rather than for bravery, and fitted nicely into the War Merit Cross series. Because of these award criteria the medal is much rarer in this form than the gold version. Contrary to popular belief both grades could be worn together, but this was a most unusual occurrence.

The reverse again had normally four ball rivets, but a six-ball version known as the Austrian type also existed. However, the six-ball rivets were smaller in this version. Approximately 1,200 badges were awarded, the army and Waffen SS receiving 900, the Luftwaffe and navy 300.

The badge was awarded with two Citations, the smaller preliminary one and the larger formal one. Both of these have already been fully described, the only difference being in the colour of the badge on the large document. The wreath was silver in this case. The box again was identical to the one previously described.

D.031 German Cross in Silver—Cloth Version—Air Force Blue
D.032 German Cross in Silver—Cloth Version—Navy Blue
D.033 German Cross in Silver—Cloth Version—Field Grey

These three badges were identical in all respects to the cloth versions of the German Cross in Gold but were embroidered in silver wire cord, the central wreath also being silver and containing the date of institution, 1941.

D.034 War Merit Medal

For neatness of collecting I have put this medal out of chronological order of instigation, but I hope the reader will forgive this foible. The medal was designed by Richard Klein of Munich, and was introduced on 19 August 1940. It comprised a round medal with a facsimile of the War

Merit Cross without swords on the obverse, and on the reverse 'FUR KRIEGS VERDIENST 1939'. The medal was made of bronze and was usually very well produced.

It was introduced for the reward of civilians who were aiding the war effort. It was also conferable upon non-Germans engaged in Germany's war effort, although this was changed on 15 May 1943 with the non-Germans being awarded the Eagle Order Medal either in the Bronze or Silver class (this order will be fully described in a subsequent volume which will cover political awards). The medal was suspended from a ribbon comprising of stripes made up of red, white, broad black with a red central line, white and red. It was issued with a Citation which was a simple white paper affair that came in many varieties. The container in which the badge was issued was either a blue, brick red or buff packet with the name printed on the front in black.

War Merit Medal (D.034).

D.035 War Merit Cross—Second Class—Bronze without Swords

On 18 October 1939 Hitler introduced a range of medals which also included D.036, D.039 and D.040, and the relationship and orders which governed their award and production will be described here to avoid later repetition. Hitler required a series of awards basically to replace the non-combatants' version of the Iron Cross, but in doing so he wished to enlarge on the method of rewarding the recipients, because he realized, due to his own experiences

in the First World War and those gained in the Spanish Civil War 1936–1939, that the scope of that grade of the Iron Cross would not fully cover the modern requirements of a fully mechanized war.

The award was to be rendered to civilians as well as to military personnel who performed outstanding service in the furtherance of the war effort, centring around bravery and service not in direct connection with military combat. For this purpose the

War Merit Cross — Second Class — Bronze without Swords (D.035).

crosses came, in all grades, with and without swords. The version without swords was awarded for service in the furtherance of the war effort and those with swords for bravery not directly connected to front-line activities. This bravery, in fact, could be of a much higher standard than that required in the front line, considering that most of these recipients would not have been fired up by the smell of battle.

Originally Hitler had decreed that neither of the grades of the War Merit Cross, that is to say First and Second Class, with or without Swords, could be worn with the corresponding grade of the Iron Cross. This regulation was rescinded on 28 September

1941, permitting the wearing of all the grades of both types with the relevant grades of the Iron Cross, but below or behind it in precedence of wear.

It was necessary to have had the Second Class awarded before the First Class could be rendered, but in exceptional cases, both grades could be conferred upon the recipient simultaneously. The War Merit Cross could be awarded to a firm or company, for example a munitions factory or shipyard. These came under the German Labour Front and were organized along military lines. The German Labour Front was responsible for this type of decoration, having awarded since 1 September 1936 Golden Flags as emblems of the efficiency of an individual company. The firm's flag could have an emblem attached to it to show that it and its workers had received a factory citation. The flag comprised a silk red banner, with a large black cog wheel in stylized form in the centre, the emblem of the DAF. In the centre, which was white, was a Swastika. The flag was fringed with silver fringing, and in the right-hand upper corner was embroidered a silver bullion War Merit Cross First Class.

The medal took the form of a Maltese Cross with a border round the edge. The field between these borders was pebbled. The centre of the cross had a stylized oak leaf wreath, with a tie at the bottom. In this, on the obverse, was a raised Swastika and in the matching position on the reverse a raised '1939'. The field behind both this reverse and obverse design was plain.

At the upper arm of the cross was

an eyelet with a ring through which the ribbon was suspended. This ribbon was of stripes of brick red, white, broad black, white and red, the reverse of the Iron Cross Second Class colours. It is estimated that 1,591,567 crosses were awarded during the period of the Second World War. The cross was awarded with a Citation that could come in a number of forms, several having a facsimile of the cross at their top. The Citations were signed by the relevant commander of military forces, or civilian authority that had awarded them. The medal was presented in a buff, blue or brick red packet, with the name and class of the cross printed on its front.

D.036 War Merit Cross—First Class—Silver without Swords

This cross was identical to the former in design and was introduced on the same date by Hitler, but the obverse was finished in a silver wash. The reverse was plain and silver-washed as well but had a large pin and hook construction. Often the maker's number was stamped in the centre of the reverse. The quality of the badge varied quite tremendously as did the material in which it was produced, which could range from real silver, usually .800 standard, through to pot or monkey metal. The hinge in some

War Merit Cross — First Class — Silver without Swords (D.036).

Citation of the War Merit Cross — First Class — Silver without Swords to William Joyce, 'Lord Haw-Haw'.

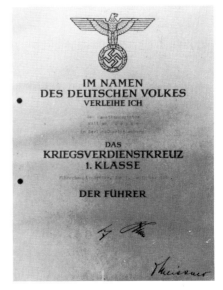

IM NAMEN
DES DEUTSCHEN VOLKES
VERLEIHE ICH

DAS
KRIEGSVERDIENSTKREUZ
1. KLASSE

DER FÜHRER

cases was exchanged for a screw post and large screw cap similar to that found on the Iron Cross First Class, D.016. One interesting recipient of this grade was William Joyce, 'Lord Haw-Haw', who received the cross for his propaganda broadcasts in September 1944. It is estimated that 91,239 awards of this cross were rendered during the period of the Second World War.

The cross was awarded with a Citation which came again in a number of varieties, signed by the relevant military or civilian authority. The box in which it was awarded, considering the number of awards, was of remarkable quality, and was black simulated leather, with a black inside lower base, with a slit to allow the badge hinge to be accommodated. The upper inner lid lining was of off-white satin or silk. The top of the outer lid of the box had either the silhouette of the badge, or a representative copy of the badge, stencilled into it.

D.037 War Merit Cross—Knights Cross—Silver without Swords

On 19 August 1940 this cross was introduced to reward the high achievements of the civilian population, civil service and political formations. It took the basic design of the War Merit Cross Second Class but was larger and usually produced in genuine silver, with silver grade ranging from .800 through to .950, but in some examples the cross was but silver-plated and these just have the maker's number on the lower arm. The upper arm had attached to it an inverted V with an eyelet at its apex. Through this eyelet was a ribbed hanger which supported the cross on the neck ribbon. As with all Knights Crosses it was worn around the neck. The ribbon was formed from stripes of red, white, broad black, white and red, and in those examples of the cross that were awarded, the ends of the ribbon had the ends turned over into a triangle, with a length of minute ribbon at each end to act as ties to secure the ribbon around the neck of the recipient.

It is very important at this point to expel a theory that has been in existence for some time, that this version came with only a plain hanger. It is, in fact, found with both *ribbed* and *plain* varieties, not only that, they are not all as long as one another. This is a new and very interesting point. If a recipient had a short neck, he required a shorter hanger for comfort. If one had a number of neck decorations (General Stopf, for example had both the Knights Cross of the Iron Cross, D.019, and the Knights Cross of the War Merit Cross with Swords, D.041) the hangers had to be adjusted for the wearer's comfort, for there was no undress version for wear for either of these orders, as had been the case of the earlier Pour Le Mérite which a number of staff officers had won in the First World War and had to wear with their Second World War counterparts.

War Merit Cross — Knights Cross — Silver without Swords (D.037). Note the ribbed hanger in this version.

Great ceremony was employed with the award of the Knights Cross decorations and the recipient was usually accompanied at the ceremony by a Knights Cross winner. Only 137 awards were rendered of this decoration, which made it very prestigious in the eyes of the Nazi hierarchy. Hitler, in fact, circulated a letter from his headquarters on 27 August 1943, outlining the criteria for award and the philosophy surrounding it and directed that 'prominent Party comrades' were not to be honoured with this decoration—a definite jibe at Reichmarschall Hermann Göring, who had coveted the award of the Knights Cross of the War Merit Cross with Swords, D.041.

It was rendered with an award Citation and was presented in a black box, with an inside black velvet base, which had a round recess into which the cross and hanger fitted. The upper part of the box above this recess was indented to accommodate the neck ribbon.

D.038 War Merit Cross—Knights Cross—Gold without Swords

On 8 July 1944 Hitler introduced this last and highest grade of the order, which was to all intents and purposes identical in every respect to the silver grade, D.037, except that it was produced only in real silver and the cross itself was then gold-plated. It had the silver grade stamped on the bottom of the lower edge of the V of the lowest arm of the cross. Only twelve awards were rendered of this decoration, which was presented with a Citation and in a black box similar to the one formerly described for D.037. Known recipients were Franz Hahne and Karl Otto Saur.

D.039 War Merit Cross—Second Class—Bronze with Swords

This cross was instituted on 18 October 1939 by Hitler and was identical in every respect to D.035 apart for the addition of swords which passed through the quadrants of the cross. These swords were

broad-bladed and double edged of the Roman Centurion or military design. This cross was awarded for bravery which occurred not in the face of the enemy. It is estimated that 6,134,950 awards of this cross were conferred during the period of the Second World War. It was awarded with a Citation which came in various forms and was presented in a packet that was either blue, brick red or buff, with the name of the order and its derivation printed on the front.

War Merit Cross — Second Class — Bronze with Swords (D.039).

D.040 War Merit Cross—First Class—Silver with Swords

This cross is identical to D.036, with the exception that it had the swords added to the cross through the quadrants of its arms. The reverse of the swords was plain, as was the rest of the reverse of the cross which had only, in some instances, the maker's number stamped in the centre.

This cross was awarded for bravery which occurred not in the face of the enemy, and it is estimated that 483,603 were rendered during the period of the Second World War. It was awarded with a Citation which was assigned as before by either the relevant military or civilian authority. It was presented in a black box, with a black base liner which had a slit to accommodate the pin as in the previous types. A screw post and screw plate was in some cases substituted for the pin. In these instances the

award boxes were recessed to accommodate this type of fastening. The lid liner was of white satin while the box top had either a silhouette or facsim-

War Merit Cross — First Class — Silver with Swords (D.040).

ile of the cross stencilled on to it in silver.

Hitler personally presented this decoration in 1942 to Konstantine Hierl, who was the leader or Reichs-arbeitsführer of the Reichsarbeits-dienstes. The point of interest is that the document cover that housed the citation for this award was similar to that of the Knight's Cross of the Iron Cross, D.018. It had on the cover the same design of a large downswept eagle which was embossed in gold. The folder was thick, as was that of the protected cover of the Knights Cross document. The design and present whereabouts of the actual inner liner and the Citation which was contained inside are unknown to this author. It is possible that it was unique to Hierl or this could have been the method of presentation to high ranking Generals and party leaders.

Hitler presenting Reich's Labour Leader Konstantine Hierl with the War Merit Cross — First Class — Silver with Swords (D.040). Note that the Citation is contained in an elaborate folder similar to those of the Knights Cross.

D.041 War Merit Cross—Knights Cross—Silver with Swords

This cross was identical to D.037, as was its date of institution, save that it had the swords added. They were the same as those described in D.039, the cross being produced in genuine silver with the grade from .800 through to .950, and sometimes the maker's mark being situated on the lower arm of the cross in the recess of the V, as in the former described position. It is estimated that 118 of

War Merit Cross — Knights Cross — Silver with Swords (D.041). Note original neckties.

these Knights Crosses were awarded during the period of the Second World War. The decoration was awarded with a Citation and was contained in a box that has already been described in D.037.

D.042 War Merit Cross—Knights Cross—Gold with Swords

This was also identical to D.037, with the addition of swords. The cross was produced only in genuine silver of grade .800 through to .950, and was gold-plated. The silver mark was situated in the lower arm in the underside of the V of that arm, as was the maker's stamp. It is estimated that this award was rendered only nine times, making it one of the rarest decorations of the Third Reich, although a considerably greater number of crosses was produced than were awarded. It was rendered with an award Citation, and was presented in a black box as previously described in D.037.

D.043 Role of Honour Clasp—Army

On 30 January 1944 Hitler instigated this clasp to reward members of the army and Waffen-SS who had been entered on the 'Honour Roll of the German Army'. This roll had been started in July 1941, to record the honourable and heroic deeds carried out by its members, but no tangible evidence of these apart from the roll existed. The clasp filled this purpose, being an outward show of inclusion on the honour roll. It comprised a finely gilded and stamped wreath of oak leaves, with a ribbon and tie at its base and a large square Swastika in its centre. The badge was finely executed and gave a definite three-dimensional appearance. The reverse took the outline exactly in negative of the obverse, being stamped. It had four pins to enable it to be secured to a piece of Iron Cross ribbon, Second Class. Approximately 4,556 awards of this clasp were rendered to the end of hostilities, making it a comparatively rare decoration. From the collector's point of view, the smallness of its size and the way that it was attached to the

Roll of Honour Clasp — Army (D.043).

tunic has made it a very difficult award to obtain.

It was presented with a Citation and was contained in a small black oblong box with a cream flocked base on which the badge sat, with the ends of the Iron Cross ribbon being tucked underneath the bed that produced the base. The lid lining was of white silk.

Hauptmann Ferdinand Frecy wearing the Roll of Honour Clasp (D.043) on its Iron Cross Second Class ribbon from his tunic button. Among his many other decorations visible are the Knights Cross of the Iron Cross (D.018), Iron Cross First Class (D.016), Infantry Assault and Wound Badges in Silver (A.002 and D.002), German Cross in Gold (D.025) and Close Combat Clasp in Bronze (A.023), as well as four Silver Badges for the Single-handed destruction of a tank (A.036).

D.044 Roll of Honour Clasp—Navy

On 13 May 1944 Grandadmiral Donitz instituted the naval version of the Honour Clasp to recognize those members of the navy who had been entered on the 'Honour Roll of the German Navy' which had been opened in February 1943. The badge was produced in a similar manner to D.043 but the gilt wreath was slightly larger and the oak leaves that comprised the gilded wreath were continuous. The central motif was an anchor surmounted by a Swastika. The reverse took the negative design of the obverse, being stamped, and had four fine prongs to attach it to the Iron Cross Second Class ribbon. It was presented with a Citation and was awarded in a black oblong box, whose base was blue flocked, while

Roll of Honour Clasp — Navy (D.044).

the lining was white silk. There are no exact estimations of the number of this type of honour clasp awarded, but it is the hardest of the three to obtain for one's collection.

D.045 Roll of Honour Clasp—Air Force

Roll of Honour Clasp — Air Force (D.045).

The first recorded instance of this clasp being awarded was 5 August 1944. Göring, in his inimitable way, did not want to be outdone by the other two Services and had belatedly introduced in 1944 the 'Honour Roll' of the German Air Force. The badge was again a gilt metal wreath of oak leaves which, in this case, had a rough appearance with the outline of the oak leaves making the border. In the centre was a flying Luftwaffe eagle, clutching in its talons a Swastika. The reverse was again the negative of the obverse, being stamped, with four lugs for the attachment to the Iron Cross Second Class ribbon. It is possible that over 30,000 clasps were rendered during the period of the war, making it quite a common award. It was awarded with a Citation and was presented in a black oblong box with an off-blue flocked base and white silk lid liner.

D.046 Medal for the Winter Campaign in Russia—1941-1942

On 26 May 1942 Hitler introduced a medal for the campaign in Russia. It comprised a round medal with, at its top, a stick genade surmounted by a German steel helmet. Round the edge of the medal was a recessed rim of approximately 1 mm. At this point there was a small lip which ran right round the medal, as a border for the central motif. The helmet and rim, on both the reverse and obverse, were silvered. The obverse was concave from the lip on the rim, and on this field was a closed winged eagle standing on a square Swastika which surmounted a branch of leaves. The whole of the design was blackened. The reverse from the rim was convex, again blackened, with, in capital letters, 'WINTERSCHLACHT', and in larger ones 'IM OSTEN' and finally the date, 1941/42. At the base was a broad-bladed sword, crossed with a branch of leaves similar to that found on the obverse.

The medal had been created by SS Unterscharführer Ernst Kraus, and I consider it to be one of the best designed of the whole series of combat awards. The period of qualification for this award was from 15 November 1941 to 15 April 1942 and, by order of the OKW, consideration for rendering of the award ceased on 4 September 1944. The region that this campaign medal was to represent stretched eastwards of the Ukraine and Ostland, or east of

the Finnish-Russian border of 1940, known as the operational area 'Finnland'.

The persons entitled to the award were:

1) Military personnel and civilians to include female personnel who were in the service of the armed forces.
2) Administration personnel.
3) Personnel killed or listed as missing in action.
4) Foreign volunteers serving in the Wehrmacht provided that the award was recommended by a divisional commander or more senior officer.
5) Civilians working in factories in the aforementioned region.

The Criteria for the award were:

Medal for the Winter Campaign in Russia — 1941-1942 (D.046).

Citation to Georg Müller for the Medal for the Winter Campaign in Russia or Ostmedaille.

1) To have been engaged in combat in the theatre of operations for two weeks.
2) Sixty days to have been spent continuously in the combat theatre of operations.
3) To have been wounded in that combat zone.
4) To have been frost-bitten for which a wound badge was awarded. (Frost-bite in Russia was very severe and this was the only occasion that a wound badge or medal could be awarded for a non-militarily or aggressively inflicted wound.)

For Luftwaffe personnel the Criterion was:

To have spent thirty days over enemy territory.

The badge was awarded with a Citation which came in various designs, and was presented in a paper packet which was either brick red, blue or buff, with the name printed on the front.

D.047 Führer Commendation Certificate

This was a paper Citation that had no outward sign of award, but after the introduction of the Honour Roll Clasp it is supposed that the recipients of the award received the equivalent clasp. It consisted of a piece of paper with a large gold eagle at its top, the details of the action and the Führer's thanks, his title and signature. The State seal is to be found in the lower left-hand corner.

Introduction to cuff bands

The German army had used cuff titles or cuff bands for a considerable time as a means of honouring a particular regiment or division. This can be illustrated by the Gibraltar Cuff Title, which had been awarded to the Hannoverian 73rd Fusiliers, 79th Infantry and 10th Jaeger Battalion which had been involved in the defence of Gibraltar, and who had been besieged by the combined armies of France and Spain from 21 June 1779 to 2 February 1783. The command of the garrison was under that of General Picton and then General Eliott and the defence was carried out by 7,000 British and Hannoverian troops. The British formations comprised the Suffolk, Dorsetshire, Essex and Northamptonshire Regiments, who were later entitled to an incorporation into their cap badge of the Gibraltar Castle or, in words, 'Gibraltar' as well. The Seaforth Highlanders and Royal Artillery who were also involved bear no visible reward for their participation, while the detachments of Royal Marines which served there during this period entitled the whole regiment to the title 'Gibraltar', which is worn on the brass belt buckle. The Hannoverians were also awarded by

General Eliott, at his own expense, a silver medal that was produced by the famous Georgian designer L. Pingo, who was incidentally responsible for the design of gold coins for George III.

The Kingdom of Hannover under George V, who had sided with Austria, came to an end in 1866 when Prussia defeated both Austria and Hannover and the Hannoverian army was absorbed into that of Prussia, as was the Hannoverian State. Along with this incorporation went the battle honours of her forces, so in the Great War units which had been as one, with the same battle honours, faced each other in the trenches.

The Nazis extended the award of cuff titles, the first major one being the 'Stosstrupp Adolf Hitler 1923', which was to commemorate the former members of the 1923 Stosstrupp. The number of these titles became legion and commemorated a wide variety of martyrs to the Nazi cause and traditional heroes of the army, Waffen-SS and Luftwaffe. The navy was the only branch of the armed forces that did not award cuff titles, possibly because of their use of cap tallies. However, they did use the many varieties of informative cuff

Typical examples of SS cuff titles: Thürin-
gen *and* Prinz Eugen *are officers' pattern
showing the two basic lettering styles,* Wiking
*is RZM pattern. SS-Oberscharfuhrer
Fredrich Olesh was the first recipient of the*
Prinz Eugen *title.*

bands that also abounded during this
period. The cuff titles described in
this section, and the one in the Spanish Civil War section, S.011 and
S.012, are the only ones that in fact
became campaign honours, and were
to be worn as such on the sleeve of
any military, paramilitary or party
uniform. The wearing of two cuff
titles at any one time was normally
prohibited, but in the case of the
campaign bands the rule was rescinded. (In parenthesese, it should be
noted that it *was* possible to wear two

of the other cuff titles in certain
circumstances, a 'Headquarters' cuff
title above an SS one for example, but
two SS cuff titles could not be worn
at the same time. An officer from a
crack division such as *Das Reich* who
was transferred to the *Prinz Eugen*
could not wear both their cuff titles,
which often had been the case until
the regulation forbidding this practice was brought into existence. For
an officer who had earned his cuff
title with the crack unit, having to
exchange it for a second-rate one
came as quite a considerable blow.
This was especially true if one had
identified personally with the particular hero who had been honoured, as
often was the case in the Waffen-SS.

When the news of the near annihilation of Sepp Dietrich's units Leib-standarte *Adolf Hitler, Das Reich, Totenkopf* and *Hohenstaufen* in Vienna reached the ears of Hitler, realizing that his order not to lose the city to the Russians had not been obeyed, he erupted in wild fury. To add to his horror, his crack SS units, completely exhausted and their will to fight nearly totally diminished, had taken refuge in the city. Hitler cancelled all promotions that he had given on 20 April 1945, which was his birthday, ordering that all the surviving members of those units must remove their prized cuff titles. Dietrich on hearing the order, summoned the four commanders of those units, SS-Brigadeführer and Generalmajor der Waffen SS Otto Kumm, SS-Standartenführer Karl Kreutz, SS-Brigadeführer and Generalmajor der Waffen SS Hellmuth Becker and SS-Brigadeführer and Generalmajor der Waffen SS Sylvester Stadler to a conference at his headquarters in Vienna. Dietrich stated categorically that not a single cuff title was to be removed and retorted to his commanders. 'There's your reward for all that you have done these past five years'. He sent a stiff reply to Hitler's headquarters refusing to implement the order. A very interesting story abounds that at the same time he packed up his own decorations in a chamber pot and sent them off to Hitler with his reply. Whether this is true is unknown, but illustrates Dietrich's feelings at the time.

Index to Campaign Cuff Titles

C.001 'Kreta' Commemorative Cuff Title   89
C.002 'Afrika' Commemorative Cuff Title   90
C.003 'Metz 1944' Commemorative Cuff Title   93
C.004 'Kurland' Commemorative Cuff Title   94

C.001 'Kreta' Commemorative Cuff Title

On 16 October 1942 this award was introduced to reward all personnel of the army, navy and Luftwaffe who had participated or helped in the capture of the island of Crete, which had been defended by British and Empire forces. This cuff band takes the form of a white cotton strip, 33 mm wide, with a border of yellow cotton. In the middle of the borders in capital letters, is embroidered the name 'KRETA'. Either side of the name title is a sprig of Acanthus in a stylized pattern. It is important to note at this point, that in the past reference works have only recognized that the material in which the band was produced was off-white cotton. There was, however, a variation, of which original examples may be found, produced on a felt off-white strip. These examples are very scarce and must be very carefully scrutinized and great caution must be exercised

Two examples of the 'Kreta' Commemorative Cuff Title, the top one in felt and the lower one cotton (C.001).

when deciding the originality, as a number of reproductions of this award have been produced in this material.

The award was to have been worn on all uniforms to include the overcoat or greatcoat. The date of termination for the award of this cuff title was 31 October 1944.

The Criteria for the award were:
1) To have been engaged in a glider or parachute landing, between the dates of 20 and 27 May 1941 on the island of Crete.
2) To have been engaged in air operations over Crete during the period of invasion.
3) In the case of the navy, to have been engaged on active service up to 27 May 1941 in the Cretan theatre of operations.
4) The army personnel who had been engaged with the naval flotilla that had put to sea on 19 May 1941 in the naval light flotilla.

The cuff title was awarded with a Citation that usually had at its top, the Luftwaffe Parachute Badge, L.014, surmounting a map of Crete which had marked upon it the place names MALEMES, CHANEA, RETMINNON and IRAKLION. The centre had ARMELBAND >> KRETA << , with the commander's signature and stamp at the bottom. There was no container for this arm band.

C.002 'Afrika' Commemorative Cuff Title

On 18 July 1941 a cuff title 'AFRIKA KORPS' was authorized for wear by members of this unit who were fighting in North Africa, by the chief of staff of the army general staff, Generaloberst von Brauchitsch. This was a cotton band 33 mm wide with 'AFRIKA KORPS' in silver block lettering on a dark green background, which was edged at the top and bottom with a band of silver embroidery, 3 mm wide. These silver bands were themselves edged in a tan coloured material. The whole of this cuff title was in fact produced, or woven, as one integral piece. It was worn on the right cuff of service, field service or uniform tunic as well as that of the greatcoat. For members of the Luftwaffe, a plain blue band was authorized with 'AFRIKA' embroidered on it in silver cotton thread for NCOs and below, and aluminium wire for officers. In this case the cuff title did not have a border. These two bands were never intended to be considered as an award, but purely a unit recognition.

The esprit de corps of the troops involved in the North African campaigns, which included their British Empire counterparts, gave rise to ex-members of the Afrika Korps, on their return from Africa, wearing either of these cuff titles as an honorarium. By this unofficial practice and wear, they thus became a form of reward. To legitimize and reward these personnel, on 15 January 1943 an official cuff title was introduced to replace the unofficial wearing of the aforementioned cuff titles. This took the form of a khaki coloured band, which was 33 mm wide and had a border on each edge of silver coloured cotton. In the centre of this band was embroidered, also in silver coloured cotton, the word 'AFRIKA' flanked on either side by a stylized palm tree. (This, incidentally, in

Below *The 'AFRIKAKORFS' cuff title should not be confused with the later decorations.*

Bottom *The Luftwaffe cuff title with white lettering on a blue background.*

The official 'AFRIKA' cuff title introduced in January 1943 (C.002) (Tim Stannard Collection).

another form which encompassed a Swastika midway up the trunk of the palm tree, had been the sign of the Afrika Korps.)

There also exists a version with a blue band, edged in gold, with gold palm trees and title as before described. The purpose of this type of cuff title is unknown, but one theory which has been put forward is that it was to reward naval personnel. After 29 August 1944, with the exception of prisoners of war, those missing in action and personnel confined to hospital due to infectious diseases who could possibly on recovery be returned to active service, no more Afrika titles could be awarded.

The Criteria for the award were:

1) To have had a minimum of six months on North African soil.

2) To have been in combat in the North African theatre of operations, that is to say on land, on the waters around North Africa or in the air.

3) To have contracted an illness while in the North African theatre of operations. This was to include personnel evacuated to the continent of Europe due to that illness, but service had to have been in excess of three months before

contracting the illness before the possible recipient could be considered for an award of the cuff title.

4) From 6 May 1943, it was later decreed by Hitler that the qualifying service time required as in 1, by those who fought in the final phases of the campaign, was to be reduced to four months.

5) The recipients of decorations awarded in this theatre of operations, to include the Iron Cross, D.013, German Cross in Gold, D.025, Goblet of Honour or Salver of Honour, would automatically be awarded the cuff title regardless of the length of service time spent in Africa.

6) Death of a member of the Afrika Korps in the line of duty again automatically qualified him for an award of the cuff title without serving the time requirement. In this case the next of kin received the award document.

The award was rendered with an award Citation which could be either quite a simple affair with, in the middle the title of the arm band, and at the bottom the commander's signature and stamp; in some cases, however, the Citation had a large palm tree with Swastika midway, the symbol of the Korps, and the name of the award at the top, but the signatures and stamps were as usual.

C.003 'Metz 1944' Commemorative Cuff Title

The US Third Army had been advancing through Europe toward Germany but had been successfully halted at the Metz Citadel by stiff German resistance. The defenders held up the US Army from 27 July to 25 September 1944. This resulted in the Third Army mounting a major offensive operation against the defenders, SS units, members of the Kampfgruppe von Siegroth. (General von Siegroth was the commander of the Wehrkreise VI officer candidate school in Metz.) From 1 July 1944 to November 1944 members of this school were also employed in the defence of the citadel. The Third Army's offensive to break the defence of Metz started on 8 November 1944 and was virtually concluded by 20 November, with the outcome that the citadel was overthrown, although some diehard SS elements continued to hold on in a region known as Fort Gambelleta and continued their resistance until 7 December.

To recognize the heroic battle of

The 'Metz 1944' Commemorative Cuff Title (C.003) (J.R. Angolia).

the period 27 July to 25 September 1944, Hitler on 24 October 1944 introduced a cuff title 'METZ 1944'. This consisted of a black silk band which was similar to those worn by SS personnel as an honour title, with silver threads numbering seven threads per border on each edge of the band. In silver embroidered wire in the centre of the band, the word METZ in block letters followed by the date 1944, again in block capitals. Until this year, 1986, the award had not been positively identified as being actually awarded, which led to the supposition that it had only been instigated but never awarded. Lieutenant-Colonel Angolia, through his keen historical detection, managed to locate an excellent photograph of Generalmajor Joachim von Siegroth wearing the aforementioned cuff title while awarding the Knights Cross of the Iron Cross, D.018, to Willi Schmuckle in March 1945, proving positively that the cuff title had been awarded during the period of the Second World War.

The Criteria for the award are unknown as are details of the Citation, if indeed one ever existed.

C.004 'Kurland' Commemorative Cuff Title

The 'Kurland' Commemorative Cuff Title (C.004).

To reward the defenders of the besieged Courland region of Latvia, Hitler introduced a cuff title on 12 March 1945, at the request of the commander of army group Courland, Generalfeldmarschall Ferdinand Schörner. This cuff title was produced locally at Kuldiga, in a weaving mill. This band was of unusual design as the reverse had a form of cross stitch which joined the two outer edges together, these outer edges having been turned over. The obverse had a bold black edge beneath which was a line of black oblong dots. Beneath this was a fine thin black line. Between these two thin lines, in capitals, was the legend, KURLAND. Before the 'K' was a shield with a black cross as its central motif, which is not unlike a Balkan Cross. The shield was square-topped with a pointed base, and was, in fact, the crest of the Grand Master of the Teutonic Knights. The other side had a similar shield but which was black, with a moose's head in white looking towards to the left from the viewer's position, this being the coat of arms of Mitau. The overall colour of the band was off-white and the material was a rough cotton.

The Criteria for the award are uncertain, as are details of the Citation. At this late stage of the war it is often found that the Citation was purely a piece of typed paper giving the details of the award.

Introduction to Arm Shields

Of all the decorations of the Third Reich these were a total innovation, and had been brought into existence to reward the personnel of the armed forces, or people in their employ. The shields rewarded their participation in a theatre of operations and were not necessarily to reward heroism or valour, although if a decoration was awarded in that theatre of operations the recipient received the arm shield. They were produced in metal which was stamped out of a thin sheet and was usually fixed to a cloth backing that corresponded to that of the branch of the Service to which the recipient belonged. The cloth backing enabled the recipient to sew it easily on to his tunic.

These shields were worn on the left arm and when two were awarded they were worn one above the other, separated by a small, approximately 5 mm, gap. In the case of the Waffen-SS the shield had to be worn above the SS arm eagle. In the unlikely occasion of three shields being awarded, the recipient placed, or attempted to place, the last two awarded shields side by side, with a 5 mm gap between them and the first one that was awarded, so when one looked at on the wearer's arm the shields were in the form of a triangle.

They were allowed to be worn on the service, walking-out and guard uniform as well as that of the greatcoat. They could be worn on the uniforms of any of the party organizations, or Allgemeine-SS. This practice, except in the case of fighting troops who had been invalided out of the armed forces, was a rare occurrence. Most fighting troops had little time on their leaves to be engaged in party rallies or events. Enjoying themselves on these all too short and very rare occasions, was their main occupation.

There is no recorded instance of the shields described in this section being produced in a cloth version. This seems strange as they were bulky to wear on the uniforms and a cloth version would have seemed a logical progression, especially in the case of the Luftwaffe where cloth badges were used on flight clothing.

Index to Arm Shields common to all Services

AS.001 Narvik Shield—Silver Class   96
AS.002 Narvik Shield—Gold Class   96
AS.003 Cholm Shield   97
AS.004 Crimea Shield   98
AS.005 Crimea Shield—Gold Class   98
AS.006 Demjansk Shield   99
AS.007 Kuban Shield   100
AS.008 Warsaw Shield   105
AS.009 Lorient Shield—First Type   106
ASV.009 Lorient Shield—First Type—Variant   107
AS.010 Lorient Shield—Second Type   107
AS.011 Lapland Shield   108
AS.012 Stalingrad Shield—First Type   109
AS.013 Stalingrad Shield—Second Type   110
AS.014 Balkan Shield   110
AS.015 Memel Shield   111
AS.016 Dunkirk Shield   112

AS.001 Narvik Shield—Silver Class
AS.002 Narvik Shield—Gold Class

This shield was instigated on 19 August 1940 and comprised a metal shield, pointed at the bottom, surmounted at the top by three lines. The first protruded beyond the shield's edges, the second was in line with the edges and the third was short of the outline of the badge. On this rested an eagle, head to the viewer's left, with exaggerated downswept wings. In its claws it was clutching a wreath which surrounded a Swastika. The body of the shield had a box with the word NARVIK and beneath this the date, 1940. The main design of the badge was a crossed single-bladed propellor and anchor, surmounted by an eidelweiss. These were the symbols of the three arms of the German fighting forces employed in the capture of Norway.

The silver grade was given to the army and air force, with a backing cloth corresponding to the branch of the Service to which the recipient belonged. The gold one was awarded solely to the navy, and is therefore only found with a navy blue backing. A total of 8,577 was awarded, being made up of 2,755 to the army, 2,161 to the Luftwaffe and 3,661 to the navy.

The Citation was a plain paper with the derivation of the badge, commander's signature and company stamp at the bottom.

Narvik Shield — Gold Class (AS.002).

Cholm Shield (AS.003) (Tim Stannard Collection).

AS.003 Cholm Shield

On 1 July 1942 this shield was introduced and consisted of a white metal shield with flat top and pointed bottom. The central design was an open-winged eagle, clutching in its talons an Iron Cross, the centre of which had a disproportionately large Swastika relative to the size of the Iron Cross. Beneath this was the word CHOLM and then the date of award, 1942. It was to reward the garrison that had held the defensive pocket that had been created at Cholm, a small town on the Lovat river in the Kalinin region of Russia. The commander was Generalmajor Scherer and it was he who made the awards to 5,500 assorted men from various units which comprised the defenders of the pocket. The awards were bestowed for the period 21 January 1942 to 5 May 1942, the last award period for this shield being 1 April 1943.

There was an improvized air strip which measured 70×25 m which the Luftwaffe used for bringing in supplies. This practice had to be reorganized because of the dangerous nature of these flights, and freight gliders and parachute drops were later employed. For the crews who actually landed on the air strip, the award of the shield was rendered. It was worn on the arm on a cloth backing piece of the colour of the branch of Service.

AS.004 Crimean Shield

Crimean Shield (AS.004).

Feldmarschall von Manstein introduced on 25 July 1942 a bronze shield that had at its top an army eagle, the wings just breaking the edge of the shield, clutching a wreath surrounding a Swastika in its talons.

On either side of the wreath were the dates 1941 and 1942 respectively. Beneath this was a map of the Crimean region, with the major rivers and six towns marked on it, and impressed on to this map is the word 'KRIM'. The badge was to reward the troops engaged in operations in this region from the period 21 September 1941 to 4 July 1942.

The Criteria for the award were:
1) To have served in the region for three months.
2) To have taken part in at least one major operation against the enemy.
3) To have been wounded whilst serving in that region.

It was awarded on a back cloth in the colour of the branch of the Service to which the recipient belonged. It is estimated that over 100,000 awards of this shield were rendered during the period of award. It came with a Citation, which in some cases had a facsimile of the shield at the top, and von Manstein's signature and rank at the bottom.

AS.005 Crimean Shield—Gold Class

This grade of Crimean Shield was awarded twice, and the badge was produced in real gold. The first award was to Marshal Antonescu of Rumania, which he received on 3 July 1943 in Bucharest from Feldmarschall von Manstein. The second was to von Manstein himself, and was presented by the members of his staff on his birthday, 24 November 1943. The exact number of shields that were produced is not known, but it is assumed that more than two examples were made, as photographs show von Manstein wearing the shield both on his tunic and his greatcoat, which accounts for at least three examples.

AS.006 Demjansk Shield

This shield was introduced on 25 April 1943. It comprised a shield with a pointed bottom and undulating sides. On the top was a box with the name in raised capitals DEMJANSK. Above the box, at either edge, was a 'pillbox' with a gun port in each. Between these pillboxes was an eagle with downspread wings, a wreath surrounding a Swastika clutched in its talons. In the main body of the shield, at the top was a single-engined observation plane, with a twin-bladed propellor, which was straight across the shield in line with the wings of the plane. It is interesting to note, at this point, that some examples encountered show this propellor as curved. Surmounting this aeroplane were large, crossed, double-edged swords, with downswept cross guards. Beneath these was the date, 1942. The badge was then placed on a backing cloth of the colour of the Service to which the recipient belonged.

This shield was to commemorate the defence of the town Demjansk by the Second Army Corps. Serving with this corps were several non-army units, including personnel of the Reichsarbeitsdienst, organization Todt, police, Russian auxiliary volunteers and the 3rd SS Panzer Division *Totenkopf*. It is interesting to note that the shield was to be worn over the SS arm eagle, in the case of award to those units.

The defence of Demjansk tied down eighteen Russian divisions for over fourteen months, for the loss of 3,335 German personnel killed and

Demjansk Shield (AS.006).

in excess of 10,000 being wounded from a garrison strength of 100,000 men. The defenders were supplied by air and the Luftwaffe crews engaged in these operations were also eligible for the award.

The Criteria for the award were:
Ground Forces—
1) To have served for sixty days in the garrison.
2) To have been wounded whilst serving there.
3) To have gained a bravery award whilst serving in the garrison.
Luftwaffe personnel—
1) To have flown fifty combat missions over the garrison and surrounding area.
2) To have flown and landed in the garrison fifty supply missions.

Approximately 100,000 awards of this shield were made and these were rendered by the garrison commander, General der Infanterie Graf Brockdorff-Ahlefeldt. It was awarded with a Citation which came in various designs, but it is interesting to note that the SS had a special version produced for the members of the *Totenkopf* Division.

AS.007 Kuban Shield

Instituted on 21 September 1943 and of a similar design to that of the Crimean Shield, this was also produced in bronze, and had the army eagle at the top clutching a wreath which was round a Swastika. Either side of the wreath was the date '19' and '43' respectively. There was a band just touching the bottom of the wreath with the word, in block capitals, KUBAN. Beneath this was a zigzag broad line to represent the bridge-head for the defence of which the badge was introduced, to reward the defenders. With the locations KRYMSKAJA in the middle, LAGUNEN at the top and NOWORD and SSIJSK at the bottom, the badge was then fitted to a back cloth of the colour of the branch of Service to which the recipient belonged.

The Criteria for the award were:
1) To have served in the bridge-head for sixty days.
2) To have been wounded whilst serving at the bridge-head.
3) To have been engaged in one major operation at the bridge-head.

Luftwaffe and navy personnel were also entitled to the award, but the exact Criteria for their service is not known to the author.

The badge was awarded with a Citation and the signature and title of Generalfeldmarschall von Kleist at the bottom, he being the officer responsible for this award.

Kuban Shield (AS.007).

Above *Presentation case for the German Cross with Diamonds (D.026)* (Philip C. Faber).

Above right *German Cross in Gold — Cloth Version — Navy Blue (D.028).*

Right *German Cross in Silver (D.030).*

Below *War Merit Medal (D.034).*

Below right *War Merit Cross — Second Class — Bronze without Swords (D.035).*

Opposite page

Top left *War Merit Cross — Second Class — Bronze with Swords (D.039).*

Top right *War Merit Cross — Knights Cross — Silver with Swords (D.041). Note original neckties.*

Middle *Two examples of the 'Kreta' Commemorative Cuff Title, the top one in felt and the lower one in cotton (C.001).*

Bottom left *Roll of Honour Clasp — Army (D.043).*

Bottom right *Medal for the Winter Campaign in Russia — 1941-1942 (D.046).*

This page

Above *The 'Kurland' Commemorative Cuff Title (C.004).*

Below left *Narvik Shield — Gold Class (AS.002).*

Below *Crimean Shield (AS.004).*

Above left *Lapland Shield (AS.011). This example is a heavy cast variety.*

Above *Dunkirk Shield (AS.016). One of the three known examples.*

Left *U-boat War Badge — First Type (N.001).*

Below left *U-boat Badge with Diamonds (N.004): this was actually Kapitän zur See Wolfgang Luth's award.*

Below *U-boat Combat Clasp — Bronze Class (N.005).*

AS.008 Warsaw Shield

This shield was introduced on 10 December 1944 and was intended to reward and commemorate those members of the armed forces under the command of SS-Obergruppenführer und General der Polizei Erich von dem Bach-Zelewski. Some of the troops employed in Warsaw were among the most notorious with their excesses being even repugnant to the German high command. Some examples of special note are Brigadeführer der SS Kaminski, a Russian deserter who formed an anti-partisan brigade named after himself. It was reported by Bach-Zelewski that he had been executed in September 1944 for his excesses in quelling the uprising. There was also Oberführer der SS Oskar Dirlewanger who also raised and commanded a brigade named after him. This brigade was made up of ex-convicts and poachers. It was for these troops who were employed between 1 August 1944 and 2 October 1944 that this shield was produced.

It consisted of a bronze, pointed-bottomed, flat-topped shield, with a large eagle that filled the field. On the eagle's neck was a Swastika and across its chest a scroll with the words WARSCHAU 1944. Its legs were astride a snake which had its mouth open, a hump in its back that rose between the spread eagle's legs, and the tail at the point of the shield was formed in a circle. The eagle's talons clutched the snake on either side of the hump in its back.

The Criteria for the award were:

1) To have been on active service at Warsaw between 1 August 1944 to 2 October 1944.
2) To have participated in a minimum of seven days' combat.
3) To have been wounded in the fighting.
4) To have performed an act of bravery during that fighting.
5) To have served for a period of 28 days in the combat zone, not necessarily involved in combat, but in a support capacity.

Luftwaffe personnel—

1) Were awarded the badge after twenty combat missions over the area.
2) After ten days' service in support of the operation.

The badge was designed by Benno von Arent and it was put into production, but the factory responsible for

A known die-strike of the Warsaw Shield (AS.008) from Berlin at the end of the war, made in heavy metal (J.R. Angolia).

its manufacture was destroyed in an Allied air-raid. The matrix or dies and the on-hand stock of prepared shields were destroyed. It is, however, possible that some examples escaped destruction.

AS.009 Lorient Shield—First Type

This shield is one about which there exists great disagreement, many collectors doubting its authenticity or very existence. This will probably continue until someone can come up with incontrovertible proof, one way or another, to its introduction and award before the end of hostilities.

It comprised a thin shield with flat

Lorient Shield — First Type (AS.009) (David Littlejohn).

top and rounded bottom. The central design was of a naked warrior with a German steel helmet on his head. In his left hand was an oval shield, with an open winged eagle clutching wreath and Swastika in its talons, impressed upon it. In his right hand was a double-edged sword. He stood astride a U-Boat pen with a submarine in it, and in the foreground were stylized waves. From behind the warrior emanated rays. Either side of the helmeted head were '19' and '44' respectively. Running round the bottom edge of the shield was the word LORIENT. This design was submitted by Marinebaurat Fehrenberg to the garrison commander, Admiral Henneke, who authorized production of the shield in December 1944. It is interesting to note, however, that when recently approached for information about the shield Admiral Henneke denied any knowledge of it.

The garrison of Lorient survived as a pocket of resistance until the end of the war, after being cut off by advancing Allied troops subsequent to the drive after the breakout from the Normandy beach-head in 1944.

The badge was produced in a local fish cannery and was purported to have been produced from various materials, the most likely being the tin plate from which the cannery produced its tins. Holes were then pierced to allow the shield to be sewn on to the uniform. It has been stated that large numbers of the shield were produced, and this has been used as an argument to prove that the badge did not exist at all because very few examples have turned up. My view is that there were only small quantities produced, making it rare, especially since a photograph of the shield being worn has so far not been found. As with the Metz Cuff title, C.003, dextrous detective work will uncover one in due course.

ASV.009 Lorient Shield—First Type—Variant

There was a variety that to all intents and purposes was identical to the badge described, but in this case the shield was raised to symbolize the defence from air attacks which the pocket received liberally.

AS.010 Lorient Shield—Second Type

This was not an arm shield as such, but an unused disc that had stamped upon it 'FESTUNG LORIENT 1944', which appeared in three lines.

Reconstruction of the Lorient Shield — Second Type (AS.010) (Drawing by Howard Reynolds, Managing Director, Artytype).

This has been reported to be an alternative design to AS.009, when it was impossible to reward the troops with that shield. This item leaves the researcher detective with a lot more enquiry and research to be done and I would like to hear readers' comments on it.

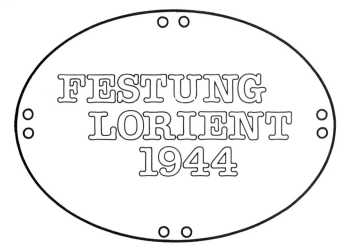

AS.011 Lapland Shield

Lapland Shield (AS.011). This example is a heavy cast variety.

This shield was instituted in or around February or March 1945, and was the last official shield to be awarded by the German high command. It comprised a round-bottomed shield with a flat top. Just below the top was a bar that ran horizontally across the shield and broke its edge. Round the edge of the shield was a rim. On the bar was an eagle, which positively looked more like a chicken! It is interesting to note at this point that the eagle did not incorporate the Swastika in its design, and in fact it was not employed at all on the badge. Another point of great interest is that the eagle looked in different ways on various badges, and I have encountered six slight variations in design and production. (I have not included a breakdown of variations at this juncture as a lot more research work is required, but I hope to include an update at a later time.) Beneath the bar was the word in capitals LAP-PLAND, and beneath this was a map of the area. It was intended to reward members of the 20th Mountain Army Group which was under the command of General Boehme who, incidentally, was responsible for the award of the shield.

The Criteria for the award were:
1) It has been suggested that six months' service in the area was required.
2) To have been wounded in that theatre of operations.
3) To have been engaged in a major offensive or defensive battle in that region.
4) To have won a bravery award in that area.

The shield was awarded with a Citation which was in script with the commanding officer's signature at the bottom. Some of these Citations were prepared and made out after the end of the war, and the official stamp with which they were franked had the Swastika removed crudely from the eagle.

AS.012 Stalingrad Shield—First Type

On 26 October 1942 Hitler ordered that a design should be prepared for a shield for the defenders of Stalingrad. Ernst Eigener, a war artist with Propaganda Company 637, was instructed to produce the artwork, Hitler's wishes having been passed to the press relations department who had authorized the design to be prepared.

This design took the form of a shield with pointed bottom and a closed winged eagle on the top, without a Swastika. The centre had a silo

Ernst Eigner's original design for the Stalingrad Shield (AS.012) **below** *was considered too morbid so von Paulus produced the second design (AS.013)* **below right** (Howard Reynolds).

admidst the ruins of Stalingrad. (These silos, which were a landmark in Stalingrad, had been the scene of many bitter encounters.) Facing it was, in profile, a dead German infantryman with a crown of barbed wire round his helmet. Across the shield at the top was a box with the word STALINGRAD in capital letters.

The high command decided that this design was too morbid for consideration and turned it down. Ernst Eigener did not get the opportunity of submitting another design, as he himself was killed the following month at Stalingrad. Perhaps his design was a premonition of his own future fate.

AS.013 Stalingrad Shield—Second Type

Feldmarschall von Paulus designed a shield, again with a pointed bottom. The top was flat and had a box in which the word STALINGRAD appeared in capitals. Surmounting this was a closed winged eagle without a Swastika. The central motif of the shield was that of the silo with the ruins of Stalingrad. Beneath this design was a stylized river, with the word WOLGA on it. The field had a background made up of snow and clouds. The similarity of both these designs gives rise to the possibility that there must have been some collusion or, if not, that von Paulus had redesigned Eigener's work into a more acceptable design. However, Stalingrad fell with a humiliating defeat for Germany, von Paulus surrendering on 30 January 1943, taking with him more than 94,000 German troops into captivity. At least 147,000 had died within the city and a further 100,000 had died outside it. Also, two Rumanian, one Italian and a Hungarian Army had been destroyed. Von Paulus' 6th Army was the first German army to surrender in World War 2. One final sting in the tail for Hitler, who had viewed Stalingrad as a personal struggle with its namesake, was that he had promoted von Paulus to Feldmarschall on 29 January 1943, only one day before von Paulus had surrendered to the Russians. This promotion was to have encouraged him in the battle.

AS.014 Balkan Shield

In January 1945 a shield was awarded for the forces who were engaged in holding the Red Army back and fighting the partisans in the Balkan region. The design for this shield was produced by Benno von Arent and took the form of a pointed-bottomed shield with a flat top. Across the top of the shield in large capitals was the word BALKAN. Beneath this was an eagle, not unlike the SS type with, on either side below the under edge of the wing, 1944 on one side and 1945 on the other. This all surmounted a map of the Balkan region.

It has always been thought that this badge was never produced or issued, but an SS Oberscharführer in the *Prinz Eugen* Division, Fredrich Olesh, stated to me that he had the job as adjutant, which he had held for some time (in fact being a personnel friend of SS Gruppenführer and Generalleutnant der Waffen-SS Arthur Phleps, to whom he was also adjutant), of awarding approximately 250 of these shields. At the same time each man received a wrist watch inscribed on the back, from Hitler. Unfortunately both the shield and watch were removed from him in an internment camp in England, while he retained his collar patch, cuff title officer's quality, black wound badge, Iron Cross ribbon, shoulder straps and rank patch, which he presented to me as a present.

Although known to be reproductions, these two badges are included to show the basic design produced by Benno von Arent and as a warning to the collector not to consider either of these badges as originals.

AS.015 Memel Shield

Little is known of this award and it is probably an unofficially recognized one, which might have been instigated by the commander of the 7th Panzer Division. It consisted of a pointed-bottomed shield, with a square top. Below the top line of the shield was the word Memel in stylized lettering. The central motif was a gatehouse with portal and two square windows above it. On each side was a stylized watch tower resting on battlements. Beneath this was a curious boat-shaped gate with Njemenfront under it, again in similar stylized Lettering. Further information about this shield would be appreciated by the author.

Reconstruction of the Memel Shield (AS.015).

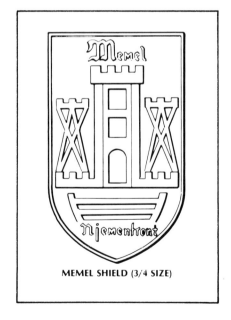

MEMEL SHIELD (3/4 SIZE)

AS.016 Dunkirk Shield

Dunkirk was surrounded by the Allies after the D-Day invasion and held out until 9 May 1945. Hitler had decided that it was most important to turn certain ports in the Channel Islands and those situated on the west coast of France into fortresses; this was in response to Admiral Krancke's telegram which contained the following paragraph, illustrating graphically the thinking of the fortress policy which encompassed La Rochelle, St Nazaire, Lorient and Dunkirk. The principle of the production of a shield in recognition of the defence of a fortress which gives rise to the production of this particular example has already been discussed. It is therefore possible, but highly improbable, that shields exist for the other two fortresses. Krancke's telegram states: 'It is abso-

Dunkirk Shield (AS.016).

lutely essential that the most important harbours on the south and west coasts are denied to the enemy for the longest possible time ... The Navy will support the defence of the fortress and the fortress areas through the use of all available naval forces, and when these are lost the weapons and the men are to be used in the defence of the landward perimeters.'

Needless to say, many of those supposedly fortress ports fell to the Allies quickly. However La Rochelle, St Nazaire, Lorient and Dunkirk remained uncaptured until the end of the hostilities. The last to surrender was Dunkirk and the German perimeter around the hinterland was reinforced by the garrisons of Nieuport and Ostend. The garrison exhibited its fighting capacity when in the dawn of 5th April Rear-Admiral Frisius opened Operation 'Blucher'. This offensive, which could be counted little more than a raid, was enacted with such ferocity that it panicked the unsuspecting British forces. The strength of the attack so confused the British headquarters that it was driven to issue orders to blow up the bridges that surrounded Dunkirk. Regaining its momentum, the British headquarters mounted a counterattack which was supported by rocket firing Typhoons, but even with this superior force they were unable to dislodge the determined German units from their newly gained front line positions.

Frisius perceived the close proximity to the final collapse of the Third

Reich and signalled the Navy high command to establish if his ad hoc forces were included in the armistice which had been signed at Luneburg. Montgomery, obviously piqued at the Admiral's pugnacious defence of Dunkirk, had demanded that Frisius should be included in the armistice agreement. The OKM had only one response to Frisius, and that was that he would be informed verbally by them when he was to surrender. Reassured by his high command that his garrison was excluded, he was able to reject the terms offered by the Allies. His military honour and that of his men was his only concern, and if he held out until the general surrender the Allies could not claim to have defeated his gallant force. Frisius signed the surrender document when the war was indeed ended, on 9 May 1945, his honour and that of his men being upheld. The last fortress along the Atlantic wall of Fortress Europe had surrendered.

The garrison comprised between 12,000 and 15,000 men made up of units of the 226th Infantry Division, Navy and Luftwaffe contingents. These were all put together into an ad hoc defensive force by Konteradmiral Frederick Frisius who commanded the overall garrison. He introduced, some time in February 1945, a small shield, produced in thin stamped brass. The bottom of the shield was rounded and the top square. The edge was gently rolled under all around, and there was a small hole in each top corner, with one centrally at the bottom. These holes were there to allow the badge to be attached to the uniform. I have seen three examples of this shield: two had no back cloth but the other one did. Whether it was to have been awarded with a back cloth or not is thus a point of conjecture. Dr Kurt Gerhardt Klietmann of 'Die Ordens—Sammlung' Berlin, has suggested that it was to have been worn on the side of the hat. My opinion is that it was to have been worn on the arm.

The central device was the watchtower of Dunkirk with stylized waves in three lines on either side of it. To each side of the tower, in line with its top, was the date 1944, two numbers on either side. Across the top in small capitals was stamped DUENKIRCHEN, and round the bottom of the shield was a chain of seven unbroken links. It is considered that there were only fifty awards of this very rare shield. It is uncertain if a Citation was rendered with the award, but an official entry was made of the award in the pay-book of the recipient to allow him to wear the shield. This entry tends to make the award a more official decoration than some of the previous unofficial ones.

It is possible that this shield was to reward members of the force who were engaged in such adventures as Operation 'Blucher' and would thus give rise to the very small number that were supposedly awarded out of a total garrison of 15,000. Equally, if this was the case, it would account for the scarcity of the Lorient Shield which would have been given for a similar type of operation.

Introduction to the Navy

With the end of the Napoleonic War in 1815, Prussia and the other German States began to draw together into trade areas or unions known as Zolveriegns. This pleased British foreign policy, because the vacuum that was left by the collapse of the French Empire and Napoleon was being filled by the two old empires, that of the Austro-Hungarians (or, as it was formerly known, the Holy Roman Empire) and the Ottoman Empire in the east. Both of these threatened British interests, particularly the Ottoman Empire which had eyes on British India and the region around it. This was also being tentatively investigated by the Russian Bear, even though she had suffered a terrible blow—but not a defeat—at the hands of Napoleon. French troops even entered Moscow but were forced to retreat, marking the turning point in Napoleon's career. Hitler and his armies faced the same situation in the Second World War.

Russia was interfering in the Afghanistan region of the Indian subcontinent and Britain felt threatened that her 'Jewel in the Crown' might be seduced by the diplomatic intrigues of Russia and Turkey. Austria was hungrily trying to infiltrate

the Balkans and particularly Greece who, in her turn, was trying to throw off the yoke of the Ottoman Empire. Asia Minor was in turmoil and it was British sea power that safeguarded our trade routes and colonies.

The German states, being totally land-orientated, had little feeling for a navy, so much so their merchant fleet, which plied mainly from the Baltic coast and Hamburg, could be threatened by a navy as small as that of Denmark. In 1848 a combined German States Navy came into existence in the name of the Reich Marine. Due to an inability to co-ordinate diplomatic aspirations between the states, the infant Reich Marine was abolished in 1852, but the Royal Prussian Navy stayed in existence to form the navy of Germany in later years.

The 'Iron Duke', Otto von Bismarck, a great friend of Britain, realized the necessity for a strong navy and it was he who was to become the father of that service. He introduced the 'Ironclads' in the 1870s and finally introduced the production of Dreadnoughts, which angered Britain and worsened relations between the two countries from the 1880s onwards. Britain felt that she had an unassailable right to patrol the sea lanes of the world and protect her shipping, colonies and territories as the policeman of the world. Germany felt that she could do the same, as her colonies in East Africa were becoming very important to her emerging economy. Britain coveted those colonies greatly and, as the period of the late 1880s and early 1890s proved troublesome to her in Africa, with the ultimate outbreak of the Boer War, Germany became the greatest threat. Britain inveigled herself into the entente cordiale with France, her oldest enemy, and a reciprocal arrangement with Russia. Germany feeling also threatened, signed an agreement with Austria and the Ottoman or Turkish Empire. The seeds of the First World War were sown.

The First World War erupted and the sea might of the two countries came together at the decisive battle at Jutland in 1916 which had the effect of defeating the German Navy and returning its capital ships to harbour. As a result Germany developed the new science of the U-boat, which they used to great effect against the British. At the end of the First World War the Germans had emerged as a U-boat nation. The capital ships which until that time had been thought invincible, were now under a threat, and naval strategy had to be rethought.

With the Treaty of 1919, Britain settled a crushing blow on the German Navy. It was to be reduced in size, the ships themselves having to be physically reduced in length. The German Navy, which had surrendered and was interned at Scapa Flow, swung at its moorings, manned by skeleton crews, waiting for its fate. Finally, the Admiral in Charge decided to regain the pride and honour of Germany and scuttled the complete Fleet at its moorings in the anchorage.

When Hitler came to power in 1933, he wished to accelerate the growth of the German Navy, which had started to be reconstructed under the Weimar Republic. The German war plans were, of course, tailored to a fleet which was basically unready for war. Hitler at this time informed Admiral Raeder that he would not precipitate a full-scale war until at least 1944. It was on this assumption that Admiral Raeder planned the German Navy's expansion. When war came in 1939, five years earlier than he had thought, many of the ships that he had hoped would be in service were still being built, or were on the drawing boards of the designers. Needless to say, he still had a formidable Navy. The three pocket battleships, which should have been 10,000 tons to keep within the regulations of the Treaty of 1919, had been secretly built to 13,000 tons and these were immediately available for any conflict. The battle cruisers *Scharnhorst* and *Gneisenau*, which were also in contravention of that treaty limit by 6,000 tons, were formidable adversaries for any navy to take on. The big 'Hipper' Class cruisers, 4,000 tons over treaty weight, were nearly ready and added to this impressive array of capital ships were 56 U-boats, of which all but ten were operational. Their crews had been well trained during the years when no U-boats were supposedly permitted. The secret training had taken place under the guise that they were undergoing anti-submarine exercises. The U-boat flotillas were admirably led by Dönitz, who was to strengthen their fighting ability and to build the 'Wolf Pack' system of attack.

Battle instructions were issued to the German Fleet in May 1939. The plan revolved round the idea of a continuous series of operations in the North Sea, to create as much havoc as possible by engaging in attacking the shipping in that area which, it was hoped, would tie down large British forces in containing them. The larger ships were instructed to cruise in the oceans of the world in a heavy and sustained attack on the merchant marine of any allied nation.

The main aim of the U-boats was to operate against convoys in the Atlantic and, especially, in the approaches to the main British ports. To offset the delay in the heavy ships still under production, it was decided that a number of merchant ships were to be fitted out as fast, heavily armoured attack ships, which were to be known as Auxiliary Cruisers. In all there were nine raiders, of which the most successful was the *Pinguin* which scored 28 sinkings and then the *Atlantis*, captained by Bernhard Rogge, with a score of 22.

In the German battle instructions one ominous phrase was inserted, which was to bode badly for the naval commanders in later years: 'Fighting methods will never fail to be employed merely because some international regulations are opposed to them'. It was a foreshadow to the unrestricted submarine and raider warfare that was to follow.

It was in this climate that the German Navy went to war and her personnel earned the badges and medals described in this section. Finally, with the collapse of Germany Admiral Raeder, who had overseen the expansion and rearmament of the Navy and directed its operations until 1943, when at his own request he relinquished command to Dönitz, was sentenced at Nuremberg to life imprisonment. Dönitz, after Göring's and Himmler's fall from favour in April 1945, was nominated by Hitler to succeed him as Head of State. Dönitz became the last Führer and had the onerous task of arranging the surrender of Germany. He received a ten-year jail sentence at the trials. His submission that he was purely a professional naval officer was partially believed by the court, which went a considerable way to reducing his sentence. This was still a light sentence compared to that of ninety per cent of the members of the all-volunteer crews of the U-boats, who now lay at the bottom of the sea entombed in their vessels.

Index to Naval War Badges 1939-1945

N.001 U-boat War Badge—First Type 118
NV.001 U-boat War Badge—First Type—Variation 119
N.002 U-boat War Badge—Second Type 120
N.003 U-boat War Badge with Diamonds for Dönitz 120
N.004 U-boat War Badge with Diamonds 122
N.005 U-boat Combat Clasp—Bronze Class 124
N.006 U-boat Combat Clasp—Silver Class 124
N.007 Destroyers War Badge—First Type 125
N.008 Destroyers War Badge—Second Type 126
N.009 Destroyers War Badge with Diamonds 127
N.010 Minesweepers, Sub-Chasers and Escort Vessels War
    Badge—First Type 128
N.011 Minesweepers, Sub-Chasers and Escort Vessels War
    Badge—Second Type 129
N.012 E-boat War Badge—First Type 130
N.013 E-boat War Badge—Second Type 130
N.014 E-boat War Badge—Third Type 131
N.015 E-boat War Badge with Diamonds 132
NV.015 E-boat War Badge with Diamonds—Variation 133
N.016 Auxiliary Cruisers War Badge—First Type 133
N.017 Auxiliary Cruisers War Badge—Second Type 134
N.018 Auxiliary Cruisers War Badge with Diamonds 135
N.019 High Seas Fleet War Badge—First Type 136
N.020 High Seas Fleet War Badge—Second Type 141
N.021 High Seas Fleet War Badge with Diamonds 142
N.022 Blockade Runners Badge 143
N.023 Blockade Runners Badge—Civilian Wear 143
N.024 Coastal Artillery War Badge—First Type 144
N.025 Coastal Artillery War Badge—Second Type 145
N.026 Naval Combat Clasp 146
N.027 Combat Badge of the Small Battle Units—Fourth Class 149
N.028 Combat Badge of the Small Battle Units—Third Class 149
N.029 Combat Badge of the Small Battle Units—Second Class 149
N.030 Combat Badge of the Small Battle Units—First Class 149
N.031 Combat Badge of the Small Battle Units—Bar—Bronze Class 150
N.032 Combat Badge of the Small Battle Units—Bar—Silver Class 150
N.033 Combat Badge of the Small Battle Units—Bar—Gold Class 150

N.001 U-boat War Badge—First Type

With the growth of importance of submarine warfare in the Great War, the Kaiser belatedly instituted, in January 1918, a War Badge to reward submarine personnel. This comprised an oval badge with laurel leaves running round its rim, surmounted by an Imperial Crown. The base of the wreath was decorated with crossed ribbons. Through this oval badge was a submarine which had been used in the First World War.

Hitler reinstituted the Submarine War Badge on 13 October 1939. It was similar to that of the 1914–1918 issue, except that the Imperial Crown was substituted by the Third Reich emblem of the eagle and Swastika and the U-boat was modified to a more modern type. Dönitz wore this badge with great pride, in conjunction with his diamond version, N.003. (Incidentally, these First World War badges had no second award status and were

U-boat War Badge — First Type (N.001).

unique in award badges in this respect. For example, a pilot in the First World War who was an operational pilot in the Second World War did not wear his first badge but the modern 1935 version.)

The construction of the badge varied due to war conditions. The best examples were of very high quality, being struck in brass, with very fine detail to the badge and segmented arms to the Swastika. On the reverse was usually found the maker's mark, being that of Schwerin und Sohn of Berlin 68, and on this type was a broad pin, with laid down hinge at the top and large hook at the bottom. The poorer quality badges were produced in pot metal with a needle pin, again with the maker's mark being stamped on to the reverse, usually just initials, eg, F.O. which represents Frederich Orth. The pot metal, which was gilded, quite often deteriorated to give a rather unpleasant appearance.

The Criteria for the award were:
1) To have been involved in a particularly successful mission.
2) To have completed or participated in more than three missions.
3) To have won a bravery decoration in one of these missions, even if it was the first.
4) To have been wounded on a mission, again, even if it was the first.
5) The badge with Citation was rendered to the next of kin of those lost at sea in a U-boat due to enemy action.

The badge was awarded in a variety

of manners. The brass high grade badges were usually awarded in a box which was hinged and was of black colour with a black or blue velvet base, with a white silk lid lining. The poorer quality badges were awarded in paper packets. These are quite rare due to the fact that they were seldom saved after the award ceremony.

There was provision for a cloth version of the badge, which came in two versions. Those for enlisted men and NCOs were gold cotton on a blue felt backing, but the officer's version of the U-boat Badge was not bullion embroidered. A few one-off examples may exist of gold bullion which is worked on to a felt padded badge, but these would be purely private purchase items. The type for officers were woven instead in Bevo style in gilt wire, on a blue silk oval backing. Both of these forms could be sewn on to naval uniforms, but from the lack of availability of examples and photographs of them in wear, it seems they must have been very unpopular with crew members.

The badge was awarded with various elaborate award documents too numerous to describe in this volume.

NV.001 U-boat War Badge—First Type—Variation

There were three or four slight variations in the production of this badge but I have, for convenience, condensed them to two. The badge as described in N.001 is normally known as the Schwerin type. The type which I have designated as this variant had three main characteristics. The first lay in the production of the eagle whose chest was a pronounced heart or shield design, surmounted by bold symmetrical fletching. The second point to notice is that the laurel leaves that produce the wreath were more pronounced, the tips of those leaves giving the impression of being worn. The central vein of each leaf was also more pronounced. The third point of reference is the submarine and there are a number of identifying points but they can be condensed down to the deck gun, flag, conning tower and waterline. Normally, the reverse was plain or with the maker's mark, F.O. for Frederick Orth, and had a needle pin. Some of the finer quality badges had a segmented Swastika, but these are quite rare.

U-boat War Badge — First Type — Variation (NV.001).

N.002 U-boat War Badge—Second Type

This badge is generally the same as the previous badge and the award Criteria was exactly the same. The German Navy being largely based in France after 1940 found it more economical in certain cases to resort to local manufacturers to produce a series of naval war badges. This is the first of that series. The rest of these French types of badges will be fully discussed at each section of the book, and there will be notations of this series which will be incorporated into the reference numbering system that I have adopted. The badge's only real difference was in the design of the wreath, which had a broader leaf. This gave it a more formal design, and a rougher appearance to the outer and inner edge of the badge. The pin construction was slightly different, comprising two slots with a pin running through them to allow the pin to open and close. It was horizontally placed across the reverse of the badge.

N.003 U-boat Badge with Diamonds for Dönitz

Below left *U-boat Badge with Diamonds for Dönitz (N.003).*

Right *Admiral Dönitz wearing the Knights Cross with Oak Leaves (D.019) and, below his ribbons, the Second World War U-boat Badge with Diamonds (N.003), Second World War Iron Cross First Class Bar (D.017), First World War Iron Cross First Class and First World War U-boat Badge (V.018).*

Grossadmiral Raeder instructed the firm of Schwerin of Berlin to produce a special grade of the U-boat badge which was to be a once only award to be rendered to Admiral Dönitz, to reward him and to show Raeder's own recognition of the successes Dönitz had achieved with his leadership in the U-boat warfare that had been particularly successful in decimating many Atlantic convoys. This beautiful badge was struck in solid gold, proofed to the gold standard of .535, and was set with a total of 21 diamonds. Nine rose-cut diamonds were set in the Swastika, and twelve larger diamonds implanted and surmounted upon the laurel wreath that formed the outside of the badge. The basic design and dimensions were the same as for the U-boat War Badge, N.001. The quality of the badge was exceptional. On the reverse was the maker's mark or logo, C.S.U.C./ BERLIN 68. This logo was produced in two lines. The badge had a wide flat pin on the reverse, the hinge at the top was of the laid down box type, and it had a massive hook at the other end.

Dönitz wore this badge in conjunction with his First World War badge and continued to wear it right up to his surrender in May 1945. He was the last leader of the Third Reich

and his rump government lasted for only approximately two weeks. Unfortunately for the numismatical world, at the end of the war the badge was removed from Dönitz and crudely de-Nazified by having the Swastika torn off.

It seems, after corresponding with Dönitz, that the badge was awarded without a Citation and the box in which it was awarded was just a plain black box with a ramp for the badge to sit on at the base. This box was similar to the one to be described in N.004.

N.004 U-boat War Badge with Diamonds

A special U-boat badge was produced to be awarded to particularly successful commanders. This badge followed the design of the previous badge, N.003, but without the diamonds in the wreath. It was made of solid silver which was then finely gilded. The Swastika was set with nine rose-cut diamonds. The firm that produced the badge was again Schwerin of Berlin, their trade-mark being placed across the reverse of the submarine, in two lines as in the former badge, and the reverse had a large pin and hinge construction as well. The Swastika in this type of badge was, in fact, surmounting the Swastika that was produced with the actual body of the badge. There was another version of this award badge which so far is quite unique. The wreath was a finer type and the eagle had a heart-shaped chest with broad

fletching. (This is in fact identical in design to the badge described in NV.001.) The legs were separated to hold the Swastika. This was also set with nine rose-cut diamonds but in this case the diamonds were set directly into the arms of the Swastika. The reverse was semi-hollow with a thin square pin which had the silver content .800 stamped into it, and the maker's mark L/21. In the example that has been examined this is in a square that has been double-struck. This badge was of particularly high quality, reminiscent of the exceptional work carried out by Godet and Son of Berlin, to whom this trade mark belonged. It is interesting that in *For Fuhrer and Fatherland* volume 1, John Angolia illustrates, on page 121, the case which held the submarine badge with diamonds presented to Wolfgang Luth, which clearly shows on the lid lining the address and trade mark of that firm.

To have qualified for the badge the recipient had to be a holder of the Knights Cross of the Iron Cross with Oak Leaves, D.019. The commanders who qualified and received this award are as follows: Fregattenkapitän Albrecht Brandi, Commander *U617, U967*; Kapitän zur See Wolfgang Luth, Commander *U138, U181*; Fregattenkapitän Otto Kretschmer, Commander *U99*; Fregattenkapitän Reinhard Suhren, Commander *U564*; Fregattenkapitän Erich Topp, Commander *U552*; Korvettenkapitän Heinrich Bleichrodt, Commander *U48, U109*; Korvettenkapitän Otto von Bulow, Com-

U-boat Badge with Diamonds by Schwerin.

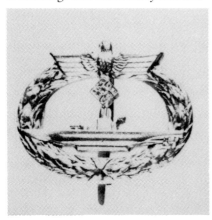

U-boat Badge with Diamonds by Godet: this was actually Kapitän zur See Wolfgang Luth's award.

Reverse of Luth's U-boat Badge with Diamonds.

mander *U404*; Korvettenkapitän Carl Emmermann, Commander *U172*; Kapitänleutnant Engelbert Endrass, Commander *U46, U567*; Kapitänleutnant Friedrich Guggenberger, Commander *U81*; Korvettenkapitän Robert Gysae, Commander *U98, U177*; Korvettenkapitän Reinhard Hardegen, Commander *U123*; Kapitän zur See Werner Hartmann, Commander *U37, U198*; Korvettenkapitän Werner Henke, Commander *U515*; Kapitänleutnant Hans-Gunther Lange, Commander *U711*; Korvettenkapitän Georg Lassen, Commander *U160*; Fregattenkapitän Heinrich Lehman-Willenbrock, Commander *U96*; Fregattenkapitän Heinrich Liebe, Commander *U38*; Korvettenkapitän Johann Mohr, Commander *U124*; Kapitänleutnant Rolf Mutzelburg, Commander *U203*; Kapitän zur See Karl-Friedrich Merten, Commander *U68*; Kapitänleutnant Joachim

Schepke, Commander *U100*; Korvettenkapitän Adalbert Schnee, Commander *U201*; Kapitän zur See Klaus Scholtz, Commander *U108*; Kapitän zur See Victor Schutze, Commander *U103*; Korvettenkapitän Herbert Schultze, Commander *U48*; Kapitänleutnant Rolf Thomsen, Commander *U1202*; and Korvettenkapitän Gunther Prien, Commander *U47*.

This prestigious award, which was only rendered 28 times, was not a government or Reich award but one which was purely from the commander of the Navy. The two types of badge that have been described indicate that there was possibly a wear version of this badge and that the type with the applied Swastika holding the rose-cut diamonds might be this, but this is purely supposition.

It has been reported that Reichmarschall Göring received a badge in acknowledgement for his award to Grandadmiral Dönitz of the Combined Pilots and Observers Badge with Diamonds, L.004. This award if it took place, would have been made begrudgingly by him, as it contravened his intended award criteria for this badge. On correspondence with Dönitz he stated he had no recollection of receiving the Combined Pilots and Observers Badge with Diamonds (L.004), or the German Order (D.024) that he also supposedly had been awarded by Hitler (to be covered in the volume on political and diplomatic decorations).

It seems fairly certain from correspondence with Korvettenkapitän Adalbert Schnee that there was no award certificate or Citation ren-dered with the badge. The badge, however, was rendered in a protective box which took the form of a black or exceptionally dark blue case, which was hinged with a press-stud holder. The base of the box had a raised plinth on which the badge sat. Through this plinth was a slit to take the pin. This lining again was of a very dark blue as in the case of the Schwerin badge that I examined, and in the case of the Godet badge, black velvet. The lid liner in both cases was of white satin, but in neither of the cases did it have the maker's name or logo stencilled in, as in the example of Wolfgang Luth.

N.005 U-boat Combat Clasp—Bronze Class
N.006 U-boat Combat Clasp—Silver Class

On 15 May 1944 the high command of the navy introduced the U-boat Combat Clasp in Bronze. This was done to follow and come in line with the army and the Luftwaffe. It was to commemorate and recognize greater

U-boat Combat Clasp — Silver Class (N.006). The silver on the U-boat has been scratched off to give constrast.

courage performed by the U-boat service. When one comes to consider that something coming close to ninety per cent of crews of U-boats were lost at sea, and that the personnel of those boats were all volunteers, it brings one to consider the bravery and valour that this decoration was

Rare picture of a group of U-boat personnel: the man third from right in the front row is wearing both the U-boat Combat Clasp (N.005) and the U-boat War Badge (N.001) (Graham Boddy Collection).

instituted to commemorate.

The badge comprised a U-boat Badge, with an eagle with downswept wings at the top of the laurel wreath. The wings of the eagle in this case, followed the line of the wreath. The ribbon ties at the base of the wreath were replaced by crossed swords, which indicated the combat worth of the decoration. The central badge, or wreath, was flanked on either side by oak leaves which consisted of three rows of leaves, two in each row. The upper and lower rows had smaller oak leaves. The maker's logo, and the designer originally of the badge, was Peekhaus and this is found on the

reverse of the badge. The pin was of a large configuration and went horizontally across the badge, usually from right to left. The structure of the pin was usually fluted.

On 24 November 1944 a silver grade was introduced for further valour. The exact details of the Criteria for the award of either of these badges is uncertain and on corresponding with Admiral Dönitz about the matter, he replied that it was 'to be something of the greatest bravery'. Gold versions of the badge were produced but they were not awarded.

The award document had a facsimile of the badge at the top and the commander's signature and stamp at the bottom. It was awarded in a plain paper packet with the name printed on the front.

N.007 Destroyers War Badge—First Type

On 4 June 1940 this badge was introduced by Grandadmiral Erich Raeder, on the demand of the Ober-

belchlshaber der Kriegsmarine, during the battle of Narvik. It was initially to reward the crews, under

Destroyers War Badge — First Type (N.007).

the command of Commodore Bonte, involved in the battle. It was awarded in conjunction with the Narvik Shield, AS.002, but was a separate distinction from the shield.

In an order dated 22 October 1940, awards and authorizations for the wear of the badge were extended to crew members of other vessels that could be described as 'destroyers' including torpedo boats and E-boats. Following the initial singular awards for participation in the battle of Nar-

vik a crew member needed to meet the qualifying requirements before he could receive the award.

The Criteria for the award were:
1) To have been wounded.
2) To have served on a ship sunk by enemy action.
3) To have participated in three separate engagements with the enemy.
4) To have completed twelve operational sorties without enemy action.
5) To have performed an heroic action for which no other decoration had been awarded.

The designer of the badge was Paul Caseberg of Berlin and it was first produced in bronze and then later, due to war constraints, in zinc or pot metal. The badge was accompanied by a Citation which had, in many cases, a facsimile of the badge at its top, the name of the badge in the centre and the company commander's signature and stamp at the bottom.

It came, in the early days of the war, in a blue box with blue velvet base and white silk lid lining, and later in a plain paper packet which can be found in the usual three or four colours, with the name printed in black on the front. This badge is also found in cloth embroidered with cotton thread.

N.008 Destroyers War Badge—Second Type

This badge was again produced in France and had the variation leaf pattern in its wreath as in other badges of this type, but in this case

the eagles that surmount the badge were identical to the one in the former, N.007. In this version the ship, which is in the form of a destroyer, was more finely worked and the detail greatly enhanced. The reverse had the French-styled pin as described formerly. Whereas on a number of these war badges the negative imprint of the obverse is found in the reverse, it is not noticed on this type.

The award Criteria for this badge were identical to that of N.007. The container in which these badges are encountered is a buff box which comprises a bottom and lid which are separate, the corners being stapled together. The badge inside is found wrapped in tissue paper.

Destroyers War Badge — Second Type (N.008).

N.009 Destroyers War Badge with Diamonds

This was a different version of the Destroyers War Badge set with nine small rose-cut diamonds placed into the Swastika, which was clutched in the talons of the eagle. The Swastika was also larger than that found on the normal badge. The badge was again similar to others which are diamond beset in that it was struck in solid silver and carried the .800 fine silver mark on the reverse. The pin was horizontal with a hook and heavy hinge. Presumably this badge was intended to recognize particularly successful destroyer captains who

Destroyers War Badge with Diamonds (N.009) (INFO magazine).

had won the Oak Leaves to the Knights Cross of the Iron Cross (D.019). However, none are known to have been awarded. One theory has it that this was to be the badge awarded to successful E-boat commanders, as they were entitled to the Destroyer War Badge (N.007) after 22 October 1940, but this badge could have been superseded by the introduction of the E-boat badge with Diamonds, N.015. That was, however, awarded later in the war.

Reverse of the Destroyers War Badge With Diamonds (N.009) showing how the Swastika is pierced to allow the light to shine through the diamonds (INFO magazine).

N.010 Minesweepers, Sub-Chasers and Escort Vessels War Badge—First Type

Grandadmiral Raeder directed Otto Placzek to create a special badge for Minesweepers. It was to take the form of a silver water spout, rising from the waves of the 'sea', which were chemically blued. The outer edge of the badge was formed by a wreath of laurels, the inner and outer edges of which took the line of the leaves that went to make up and form it. The bottom had a bow. The wreath was surmounted by a broad winged eagle clutching a Swastika in its claws.

On the reverse was a large pin which was usually vertical, but is also encountered in the horizontal position. If it was of the horizontal form there was a hook behind the eagle which helped to fix the badge to the

uniform—that is to say, it went through a small cotton stitch so that the badge would be kept flat at the top to the tunic while, if the pin became open and free from the tunic, the badge hung from the cotton loop. Usually these horizontal pins were of the thin needle type. Most badges carried on the reverse the maker's logo or address.

The quality of these badges varied, starting with the highest formed of brass, finely detailed and having a segmented Swastika, the wreath being finely gilded and the water spout (and in some occasions the sea waves) silver-plated, the waves being then chemically blued or blackened, and going down to the lesser zinc, pot or monkey metal badges which were poorly struck with a very inferior finish.

The badge was instituted on 31 August 1940 for officers and ratings of the German Navy and the civilian merchant marine personnel employed in its service.

The Criteria for the award were:

1) To have completed three operational sorties.
2) To have been wounded during an operational sortie, even if it was his first.
3) If the ship had been sunk due to enemy action.
4) For exemplary conduct in the execution of his duties over a six-month period.
5) To have completed a specially dangerous mission in a mined area.
6) A mission that comprised 25 days or more on escort duty.

The first award of this badge was made on 28 November 1940, and was rendered with a Citation. Subsequently, the Citations for the badge varied greatly but the most common encountered is that which had a facsimile of the badge at its top, its name in the middle and the commanding officer's signature, rank and official stamp at the bottom. The award

Minesweepers, Sub-Chasers and Escort Vessels War Badge — First Type (N.010). No example of the Second Type is available.

container also varied widely to include a blue box with navy blue flocking base and silk lid liner, through to the paper packet which came in various colours with the badge derivation printed on its front in black.

N.011 Minesweepers, Sub-Chasers and Escort Vessels War Badge—Second Type

This was identical to the former badge in design but once again had the distinctive French-style wreath and slightly variant eagle. It had a French-style pin and again the reverse was hollow struck. It came in a buff-coloured box with the corners stapled together and was usually wrapped in tissue paper.

N.012 E-boat War Badge—First Type

This badge was designed by Wilhelm Ernst Peekhaus of Berlin and was instituted on 30 May 1941. Its design consisted of an oak leaf wreath which had a tie at the base and was surmounted at the top by an eagle clutching a Swastika. It is interesting to note that the wings on this eagle were stubby. Both the wreath and eagle were finely gilded.

The main subject of the badge was an E-boat ploughing through the sea. The boat only came to half-way through the wreath and was finished in silver. The sea was blue-black with the crests of the waves being burnished silver. The reverse was flat, and usually had a horizontal pin. When this was the case, a small hook could be found which helped secure the badge to the uniform in the way that is described in N.010. It can also be found with a vertical pin construction. On the reverse, in rarer occasions, the maker's address or logo can also be seen.

The Criteria for the award were:
1) To have completed twelve sorties against enemy vessels or installations.
2) Outstanding leadership.
3) A particularly successful mission.
4) To have been wounded in the course of an action, even if this was the first.

The badge was awarded with a Citation document which bore the facsimile of the badge at its top, the badge derivation in the middle with the company commander's signature and stamp to be found at the bottom. The badge itself was usually presented, in this early format, in a blue box with a blue flock base, with white silk lid liner and the badge title stencilled in silver on the outer upper lid of the box. This badge was discontinued soon after its inception and is therefore considered reasonably rare.

N.013 E-boat War Badge—Second Type

This was also designed by Wilhelm Ernst Peekhaus of Berlin, but this time in conjunction with, and with the assistance of, Korvettenkapitän Rudolf Peterson. The resultant badge was introduced into service in January 1943.

The wreath of this badge had a flatter base and the oak leaves were of a smaller and more delicate design. The eagle that surmounted the wreath was much larger and, in comparison with the stumpy winged version of N.012, it had a longer wingspan. The Swastika was made in two distinct styles or types, which could either be of solid construction or cut out (ie, segmented or silhouetted) between its arms, and it was placed beneath the inner edge line of the wreath.

The other main distinguishing factor to be found is that, in this type, the E-boat, which took the form of a

E-boat War Badge — First Type (N.012).   *E-boat War Badge — Second Type (N.013).*

more modern boat, was cutting through a sea which comprised three distinct low waves. This time the boat broke the wreath so that the prow, in fact, formed part of the outer edge design. The reverse had the maker's logo or address on it with a horizontal or vertical pin. Again in the case of the horizontal pin the little hook is found at the top, which safeguarded the attachment to the tunic as described in N.010.

The Criteria for the award were exactly the same as those for N.014.

The badge was rendered with an award Citation which came in many variations but is often encountered with a facsimile of the badge at its head. As usual, the derivation of the badge was in the middle with the commanding officer's signature and stamp at the bottom. It was presented either in a blue box with blue flock base and white silk lid liner or in a paper packet in varying colours with the derivation of the badge printed in black on the front.

N.014 E-boat War Badge—Third Type

This was again of the French type with the distinctive wreath, eagle and

Swastika which surmounted it. The badge was of the same general design

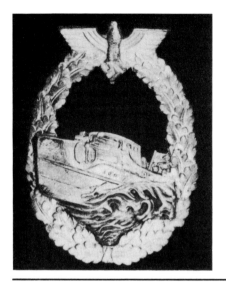

as N.012. The reverse was hollow-struck and had the distinctive French pin construction. The overall quality of this particular badge was superior to that found in the decorations of German manufacture.

The Criteria for this award were identical to those of the previous two badges, N.012 and N.013. The container in which the badge was awarded was a buff box in two parts, with the edges stapled together and the badge wrapped in white tissue paper.

E-boat War Badge — Third Type (N.014)
(Gordon Williamson Collection).

N.015 E-boat War Badge with Diamonds

This was not a national award but a personal presentation or award from the commander of the German Navy to particularly successful commanders of E-boats who were having an increasing effect on patrolling the English Channel. It took the form of the second pattern E-boat Badge, N.013, but was constructed from solid silver of .800 fine grade, and was finely gilded. The Swastika had a slightly larger format than that found in the standard badge. Nine rose-cut diamonds were set directly into the arms of the Swastika.

This badge, as far as research can ascertain, was only awarded eight times, and was to further honour the Knights Cross of the Iron Cross with Oak Leaves winners (D.019). Those

who were awarded the badge are as follows: Kapitän zur See Rudolf Peterson; Kapitänleutnant Frhr von Mirbach; Kapitänleutnant Werne Toniges; Korvettenkapitän Klaus

E-boat War Badge with Diamonds (N.015)
(INFO magazine).

Feldt; Korvettenkapitän Bernd Klug; Korvettenkapitän Friedrich Kemnade; Korvettenkapitän George Christiansen; and Oberleutnant zur See Siegfried Wuppermann.

The badge was designed by Peekhaus and was produced by the firm of Schwerin of Berlin. It was awarded at an informal ceremony after the recipient had received his Knights Cross with Oak Leaves and was not accompanied by a Citation.

Reverse of the E-boat War Badge with Diamonds carrying both the designer's and the manufacturer's names. Note that unlike other diamond awards, the Swastika is not pierced (INFO magazine).

NV.015 E-boat War Badge with Diamonds—Variation

There was a unique design of this badge which differs in that the space above the boat was solid, and the field that this created was pebbled. The Swastika was drilled as in the former badge and nine rose-cut diamonds were set directly into the body of the Swastika. The reverse of the badge was numbered M.003 and had Hitler's signature placed on it. The reason for its existence is unknown, but one theory is that it could have been the wear copy for general use. The other interesting fact about it is that it was produced in bronze, which had been finely gilded.

The type of container for either of these badges is unknown to the author but, in correspondence, Dönitz stated that the badge (N.015) came just in a protective jeweller's box.

N.016 Auxiliary Cruisers War Badge—First Type

Ernst Peekhaus of Berlin produced this badge on request from Grandadmiral Raeder. It was introduced on 24 April 1941 to recognize the armed merchantmen who were so successful in harassing Allied shipping. The badge in its early forms was constructed in two parts,

Auxiliary Cruisers War Badge — First Type (N.016).

then smoked and the highlights polished. The globe was riveted to the badge by a single rivet. The reverse was plain and it seems that few of these badges carried either the maker's mark, address or logo. It had a wide vertical pin with a hinge of the laid-down box type and a large hook at the base. The later war badges were of one-piece construction with the detail being usually less distinct and the gilding often being absorbed, giving a rather dull and lifeless appearance. These badges are usually found with a vertical pin and the maker's logo which is often that of Fredrick Orth (F.O).

The Criteria for the award were:
1) To have participated in a successful long-distance voyage.
2) For outstanding leadership.
3) To have been wounded in the course of duty on one of these long-distance voyages.

The badge was rendered with a Citation which normally came with a facsimile of the badge at its head, badge derivation in the middle and commander's signature and stamp at the bottom. The container in which the badge was rendered, in the first instances, was a blue box with a dark blue base and white silk lid lining, later awards being rendered in blue paper packets with the name printed in black on the front.

its base being of solid brass which was then burnished to give the appearance of gold. The badge consisted of a wreath of oak leaves which was secured by a tie at the base and surmounted by an eagle and Swastika. The main feature of the badge was a Viking ship on a globe showing Western Europe and part of the USA. In these early versions the globe was chrome-plated, which was

N.017 Auxiliary Cruisers War Badge—Second Type

The Viking ship on this badge had numerous small variations from the former badge, but these gave it a marked contrast, as did the design of the globe. This piece was manufactured in a one-piece construc-

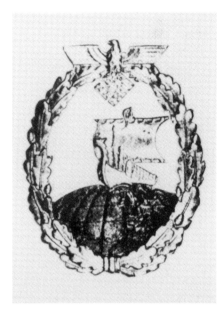

Auxiliary Cruisers War Badge — Second Type (N.017).

Auxiliary Cruisers War Badge with Diamonds (N.018) (David Littlejohn).

tion, the wreath being again in the distinctive French design with the variant eagle. The reverse was hollow struck with the French style of pin. The award criteria were identical to

those necessary for N.016 and the badge came boxed in a buff two-part box with the edges stapled together and the badge wrapped in white tissue paper.

N.018 Auxiliary Cruisers War Badge with Diamonds

This was identical to the Auxiliary Cruisers Badge (N.016) in construction but was produced in solid silver of .800 standard. The wreath and eagle were finely gilded, the ship and globe being polished. This badge was introduced by Grandadmiral Raeder in January 1942 and was to be used like the other Diamond awards of the Navy,

as a further mark of favour when the recipient had received the Oak Leaves to his Knights Cross (D.019).

One badge was awarded to the commander of the *Atlantis*, Kapitän zur See Bernhard Rogge, who had been a particularly successful raider. A second example was awarded to Kapitän zur See Ernst Felix Kruder, commander of the *Pinguin*. It is also thought that the badge was to have been awarded, albeit on paper only, to Kapitän zur See Hellmuth Ruckeschell, but it has been reported that he never actually received it.

The badge was not rendered with an award Citation and the box in which it was awarded is unknown. The only interesting variation is that Rogge had the pin of his badge removed and a screw post put on the reverse to make it more secure while he was wearing it on his tunic.

N.019 High Seas Fleet War Badge—First Type

This badge was introduced on 30 April 1941 at the direction of Grandadmiral Raeder, who at the time was Commander-in-Chief of the Navy, to recognize the sea actions in which the German Navy had been employed against the Royal Navy. The designer, and principal maker, was Adolf Bock of Berlin.

It took the form of a German Navy capital ship at full steam, passing

High Seas Fleet War Badge — First Type (N.019).

through an oak leaf wreath, with a large winged eagle at the top of the wreath. These badges by Bock and Schwerin were of particularly high quality with heavy pins and quality hinge and hook construction, while those of Frederick Orth tended to be of inferior quality, with a thin needle pin. In the case of this maker the hook was cast in with the badge and this, as the badge got older, tended to crystallize and became very prone in this brittle state to being broken off. The gilt on the wreath also tended to be absorbed, giving the appearance of having a silver wreath. This should not be confused with a variant type which had a silver wreath.

The Criteria for the award were:
1) To have completed twelve weeks' service on a battleship or cruiser.
2) This could be reduced if the recipient had been wounded during the twelve-week cruise.
3) If the cruise had been successful.
4) For service with the High Seas Fleet, but for which no other award badge could be given.

This badge was worn on the lower left breast pocket, and was awarded with a Citation which came in a number of varieties. The container in

Above *Destroyers War Badge — First Type (N.007).*

Above right *Minesweepers, Sub-Chasers and Escort Vessels War Badge — First Type (N.010).*

Right *E-boat War Badge — First Type (N.012).*

Below *E-boat War Badge — Second Type (N.013).*

Below right *Auxiliary Cruisers War Badge — First Type (N.016).*

Above left *High Seas Fleet War Badge —
First Type (N.019).*

Above *Blockade Runners Badge (N.022).*

Left *Coastal Artillery War Badge — Second
Type (N.025).*

Below left *Naval Combat Clasp (N.026).*

Below *Fourth, Third, Second and First
Class Combat Badges of the Small Battle
Units (N.027–N.030)* (Gordon Williamson Collection).

Above *Army Parachutists Badge (A.001).*

Above right *Infantry Assault Badge —
Bronze Class (A.003). This badge was found
at Bastogne.*

Right *Silver Tank Battle Badge (A.004).*

Below *Silver Tank Battle Badge — 75 Class
(A.007).*

Below right *Bronze Tank Battle Badge
(A.010).*

Above left *General Assault Badge (A.016).*

Above *General Assault Badge — 25 Class (A.017).*

Left *General Assault Badge — 100 Class (A.020).*

Below left *Close Combat Bar — Gold Class (A.025).*

Below *Army Balloon Observers Badge — Bronze Class (A.026).*

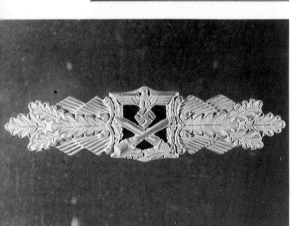

which the badge was awarded was a blue box with blue flock base and white silk lid lining, with the name of the badge stencilled in silver on the lid top, but the inferior quality badges were presented in grey paper packets with the badge derivation printed on the fronts. This badge is also found in cloth embroidered with cotton thread.

N.020 High Seas Fleet War Badge—Second Type

This was identical in all respects to that of the former badge, the difference being in the construction and in the fact that it is thought to have been produced in France. The concept of German badges being produced there is quite logical, considering that the German Navy was based right around the coast, enabling the naval personnel to purchase the badges locally.

The construction difference lay in the way that the wreath was produced. In this case the oak leaves were of a more offset pattern, giving a rougher appearance to both the inner and outer edges of the wreath. The eagle had a rounder form of fletching to the underside of the wing and the actual wingspan of the eagle which surmounted the wreath was reduced. The reverse was semi-stamped and there was a horizontal pin of the French style which has been previously described, with a hook mounted behind the eagle. Again this was to facilitate the badge's safety as well as appearance on a tunic. This range of French badges is rare and desirable.

The form of container was similar to the former in the fact that it was a

Observe and reverse of the High Seas Fleet War Badge — Second Type (N.020) (David Littlejohn).

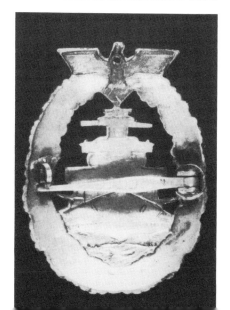

buff box with the corners stapled together, and the Criteria for the award were identical to those of N.019.

N.021 High Seas Fleet War Badge with Diamonds

An example of the first type of War Badge, N.019, was produced in solid silver of .800 grade. The Swastika in this badge was slightly enlarged and in it were set directly fourteen rose-cut diamonds. The reason for the production of this badge is unsure but it is probable that it was produced to reward Knights Cross winners with Oak Leaves who had been engaged in naval activities which would have gained them the High Seas Fleet War Badge (N.019). This would then have logically come in line with the diamond-beset medals for the other service branches, the U-boat Badge with Diamonds, N.004, and E-boat Badge with Diamonds, N.015. No action from the German High Seas Fleet facilitated the award of the Oak Leaves to the Knights Cross (D.019), so the award never become necessary, and this badge is still surrounded in uncertainty.

High Seas Fleet War Badge with Diamonds (N.021) (David Littlejohn).

Blockade Runners Badge (N.022).

N.022 Blockade Runners Badge

Hitler instituted this badge to recognize the courage of merchant navy personnel who were breaking the British blockade—a blockade which was having a disastrous effect on essential war materials getting to Germany. The badge was designed by Otto Placzek of Berlin and introduced on 1 April 1941. The first recipient was Hugo Olendorff on 1 July 1941, and he received an award document at the same time.

The badge consisted of a liner breaking a chain, which symbolized the blockade. The badge had an overall grey appearance but the chain was highlighted in white, as was the eagle which formed the prow motif of the ship. In some cases the prow motif was silver with the highlights polished. The reverse usually had the maker's motif or name and address and a broad vertical pin, but the badge is sometimes encountered with a thin needle pin which can be either vertical or horizontal. In the cases of the horizontal pin construction, a small hook is found at the top of the badge.

The recommendations for the award in the case of the merchant navy came from the Reich Commission for Sea Travel. In the case of the Navy, senior officers could recommend a man who had fullfilled the necessary criteria to be approved by the Commander-in-Chief of the Navy.

The Criteria for the award were:
1) To have brought a ship into a German or German-held port after successfully running the enemy blockade.
2) To have scuttled the ship to avoid capture by the enemy.
3) To have served aboard a ship lost through enemy action while at sea.
4) To have displayed daring courage in preventing the ship from falling into enemy hands.

The badge was awarded with a Citation which usually had a facsimile of the badge upon it. This could either be at the top of the paper or in some cases at the bottom. The relevant authority was at the bottom with its stamp and signature. The badge was awarded with a miniature version for wear on civilian clothes, in a blue box with blue lid liner and with a base that could either be of blue velvet or flocking.

N.023 Blockade Runners Badge—Civilian Wear

This badge was identical in every respect to the former, save that it was approximately one quarter of the size of the large one. There were, in fact, a considerable number of varieties of size to this miniature. However, this should not be considered the official awarded type of civilian stick-pin, but

merely that which one could buy as any other form of miniature for general wear on civilian clothing. The reverse had a vertical stick-pin and sometimes a maker's mark and this badge was to be worn on civilian or non-military clothing when one was either on a ship or off-duty.

Left *Blockade Runners Badge — Civilian Wear (N.023).*

Right *Coastal Artillery War Badge — First Type (N.024).*

Far right *Coastal Artillery War Badge — Second Type (N.025).*

N.024 Coastal Artillery War Badge—First Type

Grandadmiral Raeder decided that the land-based naval personnel required a badge to show recognition of their importance in anti-aircraft and coastal defence. The designer was the firm of Otto Placzek of Berlin and the badge was introduced into service on 24 June 1941.

It consisted of a land-based naval gun with the sea as the background. The wreath of oak leaves round the gun was surmounted by an eagle which had downswept wings and was similar to those found on the army badges. This may have been to show that these were, in fact, naval land-based personnel as opposed to their seafaring cousins. However, that observation is just a supposition. The reverse was flat with a wide vertical

pin and usually the maker's mark as well. The wreath was finely gilded and the gun of a smoked dark grey. The metal in which the badge was made in the early period of the war was of high quality nickel but as the war progressed, the usual debasement occurred with the use of pot or monkey metal. It is often found that these badges are of very high quality and have no gilding on them whatsoever, which has given rise to some collectors believing that there was in fact a silver grade. However, this is quite erroneous.

The Criteria for the award were:
1) For a display of leadership relevant to the position that the recipient held in the gun crew.
2) For any single act of 'meritorious

service' for which no other award could be rendered.

3) If the recipient had been killed in action, contracted illness or was killed by accident in the line of duty.

4) As a member of a gun crew when the crew had amassed eight points.

The points were calculated as follows: two points for shooting down an aircraft unassisted, or one point if they were assisted by another gun crew. For non-gun crew members such as searchlight, fire-control, sound locator and radio operator personnel, eligibility was the same and also required eight points. These were accumulated at the rate of half a point for each first detection of an incoming aircraft or flight.

The badge was awarded with a Citation which usually had a facsimile of the badge at its top, badge derivation in the middle and the company commander's signature and stamp at the bottom. The badge was usually presented in a paper packet which varied in colour with the name of the badge printed on the front.

N.025 Coastal Artillery War Badge—Second Type

This badge was produced in France and took the general form of the previous badge, N.024. The main difference lay in the oak leaves of the wreath, which had a rougher appearance to both its inner and outer edges. The gun was of a slightly different design and the eagle surmounting the wreath was a smaller version than that found on N.024. The reverse was semi-struck with the negative of the obverse and had a broad horizontal pin of the French style already described, and a hook behind the eagle's body. This

badge is considered to be quite rare and desirable in collecting circles.

The Criteria for the award were identical to those that were necessary for the award of N.024 and the badge came in a buff-coloured box with detachable lid, with the corners stapled together.

N.026 Naval Combat Clasp

Grandadmiral Dönitz introduced this badge to recognize further acts of valour for the holders of War Badges who would not have the chance of winning an equivalent front clasp. That is to say, he decided that a general clasp would be introduced, rather than a special clasp for each type of operational duty, as was the case of the Luftwaffe. This was to fit into the same scheme as that of the army.

The original design of the clasp was an oval centrepiece comprising a

Naval Combat Clasp (N.026). This is a factory manufactured example whose reverse is marked 11 (Tim Stannard Collection).

chain which formed the wreath or outer edge of the central motif, which was attached at the top of an anchor. The base had crossed swords and the centre was an anchor surmounted by a naval eagle with a Swastika in its talons. From the oval chain wreath on either side was an oak leaf horizontal cluster. This beautifully designed badge did not come into existence due to the lateness of its introduction, which was 19 November 1944. The badge that was in fact put into production differed quite considerably and took the form of an anchor in a plain circle, with a similar but not so striking oak leaf cluster emanating from either side. Crude

A field version of the Naval Combat Clasp constructed in two parts (D. Morris Collection).

examples of the latter badge were produced in the field. One such example varies completely from any that I have seen before and I have included it for two reasons, the first being the style and method of manufacture. The second reason is the method of its return to England and inclusion in the book, which makes a light hearted yarn and illustrates collectors' help in amassing information and items for a reference book, without which I would have this book impossible to produce.

The badge takes the form of a thin piece of copper which is shaped like the blade of a propeller for an aeroplane. In the centre is mounted a silver coloured Kriegsmarine button. The interesting point is that the copper is cut into a circle to allow the mounting of this button, on to which fits the reverse of the button perfectly. This enhances the impression of a propeller as the button gives the impression of a propeller boss.

On both the blades is tapped with fine holes the outline of the oak leaves as described in the text. On to the outline of these oak leaves is scratched the veins of the leaves.

The reverse is even more unbelievable in the method of construction, in the fact it has a complicated pin which is produced or formed like a giant safetypin. This is crudely applied to the reverse by means of large blobs of solder. In the centre is the reverse of the button which has been raised up by a uniform button securer, possibly from an officer's epaulette, which again is held fast by a large blob of solder.

If this badge belonged to some form of naval flying 'bod' is uncertain, but it gives the impression. One certain thing is that he really held it in high esteem, for the work that was entailed in its production was very much a labour of love, as was its retention, which is the second part of the story and follows as such. A Sergeant in the East Riding Yeomanry, but who at the time, May 1945, was serving in the RAC, had the task of removing items from prisoners who were surrendering at Morkeberg near Kiel. The purpose of the operation was to remove any item capable of being

Top *Naval Combat Clasp beaten out of copper.*

Above *Naval Combat Clasp crudely cast in bronze.*

used as a weapon or which could be used in suicide attempts. His comment about the experience was that he had more rings and watches than a jeweller. He reported that the prisoners had items secreted all over their bodies and kit. It has also been stated by other eye witnesses that the naval personnel were more determined and posed a greater threat than other branches of the service, even more so, surprisingly, than the die-hard Waffen-SS. This is possibly borne out by the fact that this particular prisoner had the badge concealed in a ball of darning wool. All the items taken at this particular place were thrown into a large bomb crater which subsequently was filled in, with the exception of a handful of items that this Sergeant kept as mementoes.

This item was sent to me by the collector who had extricated from the Sergeant, along with his British items and the story for inclusion in the book, as an interesting experience to share with other collectors. Recently, finely produced examples have come to light and are offered on the market-place.

The Criteria for the award were:
1) It was necessary to perform five times that which was requisite to be awarded a naval War Badge.
2) For special service or valour for which a War Badge would have been awarded.

The badge was rendered with a Citation but was presented in an ignominious cellophane wrapper.

N.027 Combat Badge of the Small Battle Units—Fourth Class
N.028 Combat Badge of the Small Battle Units—Third Class
N.029 Combat Badge of the Small Battle Units—Second Class
N.030 Combat Badge of the Small Battle Units—First Class

Fourth, Third, Second and First Class Combat Badges of the Small Battle Units (N.027–N.030) (Gordon Williamson Collection).

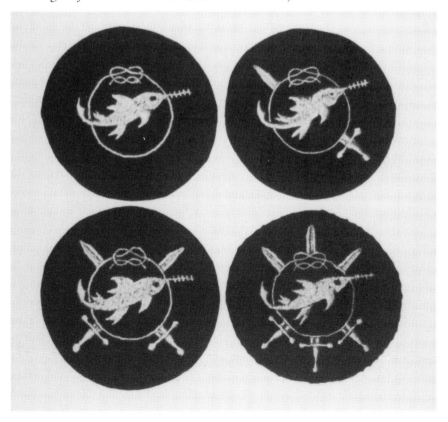

This series of badges was designed by Otlfried Neubeker and was instituted by the OKM on 13 November 1944. The Fourth Class badge was to reward service and leadership of the small battle units or frogmen groups. The badge had a blue cloth background, with a swordfish in a rope circle executed in yellow stitching. This grade was given to men who had planned an action that had ended successfully.

The Third Class badge was identical in historical detail and design and was made up, as before, of a cloth badge in blue with a swordfish in a rope circle, but in this case a sword was added at 45 degrees which passed through the badge, with the handle to the base of the badge.

The Criteria for the award of this type of badge was for bravery in action either on land or sea, as a member of a group or as an individual when part of a raiding party.

The Second Class again had the same historical details as to instigation and the design was the same, except that it had two swords crossed at 45-degree angles with the hilts both to the bottom of the badge. The Criteria were as for the Third Class Badge but at a higher level.

The First Class was identical in every respect except that it had a third, vertical sword. The criteria for its award were also the same but this badge was to reward further acts of service or valour.

There is a strong theory that the badge in all of the varying grades was available in yellow cotton for NCOs and in gold bullion for officers.

It is not know whether these badges were in fact awarded with a Citation, or just a note in the paybook of the recipient. Any further information would be gratefully received by the author.

N.031 Combat Badge of the Small Battle Units—Bar—Bronze Class
N.032 Combat Badge of the Small Battle Units—Bar—Silver Class
N.033 Combat Badge of the Small Battle Units—Bar—Gold Class

The clasps were introduced to further reward the units engaged in one-man submarines and frogmen operations. They consisted of a metal badge which had, as its central motif, a swordfish swimming to the left, the opposite of the cloth badges N.027 through to N.030, with an oval wreath made up of rope which was intertwined and ran round to produce the two sides of the oval. On either side of the oval the rope formed the elongated part of the clasp. The rope was segmented between each part so that it gave a delicate, interlaced appearance. The

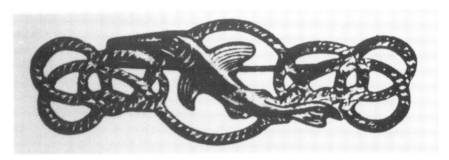

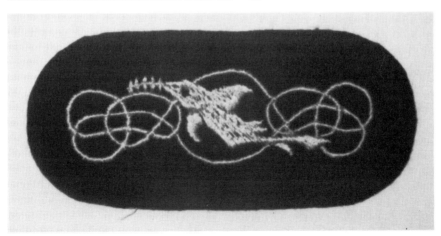

Top *Combat Badge of the Small Battle Units — Bar — grade unknown.*

Middle *Reverse of the Combat Badge of the Small Battle Units — Bar — Bronze Class.*

Above *Rare cloth version of the Combat Badge of the Small Battle Units — Gold Class* (Gordon Williamson Collection).

reverse had a long broad fluted pin that ran horizontally along the badge.

The Criteria for the award were:

1) Four actions entitled the recipient to the Bronze Class.
2) Seven actions entitled the recipient to the Silver Class.
3) Ten actions entitled the recipient to the Gold Class.

There is some doubt as to whether this badge, in any of its grades, was actually awarded. The majority of badges that turn up in collecting circles are, in fact, the 1957 version which the Federal West German government now permits, and as the design was identical in both these series it is difficult to determine which was produced before the end of hostilities in 1945.

Further information about this badge, whether it was accompanied by a citation, and details of the presentation box or packet would be appreciated by the author. There is also a cloth version of this badge which is in yellow cotton. It is therefore possible that all grades of the badge may be encountered in both cloth and bullion.

Introduction to the Army

The German Army evolved by a steady growth through the amalgamation and conquest of the former German states. Prussia had dominated this growth and its military traditions, and influenced its subsequent organization. In fact, prior to the First World War the officer corps was wholly modelled on that of the old Prussian officer school, if it was not also manned by Prussians.

After the defeat of the German Army in the war of 1914–1918 the German Army was reduced in size by the Treaty of Versailles of 1919. Europe was afraid of Germany's military image, of her goose-stepping, jack-booted soldiers who had terrorized Belgium and parts of France, or that is what the propagandists of the period would have liked us to have believed. One of these propagandists went as far as to intimate that the Hun ate babies!

The troops sidled back to their homes to find that things there were very often bleak. They looked to their former officers to give them stability and a great number of Frei Korps came into existence, to stop the spread of Communism and persecution of German minorities in the newly created Poland, and the pro-

vince of Silesia. The ill-fated Weimar government of the Republic that was created after the Kaiser's abdication rebuilt the German Army and gave the uniforms and equipment that were introduced an English look, possibly to counter the aforementioned propaganda. With the coming to power of Hitler, however, all this changed. He began the build-up of the Army and produced new uniforms in the style of the former Prussian ones, but with a National Socialist flavour.

Hitler, having come from a working-class background, found it difficult to relate to the strict upper middle-class officer corps. This unease was reciprocated by the members of that corps, with the exception of a few out-and-out Nazi Generals. This mistrust lasted right up until the 'Bomb Plot' of 20 July 1944, which convinced Hitler of his own invincibility and the ineptitude of the officer class. During the trials of the ringleaders for their part in the conspiracy against Hitler, no effort was spared to humiliate them. Feldmarschall Erwin von Witzleben, for example, had been deprived of his belt which supported his trousers. The president of the court (if this sham could be called a court) intimated that the old Feldmarschall was playing with himself while he was, in fact, trying to keep his dignity, even at this trying time, by holding up his trousers. The executions, which were most barbaric, were filmed for Hitler, and he watched them with the greatest of pleasure. This produced disgust even in some of his most ardent supporters, who had been summoned to witness the reprisals meted out to the conspirators. The special Wound Badge which Hitler introduced to reward those who were injured in the assassination attempt is described in D.004.

Not all the conspirators were hanged with piano wire on meat hooks at the same time. Admiral Canaris, for example, who had been head of the Abwehr, the German Secret Service, was sent to Flossenburg concentration camp, where he was held in the prison block. He managed to tap out on 9 April 1945, 'They are supposed to hang me tomorrow'. In fact he was garrotted with a violin string, in a grotesque ordeal that lasted half an hour.

The Army from 20 July 1944 was basically subjugated to SS. rules. The Nazi salute was introduced for all members of the Army and no General was above suspicion. Hitler's loss of confidence was only mirrored by that of his Generals who were now unable to do anything positive to stop the war but just waited and hoped for the inevitable defeat.

It is interesting to note that of all the commanders of the Army, only two were called to book at the end of the war, and these were Generaloberst Alfred Jodl and Generalfeldmarschall Wilhelm Keitel, both of whom signed the unconditional surrender of Germany. The Bomb Plot Badge illustrated in D.004 is the actual example awarded to Jodl, who gave it to his American jailor at Nuremberg before his execution. Keitel also suffered the same fate, and it is interesting to note that his was not unlike that of Canaris as the American hangman bungled his execution, which took half an hour to complete.

Introduction to the Waffen-SS

Hitler needed a Praetorian guard to protect him at rallies and political meetings so, in March 1923, from the ranks of the SA, the most reliable members were recruited to form a bodyguard for the Führer. During the next few months this unit and the 'Stosstrupp Adolf Hitler' merged into one specialist force which played an important part in the Munich Putsch of 9 November 1923. It became banned along with the Nazi Party after the failure of the Putsch and the subsequent imprisonment of Hitler and his lieutenants in Landsberg Prison. However, it did not disband but went underground where it strengthened and reorganized itself, and when the ban was lifted on the Nazi Party in 1925, emerged as the 'Schutzstaffel'. This small unit numbered only 250 members in 1926 and came under the guiding hand of its new commander Heinrich Himmler. During the next three years the membership was only enlarged by thirty members and a great deal of rivalry was created between the infant SS, because of their privileges and special position, and the numerically superior body of the original SA.

Hitler decreed that the SS should be enlarged and by 1933 it had reached approximately 152,000 members. In March of this year it was decided that a professionally trained full-time bodyguard unit was required, and the first of these was formed on 17 March 1933. In June 1933 three new companies were added to this, and in September of that year at the Nuremberg Party Rally these units were renamed 'SS–Leibstandarte *Adolf Hitler*'.

The SS was involved in the SA purge and the subsequent execution of its leader, Ernst Rohm. The debauchery and homosexual tendencies of some of the SA leaders had embarrassed Hitler and their eradication was the baptism of fire for the SS, which helped Himmler to demonstrate the SS's total loyalty to Hitler. The outcome of this purge catapulted the SS to prominence. They expanded their ideas and Himmler brought in a very stringent set of regulations for its members. Any early member who did not come up to those regulations was expelled. Himmler did not want any repeat of the Rohm purge or any scandal to be attached to his new 'Order'. Officer training schools were introduced at 'SS-Schule Tölz' and 'SS-Schule

Braunschweig'. To these were added the SS–Medical Academy and SS–Administrative School. A riding and a music school were also established. Himmler, as a former school teacher, wished to make sure that his men had the best opportunities of education, to fit them for any task on an equal footing with the other armed services. Thus the foundations of the fourth arm of the military Services was formed.

Even before the beginning of the Second World War it was decided to produce a fighting SS or, as it became known, the Waffen-SS. This initially consisted of members of the full time paramilitary formations of the SS already in existence.

It fell to Gottlob Berger to find the replacements that would soon be needed to refill the units' casualties and to try and expand the force as a whole. However, the Army was opposed to the use of the Waffen-SS and this is illustrated by the fact that the *Totenkopf* Division, although sent to France, was held in reserve, much to the annoyance of SS-Obergruppenführer und General der Waffen-SS Theodore Eicke. His troops had been used in the Polish campaign earlier but he had not gained enough importance for his division or for the Waffen-SS as a whole. He saw the French theatre as his opportunity to achieve this aim. Eicke was an empire-builder and would encourage his supply officers to raid any store of equipment for supplies, an exercise that Himmler disliked but often had to defend to his Allgemeine-SS commanders as well as to his Army General associates.

At 21:15 on 14 May 1940, as the spearhead of Army Group A prepared to break out of the Meuse bridgeheads, the operational section of OKH alerted Eicke that the moment he had been waiting for had come, and to stand by for marching orders. This order, much to Eicke's annoyance, did not come until 17 May when he was instructed to move west across the southern tip of Holland and through Belgium, to link up with General Hermann Hoth's XV Panzer Korps. The *Totenkopf* was to be flung directly into action to add depth and muscle to Hoth's fast-moving corps.

It was their subsequent fighting prowess that gained the respect, although begrudgingly, of the Army Generals but it also provoked fear in them, a fear that was to be well founded in later years. It also spawned some of the first atrocities, which in certain cases were most barbaric although, if one looks at Waffen-SS records as a whole, one finds that the atrocities tended to be restricted to only certain small groups or commanders.

One such excess was when the *Totenkopf* Division had been held up by the British at a canal. Eicke had ordered his men across, which they did, sustaining very heavy casualties. He was ordered to halt and then finally withdraw. He was enraged at the order and, in this evacuation, lost even more of his men as well as the bridging they had constructed. Eicke apparently challenged the halt and withdraw order, spluttering at Hoepner, that 'losses made no difference, and when one held a position the SS did not retreat in the face of the enemy'. Hoepner, furious with this insubordination, called the former concentration camp commander 'a butcher' to his face. The British strengthened their position and two days of mortar and machine-gun fire took a toll on men and machinery. Eicke became more irritated and finally instructed Obersturmfuhrer Harrer to lead a specially selected combat group to reconnoitre the other bank of the canal. Successfully crossing it, suddenly the SS men spotted a British motor cycle courier speeding towards them. He was dismounted by a single shot from a Mauser rifle by one of the SS men. They found him with a broken shoulder, lying in a ditch. They tried to question him, unsuccessfully. Obersturmführer Harrer finally asked the courier, in halting English, if he spoke French. When he did not reply, Harrer calmly drew his pistol and shot the motor cyclist at point-blank range through the head. His body and motor cycle were thrown unceremoniously into the ditch out of sight and the group continued on its way.

With the fall of France, the Low Countries, Denmark and Norway, Berger established recruiting officers in all the occupied territories and Axis countries. This enabled him to raise the recruits that he required without being stopped by the quotas imposed on the SS by the other three Services. So by the end of the war, the SS had been expanded to encompass not only all the nationals of Europe, including even British personnel (albeit only approximately sixty in the *Britische Freikorps*), but also Indians in the *Azad Hind Fauj* and Moslems in the *Handschar* and *Skanderbeg* Div-

isions and the Ostturkischer Waffen-Verband der SS. It is ironically reported that a Jewish brigade of the SS was in existence, with the Jewish candlestick as the motif on the collar patch ... As far as the *Britische Frei-korps* and the Irish Brigade are concerned, any use they might have had to the Waffen-SS must have been counter-productive, as illustrated by the conduct of two members of the Irish Brigade. Sent on a mission to Britain, they were found in Denmark too drunk to continue the mission, which led to it being aborted!

The SS fought with fanaticism up to the end of the war. In fact in the closing days, the cadets and officers at the school of Bad Tölz were banded together into the *Nibelungen* Division, which was supposed to fight on regardless of the outcome of the surrender, in an operation known as 'Werewolf'. This came to little, with the capture and final suicide of the Reichsführer-SS Heinrich Himmler at Luneberg. Himmler had arrived at night and by 23:00 he was dead. The SS was dead along with its master, so much so that Erich Kern, a former Waffen-SS officer, retold how a Knights Cross holder of the Waffen-SS had hung himself in a camp latrine, leaving a note stating that he could no longer live now that his Reichsführer had betrayed him.

The fanatics to the cause who still persisted in anti-partisan activities were dealt with with the greatest of severity. The fear of 'Werewolf' engendered by the propaganda of Dr Goebbels had worked. Witness the fate of Otto Teuteberg, an SS soldier who had been arrested in Duisburg and charged with shooting at

American soldiers. He was executed for these 'Werewolf' activities in Braunschweig during June 1945. In March 1945 the Americans court-martialled and sentenced to death two Hitler Youth members, aged sixteen and seventeen, who had been assigned to 'Werewolf' activities, and these executions were carried out on 6 June 1945. The Americans also meted excessively savage sentences to any SS group that comprised of 'Werewolf' or the *Frei Korp Adolf Hitler*, some boys of between the ages of twelve and fifteen being sentenced to life imprisonment.

The Thousand-Year Reich and its asphalt soldiers had passed into history with the demise of its Führer and Reichsführer. The last of the Teutonic Knights had perished in the Valhalladic fires that now abounded in Germany.

Index to Army and Waffen-SS War Badges 1937-1945

A.001 Army Parachutists Badge   159
A.002 Infantry Assault Badge—Silver Class   160
AV.002 Infantry Assault Badge—Silver Class—Variation   160
A.003 Infantry Assault Badge—Bronze Class   160
A.004 Silver Tank Battle Badge   163
A.005 Silver Tank Battle Badge—25 Class   164
A.006 Silver Tank Battle Badge—50 Class   164
A.007 Silver Tank Battle Badge—75 Class   166
A.008 Silver Tank Battle Badge—100 Class   166
A.009 Silver Tank Battle Badge—200 Class   166
A.010 Bronze Tank Battle Badge   167
A.011 Bronze Tank Battle Badge—25 Class   167
A.012 Bronze Tank Battle Badge—50 Class   167
A.013 Bronze Tank Battle Badge—75 Class   168
A.014 Bronze Tank Battle Badge—100 Class   168
A.015 Bronze Tank Battle Badge—200 Class   168
A.016 General Assault Badge   168
AV.016 General Assault Badge—Variation   168
A.017 General Assault Badge—25 Class   169
A.018 General Assault Badge—50 Class   169
A.019 General Assault Badge—75 Class   170
A.020 General Assault Badge—100 Class   170
A.021 General Assault Badge—Bronze Class   171
A.022 Army Flak Badge   171
A.023 Close Combat Bar—Bronze Class   172
A.024 Close Combat Bar—Silver Class   172
A.025 Close Combat Bar—Gold Class   172

A.026 Army Balloon Observers Badge—Bronze Class   178
A.027 Army Balloon Observers Badge—Silver Class   178
A.028 Army Balloon Observers Badge—Gold Class   178
A.029 Anti-Partisan War Badge—Bronze Class—First Type   179
A.030 Anti-Partisan War Badge—Silver Class—First Type   179
A.031 Anti-Partisan War Badge—Gold Class—First Type   179
A.032 Anti-Partisan War Badge—Bronze Class—Second Type   181
A.033 Anti-Partisan War Badge—Silver Class—Second Type   181
A.034 Anti-Partisan War Badge—Gold Class—Second Type   181
A.035 Anti-Partisan War Badge in Gold with Diamonds   181
A.036 Special Badge for Single-handed Destruction of a
       Tank—Silver Class   181
A.037 Special Badge for Single-handed Destruction of a
       Tank—Gold Class   181
A.038 Badge for Shooting Down Low-Flying Aircraft—Silver Class   182
A.039 Badge for Shooting Down Low-Flying Aircraft—Gold Class   182
A.040 Snipers Badge—First Class   183
A.041 Snipers Badge—Second Class   183
A.042 Snipers Badge—Third Class   183

A.001 Army Parachutists Badge

This badge comprises an oval wreath surmounted at the top by an eagle with downswept wings, of the Army style. The central emblem of the badge was a diving eagle grasping in its talons a Swastika which was usually unsegmented. The eagle was silver with fine fletching and spread talons. (The position of the talons is important in detecting a fake, for the rear talon should be separate and pointing backwards.) The eagle was fixed by two rivets on to the wreath. The pin on the reverse was vertical and of the needle type. It is unusual to find a maker on the reverse. When, however, it does appear it is usually C.E. JUNCKER. The badge was constructed of quality bronze or white metal with the wreath gilded and the eagle silvered. A version was also made of aluminium with a unique

Army Parachutists Badge (A.001).

hinge construction and fine ball rivets. It was produced by the firm of C.E. Juncker too and is particularly rare.

The date of introduction of the badge was 1 September 1937 and it was authorized by the commander-in-chief of the army, Generaloberst Frhr von Fritsch. The badge was discontinued when all the paratroop services were taken under Luftwaffe control in 1939, but its recipients did not have to quality for the new Luftwaffe Paratroopers Badge, L.014. Hence the rarity of this award.

The Criteria for the award were:

1) To have completed the instruction course for paratroopers successfully.

2) To have made five qualifying jumps.

3) Once having received the qualification badge, to make six jumps annually.

The badge was awarded with an award document and a jump licence, which had to have the information concerning the descents entered in it. Both these documents are rare. The box for the badge was blue with a blue flock lining and FALL-SCHIRMSCHÜTZEN ABZEICHENDES HEERES in gold on the outside of its lid.

This badge is also found in embroidered cotton for NCOs so it was presumably also produced in bullion for officers.

A.002 Infantry Assault Badge—Silver Class
AV.002 Infantry Assault Badge—Silver Class—Variation
A.003 Infantry Assault Badge—Bronze Class

This badge consisted of an oak leaf wreath surmounted by a downswept, winged eagle. Across the wreath, pointing from right to left, was a rifle, a Kar 98, with a fixed bayonet. There were many manufacturers and similarly many techniques used in the production of this badge. The general quality of the design and manufacture was of the highest quality. Considering its liberal award, the badge is a most pleasing design.

I have been able to categorize the silver badge into two main types: solid reverse and hollow stamping. Both categories were of good quality and the silver plating shiny with the highlights silver-frosted. The bronze version, on the other hand, tends to absorb its colour and does not have the same attractive appearance. In fact, the highlighted or leading edges of the badge tend to lighten and give it the appearance of being very well worn, although the metal surface may not be worn at all.

The pin construction was usually of a needle type, and of a vertical nature. Screw backs, however, are encountered, and are considered to be most rare, although this scarcity does not tend to increase the monetary value of the badge in proportion!

The badge was designed by C.E.

Infantry Assault Badge — Silver Class (A.002). Example of hollow-stamped type.

Above *An example of the solid reverse Infantry Assault Badge — Silver Type. Both these badges are constructed from high grade silver plate.*

Juncker of Berlin under the direction of the OKH and was instituted in the silver form on 20 December 1939 by Generaloberst von Brauchitsch. The bronze version was introduced on 1 June 1940 and was designed to reward the members of motorized infantry units.

Below *Infantry Assault Badge — Bronze Class (A.003). This badge was found at Bastogne, buried in the ground in a Woodbine packet, in 1983.*

The Criteria for the award were:
Silver award—

1) To have taken part in three or more infantry assaults.

2) To have taken part in three or more infantry counter-attacks or combinations of 1 and 2.

3) To have taken part in three or more armed reconnaissance operations.

4) To have been engaged in hand-to-hand combat in an assault position.

5) To have participated on three separate days in the restitution of combat positions.

Bronze award—

1) To have taken part in three or more motorized infantry assaults.
2) To have taken part in three or more motorized infantry counter-attacks or combinations of 1 and 2.
3) To have taken part in three or more motorized armed recon-naissance operations.
4) To have been engaged in hand-to-hand combat in a motorized assault position.

Left *Citation for the Silver Class of the Infantry Assault Badge to Georg Müller.*

Below *Infantry Assault Badge — Silver Class — Variation (AV.002) on the left compared with the normal badge.*

5) To have participated on three separate days in the restitution of the motorized combat position.

This badge was rendered with an award document which was a simple affair and many different types of printing and designs may be encountered. Some companies or divisions in the early days of the war even made facsimiles of the battle scene, with the badge superimposed upon it to form the award document. It was normally awarded in a simple paper packet with the designation of the award printed on it. A cloth version of this badge on printed linen was also produced.

Little is known about the variation, AV.002, but for the fact that it does exist. It was produced by the Laura firm of Nurnberg. It consisted of a similar oak leaf wreath, but surmounted by an open-winged eagle clutching a Swastika in a wreath. This eagle was of the 'political' type. It also had a rifle of the same type as the other two badges, but in this case a bolt of lightning flashing upwards from left to right. The reverse of the badge was flat with the maker's logo stamped on it, but on the reverse the badge did not have a pin. This leads one to the supposition that it was a prototype design that was not taken up because the Junkers pattern had been preferred. Another theory is that this badge was to reward the political troops of the SA who had been engaged in fighting, which would make it unique. The other consideration is that the Laura company produced mainly politically oriented awards, but all of these theories are only circumstantial and any further information regarding this or other examples of the badge, or theory to its award, would be most gratefully received by this author.

A.004 Silver Tank Battle Badge

This award consisted of an egg-shaped wreath of oak leaves, surmounted by an eagle with down-spread wings. Through the wreath a tank passed from left to right, from the viewer's position. The reverse of the badge usually followed the design of the obverse, although it does not seem to be die-stamped. The normal type of pin construction was the vertical needle pin. The general construction and manufacture of the badge was of very good quality, but the finish of the plating deteriorated with the advance of the war, early pieces being silver-plated while later versions have a grey zinc finish.

The badge was designed by Ernst Peekhaus of Berlin and introduced on 20 December 1939, by order of Generaloberst von Brauchitsch, and could be earned or awarded to drivers, radio operators, gunners and tank commanders.

The Criteria for the award were:
1) To have taken part in three armoured assaults, on three different days.
2) To have been wounded in an assault.
3) To have won a decoration for bravery in an assault.

The badge was awarded with a document which was a relatively sim-

ple piece of paper, printed in black type, having the company commander's signature at the bottom, with the unit's number beneath and in the left-hand corner, the company stamp. The badge was awarded in a simple paper packet which comes in varying colours, with the name printed on the front.

Left *Silver Tank Battle Badge (A.004).*

Right and far right *Observe and reverse of the Silver Tank Battle Badge — 25 Class (A.005) — awarded to Major Walter Pössl.*

Below right *Major Walter Pössl.*

Below far right *Silver Tank Battle Badge — 50 Class (A.006).*

A.005 Silver Tank Battle Badge—25 Class
A.006 Silver Tank Battle Badge—50 Class

In June 1943 it was considered that the tank badge did not properly recognize the competence of the long-serving members of the armoured forces. Two new designs were introduced to remedy this deficiency. The first was the A.005 and A.006 type, and consisted of a wreath of oak leaves with a box at the apex. This box was oblong, and contained a number, either 25 or 50, representing the number of engagements in which the recipient had been involved.

The numbers were raised in Arabic numerals and gilded, while the field was in relief and painted black. The top of the wreath was surmounted by

a finely detailed eagle. The wreath itself was silvered, while the tank was of a blackened oxidized finish. The badge was of a two-part construction, while the tank was larger than in the former unnumbered version.

The reverse took two distinct variations of manufacture. The first, and more desirable version from a collector's point of view, had the manufacturer's logo, R.K. and J.FS. The tank was secured to the wreath by two ball rivets. The pin was vertical and the hinge construction of an unusual type, the wreath being cut to let the pin shank fit beneath the cut, and then the piece of metal of the wreath

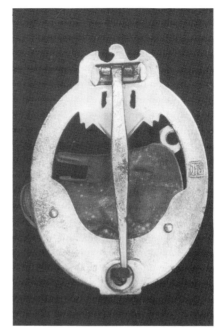

being folded on to the shank. The hook at the bottom was held in a round ball. The manufacturer's logo was usually placed on the viewer's right-hand side of the wreath, on the reverse.

The second type of reverse was found on the 'GB' type, the wreath in this version being pressed out (known as the hollow reverse) with the tank also being pressed out and fixed on to the wreath with hollow rivets. The pin in this case was a needle type with the normal hinge and hook construction.

The badge was rendered with an award document, again of a plain nature, and presented in a plain paper packet of various colours, with just the name of the badge printed on the front.

A.007 Silver Tank Battle Badge—75 Class
A.008 Silver Tank Battle Badge—100 Class

As the war progressed the need for even higher numbers gave rise to the inception of this type of badge. It had a totally different style of construction to A.005 and A.006, in that the oak leaves which formed the outer edges of the wreath actually were cut out, so that both the inner and outer edges of the wreath took the line of the oak leaves, giving it a rough appearance. The bottom was also flatter, with an oak leaf spreading horizontally from each side of the box containing the numbers. The numerals were again Arabic and raised, while the field was recessed and blackened. The wreath was gilded while the tank was silver. The reverse can again be found in the two types as previously described. The badge was presented with an award document, but the precise nature or description of this is unknown to the author. The badge was presented in a simple paper packet in varying colours with its name printed on the front.

A.009 Silver Tank Battle Badge—200 Class

Little is known of this badge or its recipient, or even whether it was awarded or not. I include a direct quote from *For Führer and Fatherland*, volume 1, by Angolia: 'This specimen bears a 200 device, is hallmarked on the reverse and is known to have been awarded in at least one case'. In conversation with the author, Lieutenant Colonel Agolia said that the recipient went into his shop and showed him the badge as well as the entry in his paybook, but was not prepared to part with the items.

Silver Tank Battle Badge — 75 Class (A.007).

Bronze Tank Battle Badge (A.010).

A.010 Bronze Tank Battle Badge

This badge was instituted for the crews of armoured vehicles other than tanks, which comprised self-propelled gunners and the like, the Panzergrenadier personnel and the support units, including medical personnel who were engaged in helping the battlefield wounded. It was in all respects the same as the silver award A.004, and was introduced on 1 June 1940. The badge was awarded with a document which again takes many different formats, but basically was printed in black with the company commander's signature at the bottom. In the left-hand bottom corner was the company's stamp. The badge was presented in a paper packet which came in varying colours, with the badge type printed on the front.

A.011 Bronze Tank Battle Badge—25 Class
A.012 Bronze Tank Battle Badge—50 Class

This was again identical to the equivalent silver grades, A.005 and A.006, except that the wreath was finished in bronze and the tank in silver. The reverses were to be the same. It was presented with an award document and came in a paper packet in varying colours, with the badge type printed on the front.

A.013 Bronze Tank Battle Badge—75 Class
A.014 Bronze Tank Battle Badge—100 Class

Again identical to the equivalent silver grades, A.007 and A.008, except on this occasion the tank was bronze and the wreath gold. The reverses are encountered once again with the same variations as on the equivalent silver grades. The badge was presented with an award document, and was housed in a paper packet, with the type printed on the front.

A.015 Bronze Tank Battle Badge—200 Class

This badge has yet to be proved to have existed, and is included to stimulate a positive response from the reader.

A.016 General Assault Badge
AV.016 General Assault Badge—Variation

The design of this badge consisted of an egg-shaped wreath with oak leaves running around it. The central device was that of the Army eagle clutching a Swastika in its talons, surmounting a bayonet and crossed grenade. The reverse was either solid or hollow stamped with a needle pin. A private purchase version was available with a screw back plate, the hinge and hook being replaced by a screw post. This type is quite rare.

The badge was designed by the firm of Ernst Peekhaus of Berlin, and was instituted by General von Brauchitsch on 1 June 1940. It was originally intended as the Engineers Assault Badge, but was quickly redesignated to include members of the artillery, anti-tank and anti-aircraft units who served with the infantry and armour in the auxiliary role during an assault. As well as the original engineers, medical personnel treating the battlefield wounded were entitled to be awarded this badge.

The Criteria for the award were:
1) The recipient must not be eligible for the Infantry Assault Badge. A.002 or A.003.
2) To have taken part in three infantry or armoured assaults on three different days.
3) To have taken part in three infantry or armoured indirect assaults on three different days.
4) To have been wounded in either 2 or 3.
5) To have won a decoration in either 2 or 3.

This badge was awarded with a certificate or Citation which sometimes had a facsimile of the badge at its top. It was printed on white paper

General Assault Badge (A.016).

General Assault Badge — Variation (AV.016) (Mohawk Arms via J.R. Angolia).

with black lettering, again with the usual commanding officer's signature at the bottom and the unit to which the recipient belonged, and the company stamp in the lower left-hand corner.

The badge was presented in a plain paper packet which could be in varying colours, depending on manufacturer and availability, with the designation of the badge printed on the front. It has also been known for it to come in a lowly cellophane packet.

Like AV.002, AV.016 again is a prototype made by the firm of Laura. It consists of a wreath of oak leaves surmounted by a standard Army eagle with, at its base, a tie produced of an outer single ribbon with, in the centre, five round dots as opposed to two outer ribbons and five dots as in the former badge. At the base are a crossed bayonet and grenade with three bolts of lightning emanating from the Swastika which is held in the eagle's talons.

A.017 General Assault Badge—25 Class
A.018 General Assault Badge—50 Class

There was a need to upgrade the General Assault Badge, A.016, to recognize the military skill of the veterans, so on 22 June 1943 four

General Assault Badge — 25 Class (A.017).

General Assault Badge — 50 Class (A.018).

new grades were introduced. The design of the first two were identical except for the number in the box. It consisted of a wreath of oak leaves similar to the unnumbered badge but which was silvered. The eagle in this case was larger and very finely executed. Once again it was clutching in its talons a Swastika and surmounted the crossed bayonet and grenade. This central motif was finished in a black oxidized finish and was separate from the wreath, to which it was attached by four ball rivets. The pin was of the broad blade type and the hinge was held on to the wreath by part of the wreath being cut and then turned back on to the hinge. The hook was held in a ball at the base of

the wreath. The makers were usually R. K. and J. F. S.

A retrospective credit was given for service in Russia and was taken to the start of the Russian campaign on 22 June 1941. The 'credits' were:

1) Eight months service equalled ten actions.
2) Twelve months service equalled fifteen actions.
3) Fifteen months service equalled 25 actions.

The Citation that accompanied the award was a plain affair, only stating the grade of the badge. Once again the company commanding officer's signature was at the bottom with the unit and the usual company stamp in the lower left-hand corner.

A.019 General Assault Badge—75 Class
A.020 General Assault Badge—100 Class

These badges were introduced at the same time as the preceding two, again

to recognize the service of the combat veterans. They were identical

General Assault Badge — 100 Class (A.020).

but this time the edges of the leaves formed the edge of the wreath, the base of which was flat. The eagle was larger than the numbered 25 and 50 grade, with segmented legs clutching in its talons a Swastika, which was also slightly larger than in the preceding badges. It surmounted a crossed bayonet and grenades. This device was separate from the wreath and was joined to it by four ball rivets. It had a broad pin with hinge attached to the wreath by the wreath being cut, and then turned back on to the hinge fitting. The hook was held in a ball at the base of the wreath. The makers were usually R.K. and J.F.S.

The Citation for these awards is unknown to this author but it is presumed that they would take the format of the former citations. Again the packets for these badges were paper with the grade printed on to them.

except for the numbers in the boxes, which were in Arabic numerals and were proud and gilded with a flat field, which was painted black. The wreath was constructed of oak leaves

A.021 General Assault Badge—Bronze Class

Little is known of this badge, except that it was awarded. An original is in the author's collection which had been removed from a prisoner of war in England. The prisoner's name was Erik Verling. I have encountered a number of variations of maker, so the theory of a faulty batch or a maker's variant is disproved. One possibility is that it was to reward members of assault gun, tank and self-propelled anti-tank units, as they became eligi-

ble for the award of the General Assault Badge, A.016, on 22 June 1943. In the case of these personnel the badge was also to signify the single-handed destruction of an armoured vehicle using a hand-held weapon. This may give rise to examples of the four numbered grades in bronze, to coincide with the silver grades already described. Any further information would be gratefully received by the author.

A.022 Army Flak Badge

This also consisted of an egg-shaped wreath made up of oak leaves, sur-

mounted by an eagle with folded wings of the Army type. The central

Army Flak Badge (A.022).

device was of an 8.8 cm gun, pointing to the viewer's right. The overall finish was silver with the reverse being flat with a needle pin, and sometimes the maker's mark.

It was designed by Ernst Wilhelm Peekhaus of Berlin and instituted on 13 July 1941. The badge can be found in a number of metals ranging from aluminium through to pot metal. It is considered uncommon and there have been a few good reproductions, so care is necessary when purchasing one of these badges.

The Criteria for the award were:
1) Any act of bravery or merit while performing anti-aircraft duties.
2) Being wounded during anti-aircraft duties.
3) Commanders of batteries received the badge when half the men in their command had received the award.
4) On the accumulation of sixteen points.

Points were calculated as follows: four points for destroying an enemy plane without support, or two points for destroying an enemy plane in conjunction with another unit. Sound locator and searchlight crews credited with first location received one point.

The badge was awarded with a certificate which had the derivation at the top, and in some cases a facsimile of the badge. The company commander's signature and the unit were at the bottom, and the company stamp in the left-hand lower corner. It was presented in either a box or paper packet with the name stencilled or printed on the front.

A.023 Close Combat Bar—Bronze Class
A.024 Close Combat Bar—Silver Class
A.025 Close Combat Bar—Gold Class

The date of introduction of this badge was 25 November 1942 and it was instigated by Hitler. He considered it the highest infantry decoration, and reserved the right to award the gold version personally. This he did for the first time on 27 August 1944, when he awarded fourteen officers of the army and Waffen-SS at his headquarters. By the end of the war, only 403 awards of the gold bar had taken place to the ground forces who qualified. The bar was worn above the ribbon bar in order to show

Combat Medals of the Third Reich

Above *Anti-Partisan War Badge — Bronze Class — First Type (A.029).*

Above right *Snipers Badge — First Class (A.040).*

Right *Air Crew Badge (L.001).*

Below *Pilots Badge (L.002).*

Below right *Combined Pilots and Observers Badge in Gold with Diamonds (L.004).*

Josef 'Sepp' Dietrich, commander of the 1st SS Panzer Division Leibstandarte Adolf Hitler, *in conversation with Heinrich Hoffmann (who is wearing his gold Party Badge). Believed to have been taken in Normandy in 1944, this unique photo shows Dietrich wearing his Blood Order ribbon on his right breast; Ostmedaille, golden Party Badge, a rare tank badge from the 1920s, Knights Cross with Oak Leaves, Swords and Diamonds and his Combined Pilots and Observers Badge in Gold with Diamonds. It is interesting that he is* not *wearing his Iron Cross — First Class.*

Above *Observers Badge (L.007).*

Above right *Radio Operators and Air Gunners Badge (L.008).*

Right *Glider Pilots Badge — First Type (L.011).*

Below *Flyers Commemorative Badge (L.013).*

Below right *Parachutists Badge (L.014).*

Above left *Anti-Aircraft War Badge (L.015).*

Above *Ground Combat Badge (L.016). A poor photograph of a 25 Class award shows the tie at the base replaced by a box with the number in it, flanked by an additional oak leaf each side giving the medal a flat-bottomed appearance.*

Left *Bomber Operational Flying Clasp — Gold Class (L.041).*

Below left *Reconnaissance Operational Flying Clasp — Gold Class with Anhanger (L.044).*

Below *Long Range Day Fighters Operational Flying Clasps: top, Silver Class (L.049); bottom, Gold Class with Anhanger (L.050).*

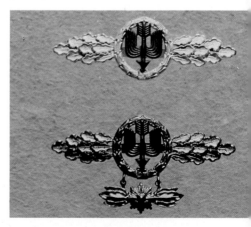

Top *Close Combat Bar — Bronze Class (A.023).*

Middle *Close Combat Bar — Silver Class (A.024).*

Above *Close Combat Bar — Gold Class (A.025).*

the high esteem in which the award was held.

The designer was Ernst Wilhelm Peekhaus. The three bars were identical except for colour and were made up of a square box with a black back plate. There was an Army-style eagle surmounting crossed bayonet and grenade at the top, the sides of the box being constructed of two oak leaves. From the box, equally on either side, emanated two sets of arrowheads made up of lines. Surmounting these on either side were four oak leaves. Adjacent to each square where the oak leaves joined were two small acorns on each side. The reverse was flat save for the maker's logo, which was usually found in two parts on either side of the back plate. The pin's hinge was an integral part of the blade, and the pins were usually of a broad type and made in a corrugated construction.

The Criteria for the award were:

1) The man must have been engaged in hand-to-hand combat when supported by armour.

2) A bronze Bar required fifteen days of close combat, which could be reduced to ten days if the man had been wounded.

3) A silver Bar required thirty days which could be reduced to twenty if he had been wounded.

4) A gold Bar required fifty days which could be reduced to forty if he had been wounded.

For service in Russia a restrospec-tive credit was introduced back to June 1941 with a service ratio of: five combat days being represented by eight months' service; ten combat days being represented by twelve months' service; and fifteen combat days being represented by fifteen months' service.

The badge was accompanied by an award certificate which was similar to the others already described in the book, and it was presented in a plain paper packet with the name printed on the front. As the war progressed this paper packet was replaced by a lowly cellophane one.

A.026 Army Balloon Observers Badge—Bronze Class
A.027 Army Balloon Observers Badge—Silver Class
A.028 Army Balloon Observers Badge—Gold Class

The badge was introduced on 8 July 1944 by the OKH to recognize the bravery of the balloon observers who had been extensively used by the Army for artillery and other observations on the eastern front. The badge was produced by a firm in Dresden and consisted of a wreath of oak leaves, with two acorns at its base and surmounted by a closed-winged Army eagle. This eagle looked to the viewer's right and the beak was joined to the wing, giving it a bearded effect.

Army Balloon Observers Badge — Bronze Class (A.026).

The centre was a balloon with a Balkan cross on it. It looked like a barrage balloon. The reverse was a negative of the obverse with a needle pin. The quality of the striking of this badge is of the highest order. The gauge of the metal is fairly thick which makes the badge quite heavy. The quality of the badge cannot be justifiably recognized from photographs in reference books.

The Criteria for the award were on a points basis, but how the points were accumulated is not known to this author. A bronze badge required twenty points, silver 45 and gold 75. The award of the bronze and silver badges is confirmed, but the gold award does not appear to have been given. The recipient of a gold award must have been either slightly insane or had a death wish!

This is one of the most difficult badges to obtain. The Citation is also unknown to this author and any further information would be gratefully received.

A.029 Anti-Partisan War Badge—Bronze Class—First Type
A.030 Anti-Partisan War Badge—Silver Class—First Type
A.031 Anti-Partisan War Badge— Gold Class—First Type

Anti-Partisan War Badge — Bronze Class — First Type (A.029).

This badge was introduced on 30 January 1944 by Hitler to reward members of the security forces who had been involved in anti-partisan operations. Up until October 1942 this had been the responsibility of the Army, but after this date the Waffen-SS undertook its direction with SS-Obergruppenführer von dem Bach-Zelewski becoming the chief of staff for anti-partisan warfare operations.

Himmler expressed a wish that he should present the gold awards personally. This he did when he invested the first four gold awards on 15 February 1945. One of the recipients was SS-Obersturmführer Erich Kuhbandner. The badge he received was probably the same as the other three

Anti-Partisan War Badge — Silver Class — First Type (A.030).

and outer edges of the badge were pronounced. The oak leaves which comprised the wreath were well pronounced, as were the skull and bones at the base which appear to lie on a bed of oak leaves. The handle of the sword had four pronounced spots, and the sun wheel that formed the cross-bar or hilt of the sword was crisp. The reverse of the badge was flat and slightly concave and the pin could be either of the pin or broad flat form. Another point when observing the two types of badges together is that the heads of the snakes in this badge can be easily identified from the other designs of the badge.

The Criteria for the award were:
1) Bronze Award—thirty combat days.
2) Silver Award—75 combat days.
3) Gold Award—100 combat days.
Luftwaffe personnel—
4) Bronze Award—thirty operational sorties.
5) Silver Award—75 operational sorties.
6) Gold Award—150 operational sorties.
7) Being shot down counted as three sorties.

The Citation for this badge is unknown, the only known example being that of the one awarded to Erik Kuhbandner, and it is assumed that this was a hand-produced item for this special presentation. Again, any information as to the form of Citation would be greatly appreciated. The type of container for the award is also unknown, but it is believed to have been a green box with a burgundy flock base and white silk lining.

awarded at that ceremony. On inspection it was found to be unique in the fact that it was hand-finished and gilded with a chemically blued sword blade. At this point it is worth saying that there are approximately eleven variations in this series of badges, but I have condensed them all into two distinct types. The Criteria for the award of both these types of badge were identical, and this badge was awardable to all the Services involved in anti-partisan warfare.

This type was produced by the firm of Juncker and production carried on until the firm was bombed out. The main ingredient of this badge was a silhouetted snake's head, with fine scales on its head and body. The inner

A.032 Anti-Partisan War Badge—Bronze Class—Second Type
A.033 Anti-Partisan War Badge—Silver Class—Second Type
A.034 Anti-Partisan War Badge—Gold Class—Second Type

This badge was identical in general design to the previous three badges, but after the bombing of the Junkers factory new dies had to be produced which gave rise to this different variety. The oak leaves in this badge were more pronounced and filled the wreath. The scales of the snakes were not as well engraved as in the former design, nor was the skull, which in this version gives the impression of a monkey's face. The bones and oak leaves which it surmounted were not so well defined either. The reverse was hollow and took the shape of the obverse, and in this case the holes which silhouetted the snake's head were rough. The pin in this version could be of either the pin or flat broad blade type.

A.035 Anti-Partisan War Badge in Gold with Diamonds

There were supposedly twenty examples of this badge produced, and it is probable that these were produced to reward those members of anti-partisan warfare groups who had been awarded the Knights Cross with Oak Leaves (D.019) in this type of operation. The design of the badge is assumed to have been the same as previously described but made in silver which was gilded, with nine rose-cut diamonds set in the sun wheel that produced the hilt of the sword. These badges were made by the firm of C.E. Juncker of Berlin.

A.036 Special Badge for Single-Handed Destruction of a Tank—Silver Class
A.037 Special Badge for Single-Handed Destruction of a Tank—Gold Class

On 9 March 1942 a new badge was introduced to reward the destruction of armoured fighting vehicles or tanks. It was not for members of anti-tank units, but for other Service personnel who destroyed a fighting veh-

Special Badge for Single-Handed Destruction of a Tank — Silver Class (A.036) Tim Stannard Collection).

icle single-handed. By 18 December 1943 the need for a higher grade of the award was recognized, so the gold class was brought into being. The badge comprised a Russian T-34 tank on a silver or gold card background.

The Criteria for the award were:

1) One silver emblem was awarded for each fighting vehicle destroyed.

2) Four awards could be worn at any one time, being worn one directly above the other on the upper arm of the tunic.

3) On the fifth award, the five badges were exchanged for one gold one.

4) This process was continued with a gold award with silver badges beneath it until the tenth badge was awarded, when the silver ones were replaced by another gold. This process continued with silver awards being given until the fifteenth, and so on.

A.038 Badge for Shooting Down Low-Flying Aircraft—Silver Class
A.039 Badge for Shooting Down Low-Flying Aircraft—Gold Class

On 12 January 1945 these two badges were introduced for destroying low-flying aircraft by means of small arms or machine-gun fire. The badge comprised a small single-engined plane surmounted on a piece of either silver or gold cloth backing. The award of either of these badges is very uncertain, but an actual example of the emblem produced prior to 1945 was returned from Germany in 1948 by my uncle. This emblem comprised a silver metal 'plane. On the reverse of the 'plane, which seemed to be stamped out, was a round pin like a pop stud which enabled it to be secured to the backing.

Badge for Shooting Down Low-Flying Aircraft — Silver Class (A.038).

A.040 Snipers Badge—First Class
A.041 Snipers Badge—Second Class
A.042 Snipers Badge—Third Class

On 20 August 1944 this series of badges was instigated. They were

Snipers Badge — First Class (A.040).

Snipers Badge — Third Class (A.042). Since it lacks the usual acorn, it may be a manufacturer's variation, but is not a normal variation (J.R. Angolia Collection).

initially only awarded to accredited Army snipers, but as the war progressed it was later made available to snipers of all branches of every Service. 1 September was the starting point for the accumulation of points and retrospective kills were not allowed to be taken into account, as this would have involved too much paperwork and verifications. The badge was made in cloth and consisted of a grey oval patch, on which was a black eagle's head with a bright yellow beak and eye, surmounting three light green oak leaves and one acorn. The Second Class badge had a silver cord surround, First Class a gold cord. The badge was to be worn on the right cuff of the jacket above any other insignia that were to be worn there.

The Criteria for the award were:
1) Third Class—twenty kills.
2) Second Class—forty kills.
3) First Class—sixty kills.

Introduction to the Luftwaffe

The halcyon days which preceded the First World War in Europe saw the armies of most European nations becoming more resplendent in their uniforms. Since 1853 and the Crimean War there had not been a real war to fight. The only other major conflagration had been the Franco-Prussian War and this had been an unequivocal German victory over the French, who suffered not only a rout but a humiliating defeat. So the Generals and Admirals of the armed forces, who were of the 'General Blimp' brigade, had to content themselves with designing ever more flamboyant uniforms and grander pageants to show off their new creations, while the administrative and boffin types busied themselves with new military inventions. So bizarre and crazy were some of these inventions and ideas that, for instance, the Russian Navy designed round battleships to fight the Japanese in the war in which they were engaged in 1904.

While the Generals busied themselves with their preoccupations, the junior officers amused themselves with cafe society in the broad boulevards of Paris, linden-lined Strasses of Berlin and the gentlemen's clubs of St James' in London. While these aspirant young officers were not involved in socializing, they were possibly on exchange visits to one another's respective countries, perhaps enabling themselves to collect another jubilee medal or gong for the service of just being there! It was in this climate of military ineptitude that two major revolutionary military advances emerged. The first was the submarine which has already been considered in the introduction to the Navy, and the second and more junior was that of flight.

At the turn of the century all of Europe was taken up with the enthusiasm of powered flight and no little interest was shown in Germany. A system of pilots' licences was introduced in 1910 by the German Aviation Association and the Inspectorate of Transport for Military Troops and Civilian Pilots. The first individual to gain one of these licences was August Euler on 1 February 1910. To reward military pilots and to give an outward recognition of their prowess the Kaiser introduced, on 27 January 1913, the Military Pilots Badge.

At the outbreak of the First World War in August 1914 the importance of aerial warfare was overlooked. It was considered a toy of little importance and those in the infant air services, backsliders who had found a way of avoiding real action. This contemptuous view was held by most of the general staffs of the combatant nations entangled in the war. However, the esprit de corps of the fledgling air forces of the two opposing alliances, enhanced by their 'knights of the air' and 'riders of the skies' attitudes, soon led to their proving their military worth, especially after the technical breakthrough of synchronized machine-guns which were able to fire through the propellers of their machines. By the end of the First World War new fighting forces on both sides had been welded together in the forges of aerial combat and the burning wreckage of crashed war planes.

The importance of aerial warfare was so much felt that the Peace Treaty of 1919 banned the German air force. Its 'planes were confiscated or broken up and the production of aero engines prohibited. Sports clubs sprang up all over Germany which undertook to teach the aeronautically minded Germans the art of flying. However, the Reichswehr, fearing that it was being left behind in its capacity to defend itself, secretly negotiated with the Red Army early in 1923 and finally signed an agreement in April 1925, which made the Lipezk Airfield in Russia available for German military training. In 1926, besides the fighter pilot training that was already underway, observer training began. Added to this, a special unit for testing new aircraft and weapons was also included.

Between 1925 and 1933 approximately 120 officers returned from this flying school in Russia fully trained as fighter pilots. Those who returned during this period kept up their skills by being incorporated as civilian pilots flying for the Lufthansa Airline. Incidentally, the airline also employed the best veteran pilots from the First World War, so the old and new pilots of Germany flew together and gained experience from one another.

When Hitler came to power in 1933 he introduced, in that year, the Deutscher Luftsport-Verband. This organization was to stimulate airminded young men. The club offered its members, most of whom had been in the armed forces, the active disciplined life for which they yearned, to such an extent that on 10 November 1933 Hitler introduced for the DLV a special uniform with rank and trade insignia. Under the direction of this organization the members learned the three main aeronautical skills, those of balloon, glider and powered flight. Hitler also abandoned the school at Lipezk and relied on the DLV to train the new personnel of his clandestine Luftwaffe.

As the NSDAP began to flex its political muscles, Hitler became more confident and on 26 February 1935 announced the official formation of the new Luftwaffe and all the secrecy that had surrounded it was blown away, as if as a prelude to events that were to come, by the winds of war.

The DLV was disbanded and all its former members encouraged to join the new National Sozialistische Flieger Korps (NSFK) that was introduced in its place. In this manner the Party brought together under its control all of the country's flying clubs into one organization which, in fact, was paramilitary. The NSFK could thus operate with the fledgling Luftwaffe and both could grow and gather strength together.

In April 1935 the first German fighter squadron emerged under the command of Major Ritter von Greim, and bore the title Jagdgeschwader Richthofen 2. The fighters made their first public display during the occupation of the Rhineland on 7 March 1936. The first Luftwaffe fighter school was established at the Deutsche Verkehrsfliegeschule (German Commercial Pilots School), at Schleissheim, thus completing the formation of the new Luftwaffe and the National Sozialistische Flieger Korps. This produced a need for the introduction of Luftwaffe qualification badges which are described in this section (those for the NSFK will be described in a later volume).

Hitler's conjuring trick had worked, through skillful propaganda and deception an astonished world was convinced that he had been able to produce a force as technically advanced as the Luftwaffe virtually out of a hat. This feat added to Hitler's international diplomatic aura and, as the Luftwaffe gained experience in Spain in the Civil War, the fear of this 'terror machine', which was interlaced with the chivalry of those knights of the air from the former days, often settled a diplomatic disagreement.

Herman Göring was to emerge, with the growth of the Luftwaffe, as Reichsmarschall of the Third Reich, resplendent with medals, instigating more to reward the heroic deeds of his aces, to himself receive the highest grade of the Iron Cross, the Grand Cross (D.024) itself, which he received on the Luftwaffe's behalf for their victory over France and the Low Countries in 1940. Later he would mirror the defeat of that Luftwaffe, which he so dearly loved, with his own surrender, final trial and suicide.

Index to Luftwaffe War Badges 1933-1945

L.001 Aircrew Badge   190
L.002 Pilots Badge   191
LV.002 Pilots Badge—Variation   193
L.003 Combined Pilots and Observers Badge   194
L.004 Combined Pilots and Observers Badge in Gold with Diamonds   194
L.005 Combined Pilots and Observers Badge in Gold with Diamonds
         —Dress Copy   197
L.006 Combined Pilots and Observers Badge in Gold with Diamonds
         (Female Class)   198
L.007 Observers Badge   198
L.008 Radio Operators and Air Gunners Badge   201
L.009 Air Gunners and Flight Engineers Badge   202
L.010 Unqualified Air Gunners and Flight Engineers Badge   203
L.011 Glider Pilots Badge—First Type   204
L.012 Glider Pilots Badge—Second Type   204
L.013 Flyers Commemorative Badge   206
L.014 Parachutists Badge   206
L.015 Anti-Aircraft War Badge   207
L.016 Ground Combat Badge   208
L.017 Ground Combat Badge—25 Class   209
L.018 Ground Combat Badge—50 Class   209
L.019 Ground Combat Badge—75 Class   209
L.020 Ground Combat Badge—100 Class   209
L.021 Close Combat Clasp—Bronze Class   210
L.022 Close Combat Clasp—Silver Class   210
L.023 Close Combat Clasp—Gold Class   210
L.024 Silver Tank Battle Badge   211
L.025 Silver Tank Battle Badge—25 Class   211
L.026 Silver Tank Battle Badge—50 Class   211
L.027 Silver Tank Battle Badge—75 Class   211
L.028 Silver Tank Battle Badge—100 Class   211
L.029 Black Tank Battle Badge   212
L.030 Black Tank Battle Badge—25 Class   213
L.031 Black Tank Battle Badge—50 Class   213
L.032 Black Tank Battle Badge—75 Class   213
L.033 Black Tank Battle Badge—100 Class   213
L.034 Sea Battle Badge   213
L.035 Day Fighter Operational Flying Clasp—Bronze Class   214
L.036 Day Fighter Operational Flying Clasp—Silver Class   214
L.037 Day Fighter Operational Flying Clasp—Gold Class   214

L.038 Day Fighter Operational Flying Clasp—Diamond Class   215
L.039 Bomber Operational Flying Clasp—Bronze Class   216
L.040 Bomber Operational Flying Clasp—Silver Class   216
L.041 Bomber Operational Flying Clasp—Gold Class   216
L.042 Reconnaissance Operational Flying Clasp—Bronze Class   218
L.043 Reconnaissance Operational Flying Clasp—Silver Class   218
L.044 Reconnaissance Operational Flying Clasp—Gold Class   218
L.045 Transport and Glider Operational Flying Clasp—Bronze Class 220
L.046 Transport and Glider Operational Flying Clasp—Silver Class 220
L.047 Transport and Glider Operational Flying Clasp—Gold Class 220
L.048 Long Range Day Fighter Operational Flying Clasp—
       Bronze Class   220
L.049 Long Range Day Fighter Operational Flying Clasp—Silver Class 220
L.050 Long Range Day Fighter Operational Flying Clasp—Gold Class 220
L.051 Long Range Night Fighter Operational Flying Clasp—
       Bronze Class   221
L.052 Long Range Night Fighter Operational Flying Clasp
       —Silver Class   221
L.053 Long Range Night Fighter Operational Flying Clasp
       —Gold Class   221
L.054 Short Range Night Fighter Operational Flying Clasp
       —Bronze Class   222
L.055 Short Range Night Fighter Operational Flying Clasp
       —Silver Class   222
L.056 Short Range Night Fighter Operational Flying Clasp
       —Gold Class   222
L.057 Air to Ground Support Operational Flying Clasp—Bronze Class 223
L.058 Air to Ground Support Operational Flying Clasp—Silver Class 223
L.059 Air to Ground Support Operational Flying Clasp—Gold Class 223
L.060 Air to Ground Support Operational Flying Clasp
       —Diamond Class   224

L.001 Air Crew Badge

The introduction of this badge into service is a little difficult to determine and understand, as is its role. The known references give its introduction as 1933 and state that it was used for the reward of pilots and observers in the clandestine Luftwaffe or the qualified members of the German Airsports Association. It did not gain official sanction, however, until 1 April 1934 and on 19 January 1935 it became the official Combined Pilots and Observers Badge. It became supplanted by the new version in November 1935 and was removed

totally from circulation. This is illustrated by a letter authorizing the return of the badges to the manufacturer for credit. However, the Luftwaffe Diary for 1942 for use by Luftwaffe personnel as a form of text book, still shows the badge in the order of badges. This gives rise to the assumption that, like that of the Army Parachutists Badge (A.001), it was still to be worn and a new badge did not have to be re-sat for.

The description of the badge is that it consisted of an oval wreath formed of oak leaves on the right and laurel leaves on the left. This was surmounted by an eagle holding a Swastika in its talons. On the reverse was a horizontal pin. The badge came in

Air Crew Badge (L.001).

Cloth version of the Air Crew Badge (L.001).

two types. The first, and possibly the more common, was in nickel silver. The eagle was riveted by two ball rivets, one through either wing into the wreath. The pin was of a broad-blade type. The badge can be totally devoid of any maker's mark or has the Junkers trade mark, which is CJJ in a box. It is believed there are approximately only eight examples known in existence.

The second type was made of aluminium, with the eagle sweated on to the wreath. In this version the wreath was die-stamped, as was the eagle. The reverse was formed with two holes, with one at either end of the badge. In the holes were countersunk the hinge mounting and hook mounting. The pin in this type was of a thin needle variety.

There was a cloth version of this badge which came in cotton thread, white cotton for the wreath and black cotton for the eagle. The fletching on the eagle's wings was picked out in white cotton.

The box for this badge was blue with a blue velvet base and blue silk lining. The Citation is unknown to this author, but one would assume was just an ordinary piece of paper giving details in black print, and the commanding officer's signature at the base.

L.002 Pilots Badge

The original instruction for this badge came on 27 May 1935, although the badge was not brought into being by Göring until 12 August

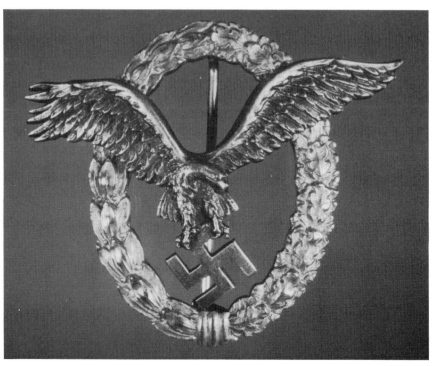

Above *Pilots Badge (L.002).*

Below *Presentation box for the Pilots Badge. In this LDO version the lettering is white instead of gold.*

Below *The 1935-1936 Pilots Badge on a round wreath.*

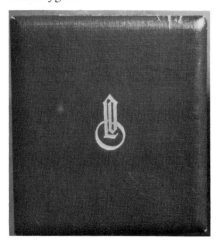

1935. On 27 November 1935 the regulations giving the exact specification for the badge were made public. It was an oval, slightly convex, silver-plated wreath, the right half of laurel and the left half of oak leaves. (This was reversed on the Air Crew Badge (L.001).) The wreath had mounted upon it an eagle in flight, oxidized and old silver-plated, clutching a Swastika in its claws. The eagle was riveted to the wreath on each side. The protruding, or raised surfaces, of the wreath were highly polished. On the reverse was a vertical hinged pin, which was soldered on. This badge was found in nickel silver or aluminium and as the war progressed, pot metal or monkey metal.

The badge was awarded on completion of flying training and when the pilot received his flying licence and Citation.

Dr Heinrich Doehle gave the institution of the badge as 26 March 1936 and this has been widely considered the official date, which gives rise to an interesting theory that the Pilots Badge from 12 March 1935 to 26 March 1936 had in fact been as described, but on a round wreath. The basis of this is that a new Combined Pilots Badge (L.003) was to replace the old Air Crew Badge (L.001) and it would be logical to have one badge for the two purposes with both the Air Crew and the round Pilots Badge (LV.002) being replaced by the new-style badge.

badge which took the form of the metal badge, but were embroidered in relief. The wreath was worked in silver on the officers' version, the eagle in oxidized silver, and the Swastika in dull aluminium thread. The NCO version was identical but expedited in cotton thread. The badge was worn on the left upper pocket of the Service uniform or flying jacket. It was issued in a box with the badge designation stencilled in gold block letters on its lid. The Citation was a plain piece of paper which sometimes had a facsimile of the badge at the head of it. The printing was in black with the commanding officer's signature at the bottom.

LV.002 Pilots Badge—Variation

The reason for this variation is unknown although I have put forward a theory for its possible use in L.002 above, but at this point I will only describe the badge and its construction leaving the theories open to comment by the reader.

In this case the wreath was round and comprised of oak leaves on the right and laurel leaves on the left as was the case in L.002. The base had a ribbon comprising three parts. The apex had a number of small berries and the overall quality of the striking was indistinct. The eagle was mounted at the top of the wreath at approximately ten to two and was identical to that found in L.002. The appearance of the Swastika was in a relatively similar position to that found in L.002, but because more dominant in the design of this badge. The space above the eagle's wings was reduced to a gap so that the apex of the wreath and the wings of the eagle nearly formed a straight line. The reverse was quite different in that the wreath was semi-dished and the eagle held on by two ball rivets as in the former badge, but at the top. The hinge was of the barrel type with a needle pin and large hook at the bottom.

All the examples that I have encountered follow this form of construction, giving rise to the possibil-ity that it was produced by one manufacturer, this design not being taken up by the Luftwaffe. One theory that has been put forward is that it was to recognise jet pilots who were being trained and came into service at the closing stages of the war. This theory I highly discount but look forward to a reader sending me a photograph of the actual piece in wear.

L.003 Combined Pilots and Observers Badge

On 26 March 1936 this badge was introduced to replace the older Air Crew Badge (L.001). It took the same format as the former badge, but the eagle was bright silver and the wreath was gilt, with the high parts of the gilt wreath polished and the indentations matt. This badge was again made in aluminium and, later in the war, pot or monkey metal. The quality of these badges varies widely from a purely silvered and gilded Pilots Badge (L.002), to a super struck and silver-plated and gilt-plated example.

The badge was awarded on completion of both the pilots' and observers' courses and was presented with licence and certificate in a blue box with blue silk lining and blue velvet badge, stencilled in blocked gold letters.

The cloth version was again identical to the pilots' form but with the colours conforming to the metal badge. The officers' version was executed in silver and gold bullion while the NCOs' version was in cotton.

The Citation was a plain piece of paper which sometimes had a facsimile of the badge at its head. The printing was in black with the commanding officer's signature at the bottom.

L.004 Combined Pilots and Observers Badge in Gold with Diamonds

This badge was possibly the most exciting flying badge of any country. Apart from its obvious beauty, the rarity and the people to whom it was awarded, notably Herman Göring himself, it also rewarded some of the bravest of the Luftwaffe pilots. It was produced by the Vienna jewellers Rudolf Stubiger.

On correspondence with the firm

Above *Combined Pilots and Observers Badge (L.003).*

Below *Presentation case of the Combined Pilots and Observers Badge.*

Right *The Combined Pilots and Observers Badge inside its case.*

Combined Pilots and Observers Badge in Gold with Diamonds (L.004).

appearance of the fletching. The general appearance of the eagle was larger and the legs were spread with a gap between them. The legs of the eagle were also finely detailed. There were 36 diamonds in the right wing and 31 in the left. A total of nineteen were inlaid in the eagle's trunk or body. Eighteen small diamonds were inlaid in the arms of the Swastika. The whole of the eagle's frame was constructed in platinum while the wreath was made of real 22 carat gold. The eagle was held on to the wreath by two massive screws. The pin was of a thin, needle type and was retained in a unique holder that acted as a safety catch.

The first award of the badge was to the chief of the Luftwaffe General Staff, Generalleutnant Wever, on 11

Citation cover for the Combined Pilots and Observers Badge in Gold with Diamonds; blue leather with gold trim (Stump via J.R. Angolia).

of Rudolf Stubiger, his son indicated that they produced seventy of these badges. On the first only the shop number was scratched on the reverse of the badge in the position of the hinge. After 1938, when Austria became part of the Greater German Reich, they placed their logo on the reverse of the eagle. This information gives one a good clue to the period and therefore the person to whom a badge was possibly awarded.

The construction of the badge was quite unique and entirely hand-produced. The eagle was constructed to allow the stones in the wing to have light coming from behind, which enhanced the fire of the diamonds. The edges of the feathers were all slightly pebbled, as was the outside of the Swastika. The upper part of the wings was highly polished, which complemented and enhanced the

November 1935 and led to the award of 55 other persons.

The known recipients were: Antonescu, Balbo, Baumbach, Baur, von Below, von Blomberg, von Brauchitsch, Bodenschatz, Christiansen, Dietrich, Dönitz, Fraff, Franco, von Gablens, Galland, Gollob, Göring, von Greim, Harlinghausen, Hartmann, Himmler, Horthy, Jeschonnek, Kammhuber, Kastner, Keller, Kesselring, Korten, Lent, Loerzer, Lohr, Mannerheim, Marseilles, Milch, Mölders, Mussolini, Naurasil, Nowotny, Parani, Peltz, Pflugbeil, Ramcke, Reitsch, von Richtofen, Rommel, Rudel, Skorzeny, Sperrle, von Stauffenberg, Student, Stumff, Trettner, Udet, Valle and Wever.

Many misbeliefs have arisen around the award of this prestigious decoration and why some of the officers were awarded the badge. The essential Criteria for the award was that each recipient had to be the holder of a pilot's licence. This licence could have been in the civil form and just encompass single-engine aeroplanes, or even to have been a glider pilots licence. Either would have qualified them for the badge, which explains some of the more unusual bestowals such as Himmler and Dietrich.

The box for this decoration is uncertain and it is considered that it was just a jeweller's case which transported the badge to the award ceremony.

For many years it appeared there was no Citation to accompany this award. Correspondence with a number of Combined Pilots and Observers Badge holders confirmed that they received neither a presentation box nor a Citation. However, the authenticity of the folder illustrated is unquestionable. Awarded to Milch, this Citation cover was accompanied by a plain square box wrapped in white parchment skin and had an Air Force blue velvet liner and matching silk lid liner. On the death of the holder this award had to be returned to Göring or his award office. This was the case with Generaloberst Korten, chief of the OKL, who was killed in the bomb plot (see D.006).

L.005 Combined Pilots and Observers Badge in Gold with Diamonds—Dress Copy

This badge is identical to the previous award but was produced in silver, with the diamonds being replaced with white sapphires. The gold parts of the badge were gilded or gold-plated and the eagle remained silver. The white sapphires were mounted in a slightly different manner. The reverse had the jeweller's mark Rudolf Stubiger Vienna 6 and the silver mark for Vienna. It had a broad-bladed pin with semi-circular end. It has been stated that every recipient received a dress copy when they were awarded the decoration. I have not been able to substantiate this and the correspondence with the recipients indicate that, and I am convinced that

this badge was a private purchase item to wear every day to protect the original. The reverse had also stamped on it 'IMIT' to identify it.

Left *Combined Pilots and Observers Badge in Gold with Diamonds — Dress Copy (L.005).*

Right *Hanna Reitsch wearing her unique 'Female Class' Combined Pilots and Observers Badge in Gold with Diamonds, its diamond-studded bar clearly visible, together with her Iron Cross First Class (D.016) and Second Class ribbon (D.013). This photograph was sent to the author specifically for this book shortly before Hanna Reitsch's death.*

L.006 Combined Pilots and Observers Badge in Gold with Diamonds (Female Class)

This badge was identical to the awarded type, being produced with real diamonds in platinum, with a gold wreath. It was produced about one third of the size and was mounted on a diamond bar. The only recipients of this exclusive award were Flugkapitän Hanna Reitsch and Frau Grafin von Stauffenberg. The former lady was a test pilot to the German airforce, who flew everything from a V1 to a Gigant. She also held the unusual honour as a woman to have had bestowed upon her both the Iron Cross Second Class and First Class of the 1939 series. In correspondence with her she stated that she received only the described Bar and not the normal award type as described in L.004, nor did she receive a dress copy as in L.005.

The box in which the badge was awarded was again only a jeweller's protective one, and she stated that no Citation existed for the grade of badge she was awarded.

L.007 Observers Badge

On 27 November 1935 the Reichminister published an order giving the details of this badge, which were for a metal design with an oval wreath, slightly convex, silver-plated with the right-hand side being of laurel and the left-hand side of oak leaves. The wreath which this com-

Above *Observers Badge (L.007).*

Below *Cloth versions for NCOs of, from left to right, the Pilots Badge (L.002), the Observers Badge (L.007) and the Radio Operators/Air Gunners Badge (L.008)* (Tim Stannard Collection).

prised had mounted upon it an eagle in a watching stance or position. This eagle had a finish of oxidized old silver plating. The eagle clutched a Swastika in its talons. The Swastika was generally darker than the rest of the badge. The eagle was riveted on to the wreath on each side of the wing tip by two ball rivets. The reverse was plain but on certain examples the maker's mark was struck into the reverse of the body of the eagle. It had a vertical hinge pin construction.

The original metal composition was of genuine German silver, with nickel content of twelve per cent. The badge was found in aluminium as well. In either form this badge is very rare. As the war progressed, the badgee declined to pot or monkey metal. As with the previous badges the actual date of institution was 26 March 1936.

The Criteria for the award were:

1) It was awarded upon completion of two months' qualifying service or after five operational flights in the capacity of observer, navigator or bomb aimer.

2) If the individual was wounded during the period of that service he was automatically awarded the badge.

The badge was awarded in a blue box with blue silk lining and blue velvet base, the title being stencilled into the lid of the box in silver block capitals. The embroidered form was identical in size to the metal badge, being embroidered in relief, the wreath worked in silver, the eagle in oxidized silver and the Swastika in dull aluminium threads for officers. The NCOs' form was executed in a similar manner, but cotton threads were substituted for aluminium.

The Citation again had the facsimile of the badge at its head, the lettering in black with the signature of the commanding officer or the officer in control of the award being placed at the bottom.

L.008 Radio Operators and Air Gunners Badge

On 27 November 1935 the published regulations for this badge described it as an oval metal badge which was to

Radio Operators and Air Gunners Badge (L.008) with type 'c' Swastika.

be slightly convex and which was silver-plated, the right half being of laurel leaves and the left of oak leaves. In the centre of the wreath, at the bottom, was a Swastika.

At this stage, it is interesting to note that there were three distinct designs which are marked by changes in the Swastika. The early, or first version, which we could nominate as type 'a', has a fully segmented Swastika. The second, which can be nominated 'b', a semi-segmented Swastika, and the last version, to be nominated 'c', a totally unsegmented Swastika. These three types hold true for all the badges of this wreath design.

In the centre of the wreath was an eagle in flight, clutching in its claws a pair of arrow-headed bolts of lightning. The eagle was flying from right to left, in a downwards direction. The projecting areas of the badge were highly polished and the reverse was flat, with a vertical pin, the eagle being held on to the wreath by two rivets, one from each wing tip. Again,

the changes through a, b and c alter with the period of construction. The badge initially was made in nickel silver or aluminium and later in monkey or pot metal. A cloth version of the badge was instituted for officers in silver bullion, and for NCOs in cotton thread in colours to correspond to those found in the metal badge.

To qualify for this badge the recipient had to have successfully completed two months' training, or to have participated in one of the positions in a minimum of five operational flights. The badge could be awarded sooner should the recipient have been wounded on an operational flight.

This badge was first introduced on 26 March 1936, and was awarded with a Citation and a flying book. The badge was presented in a blue box with a blue silk lining and blue velvet base while the badge's identification was stencilled in silver block letters on the lid.

L.009 Air Gunners and Flight Engineers Badge

This badge was instituted on 22.June 1942 and was constructed in the same manner as the former badge. It is found in the same three forms of Swastika cut-out, that is to say 'a', fully segmented, 'b', semi-segmented and 'c', unsegmented. The badge was originally constructed in nickel silver or aluminium. As the war progressed the standard deteriorated and it is found in pot or monkey metal. The badge had a vertical pin on the

reverse.

The qualification Criteria for the badge were the same as for L.008 and it was awarded with a Citation and flying book, in a blue box with blue silk lining and blue velvet base. The name again was stencilled on to the lid of the box in silver block capitals. The cloth versions were the same as those found for the former badge, L.008.

Air Gunners and Flight Engineers Badge (L.009) with type 'c' Swastika.

Unqualified Air Gunners and Flight Engineers Badge (L.010) with type 'c' Swastika.

L.010 Unqualified Air Gunners and Flight Engineers Badge

On 25 April 1944 a badge was introduced for anyone who had taken part in at least ten operations, or had been wounded in the course of his duty in these operations. The badge was to reward personnel who had been flying to replace casualties in the closing stages of the war, but who had not qualified for the aforesaid badge L.009. This badge was identical to the qualified version, but the colours were reversed, so that the wreath was darkened and the eagle was silver. It is presumed that the badge was only produced in form 'c' and it has only been encountered in zinc and pot or monkey metal.

The box for the badge is very rare and it is assumed that it took the form of the aforementioned Luftwaffe presentation boxes. No cloth insignia for either officers or NCOs has been encountered by this author, but it is logical to assume that they were produced in both bullion and cotton thread.

The Citation for this badge is unknown, but as the badge was a retrospective award, that is to say one completed the combat experience before the badge was awarded, it seems unlikely that anything more than an entry in a soldier's book was occasioned. Any further information would be gratefully appreciated by the author.

L.011 Glider Pilots Badge—First Type

On 8 July 1940 the firm of Willhelm Ernst Peekhaus submitted their design for this badge. It was approved on 16 December 1940 and was produced by the firm of C.E. Junkers of Berlin. It consisted of a wreath of oak leaves on both sides, which met at the bottom with a Swastika. Again the Swastika existed in three forms.

On the wreath was a soaring eagle, flying left to right. The wreath was produced in polished silver and the eagle in oxidized silver. The reverse was flat and the eagle was held on to the wreath by two ball rivets, one through either wing tip. However, as the war progressed the quality of the badge deteriorated, not so much in the stamping of the individual wreath and eagle, but the eagle was sweated on to the wreath. The badge was made in nickel silver or aluminium and then zinc, pot or monkey metal. The badge was awarded on completion of a glider pilot's training and was issued with a Citation and pilot's licence. It was presented in a blue box with blue satin liner and velvet base, with the name stencilled in silver on the lid. Cloth versions of this badge were produced for both officers and NCOs in the manner already described.

The Citation was a plain piece of paper with either a facsimile of the badge at its head, or just a plain black typed heading, with the commanding officer's signature at its base, and in the left-hand corner the stamp of that unit.

Above right *Glider Pilots Badge — First Type (L.011) with type 'b' Swastika.*

L.012 Glider Pilots Badge—Second Type

Little is known about this badge except that it existed. It is considered merely a design variant, but it has been photographed in wear. It consisted of a wreath as did the other Glider Pilots Badge, but the eagle was larger and more definite. The talons were outstretched and the wings considerably broader. The angle of the flight of this eagle gave the impression of powered flight, rather than that of soaring as with the other badge. The reverse was flat with a needle pin, and two small ball rivets, one each where the eagle was attached to the wreath.

Above far right *First proof positive of the Second Type of the Gliders Pilots Badge (L.012) actually having been awarded — Alfred Ruli.*
Right *Glider Pilots Badge — Second Type (L.012) with type 'c' Swastika.*

L.013 Flyers Commemorative Badge

This badge was again introduced on 26 March 1936 and consisted of a wreath of oak leaves with, at the bottom, a Swastika. The Swastika was produced in the three forms 'a', 'b' and 'c'. Unlike most flying awards this badge was struck in one piece. The centre consisted of an eagle perched on a rock, with its wings furled downwards and looking to the left. The whole badge was of a smoked appearance with polished highlights. In this author's opinion it is one of the most meaningful designs, giving a wistful gaze of retirement. The reverse was flat with a needle pin and the badge was made in nickel silver, aluminium, zinc and pot or monkey metal.

The badge was to reward both active and reserve personnel who had served as flyers during the First World War for four years' flying service, or those who had been discharged from flying duties after fifteen years' service, or had been invalided out of the service as a result of an air-associated accident. In the event of a person being killed in the course of his flying duties, the badge was awarded to the next of kin. This badge again was produced in both cloth versions, and the metal badge was presented in a blue box in the same manner as before.

The Citation usually bore a facsimile of the award badge at its head and the signature of the commanding officer at its base, and the stamp of the relevant unit in the left-hand corner. This badge is one of the rarest of all the flying awards of this period.

L.014 Parachutists Badge

In January 1935 a badge was introduced for parachutists who were members of the Luftwaffe, and on 5 November of the same year, it was extended to be awarded to all qualified military parachutists, so replacing the Army Parachutists Badge (A.001).

On 2 May 1944 the badge became eligible for medical, administrative and legal personnel who had made one combat jump. The badge consisted of a wreath of laurel leaves on the left hand and oak leaves on the right. A garland was at the bottom. The wreath was oxidized silver and on it was placed a diving eagle clutching a Swastika. This eagle was finely executed and was gilded. The reverse of the badge was flat with two rivets where the eagle was attached to the wreath. The needle pin was fitted horizontally on to the reverse.

The awarding of this badge was made with a certificate and jump book, and was presented in a blue box as described before, with the badge name stencilled in block letters in silver, on the lid. Again, the badge is found in the two cloth forms for both officers and NCOs.

The Citation for this badge came in a number of varieties too numerous to list in this book.

Flyers Commemorative Badge (L.013) with type 'b' Swastika.

Parachutists Badge (L.014).

L.015 Anti-Aircraft War Badge

On 19 July 1940 the firm of Willhelm Ernst Peekhaus submitted to the air force ministry, for their approval, a metal badge which consisted of a wreath of oak leaves with a block at the base. Surmounting this wreath was a flying Luftwaffe eagle clutching a Swastika, which was sweated on to the wreath. The central design of the badge was made up of an 8.8 cm anti-aircraft gun, pointing upwards and to the right. The reverse was flat, with a vertical needle pin. The earliest badges were constructed in nickel silver or very rarely, aluminium, but as the war continued the badge was made in zinc, pot or monkey metal.

The badge was approved and instigated on 10 January 1944 and the Criteria for its award was on a points basis. Sound locator and searchlight crews were also eligible for the award. One point for each detection was awarded, sixteen points being required for the award of the badge. The Criteria for the anti-aircraft batteries were:

1) Shooting down an aircraft unaided—four points.
2) Shooting down an aircraft aided by another crew—two points.
3) Five unsuccessful engagements with enemy targets.
4) Three actions where an aircraft was downed.
5) Any single act of bravery or merit which occurred in the course of air defence.
6) Three successful ground engagements against ships, tanks or

fortifications.

7) When the battery commander had half of his company awarded this badge, he then became eligible himself for the award.

The badge was awarded either in a blue box as described before, with the title stencilled on its lid in silver, or in a paper packet with just the badge name printed on it.

The Citation again came in numerous variations.

Left *Anti-Aircraft War Badge (L.015).*

L.016 Ground Combat Badge

This badge was instigated on 31 March 1942 to reward the members of the German air force who were engaged in military operations in support of the Army. These units consisted of 22 field divisions and were known as the 'Luftwaffe Replacement Army'. One of the most famous parts of this army was the *Herman Göring* Division. Control was vested in the hands of Herman Göring himself until July 1944.

If, prior to the instigation of this badge, an Army award badge such as the General Assault Badge (A.016),

Right *Ground Combat Badge (L.016). A poor photograph of a 25 Class award shows the tie at the base replaced by a box with the number in it, flanked by an additional oak leaf side giving the medal a flat-bottomed appearance.*

Infantry Assault Badge (A.002/A.003) or Tank Assault Badge (A.004/A.010) had been awarded, it was to be exchanged for this badge.

The badge comprised a wreath of oak leaves, with a tie at the base, with a black massed cloud at the top. Surmounting this was a silvered Luftwaffe eagle. This eagle was usually a separate piece pressed out and riveted to the badge. From the cloud was a bolt of lightning with an arrow tip striking the ground, symbolizing the striking power coming from the air.

The Criteria for the award were:

1) Being involved in three engagements on different days.
2) Being wounded in one of the actions for which this badge could have been awarded.
3) To have been awarded a decoration in one of these actions.

There was a cloth version of this badge in bullion for officers and presumably in cotton for NCOs, but both are extremely rare.

The badge was awarded in either a blue box with silk liner and velvet base (the base is sometimes encountered in a form of brushed cardboard), or in a paper packet with just the badge's derivation printed on it.

The Citation again came in a number of variations and was printed on a small piece of paper as described for previous Luftwaffe badges.

L.017 Ground Combat Badge—25 Class
L.018 Ground Combat Badge—50 Class
L.019 Ground Combat Badge—75 Class
L.020 Ground Combat Badge—100 Class

As with the assault badge for the Army and the Waffen-SS, there was a greater need to reward the achievements of the Luftwaffe ground forces. So on 10 November 1944 the higher grades were introduced. All four types were larger than the unnumbered type and comprised an oak leaf wreath with a flattened bottom. Between the two parts of the wreath was a panel for the appropriate number. These numbers were polished brass with a blackened field. It is interesting to note at this point that, unlike the Army numbered assault badges which were in two distinct designs, one for 25 and 50 and the second for 75 and 100, these badges for all grades were identical. The lateness in the war obviously dictated economies and therefore a standardization of the badge. Again the black cloud was surmounted by a separate Luftwaffe eagle, riveted to the badge with the black thunderbolt coming from the clouds.

It is uncertain if these badges were ever awarded before the end of the war although they were definitely produced. Any documentation or photographs proving their award would be gratefully received by the author.

The box and Citation are unknown.

L.021 Close Combat Clasp—Bronze Class
L.022 Close Combat Clasp—Silver Class
L.023 Close Combat Clasp—Gold Class

This badge was introduced on 3 November 1944 to reward the ground forces of the Luftwaffe. This reflected the importance of the ruthless fighting of the *Herman Göring* Division. The fighting in the Russian theatre of operations involved an enormous amount of hand-to-hand combat. The design of this badge took the form of a round wreath of laurel leaves with a tie at the bottom. From each side of this wreath was a sprig of oak leaves. In the centre of the wreath was a Luftwaffe eagle with a Swastika in its talons surmounting crossed grenade and bayonet. The reverse had a horizontal pin.

The Criteria for the award were:

1) The recipient must have been engaged in hand-to-hand combat when supported by armour.

2a) The bronze bar was for fifteen days on continuous combat but this was to be reduced to ten days if a man had been wounded in that time.

2b) The silver bar was for thirty days on continuous combat and this was to be reduced to twenty days if he had been wounded in that time.

2c) The gold bar was for fifty days on continuous combat and this was to be reduced to forty days if he had been wounded in that time.

3) For service in Russia a retrospective credit was introduced, to complement the Army version of this badge, on the basis of a service ratio of five combat days being represented by eight months' service, ten combat days being represented by twelve months' service and fifteen combat days being represented by fifteen months' service.

The award of the gold bar was accompanied by a special 21 days'

Close Combat Clasp.

leave. It is not known if, with the award of the silver or bronze, leave was granted, but presumably leave of seven days for a bronze and fourteen days for a silver would not be inconceivable. One of the first gold awards was won by an NCO in January 1945 and one of the first bronze awards on 19 December 1944 went to a *Herman Göring* Division member, Obergefreiter Albert Mahlmann.

It is not known how the badge was awarded or what the Citation was either. Again any information on either of these items would be gratefully received.

L.024 Silver Tank Battle Badge

This badge was introduced on 3 November 1944 to reward the tank crews of the Luftwaffe army and took the form of a wreath of oak leaves with a tie at the bottom. A flying Luftwaffe eagle was at the top and a tank formed the central motif. The wreath was silvered and the tank was blackened. It had a vertical pin on the reverse and the reverse was also plain and devoid of any maker's mark. The example that I inspected was made of pot metal.

The Criteria for the award were:
1) Three combat engagements on three separate days for tank commanders, drivers, gunners and radio operators.
2) Three engagements on three separate days by service engineers protecting their fortifications while repairing tanks in the front line.
3) Three engagements on three separate days by medical personnel attached to armoured units while serving at the front.

The Citation for this war badge is unknown to this author as is the form of container, but it is assumed to be a paper packet with the name of the badge printed on it.

L.025 Silver Tank Battle Badge—25 Class
L.026 Silver Tank Battle Badge—50 Class
L.027 Silver Tank Battle Badge—75 Class
L.028 Silver Tank Battle Badge—100 Class

On 10 November 1944 the higher grades of this badge were introduced to further reward the Luftwaffe tank crews. These badges were slightly larger than the unnumbered version, again with an oak leaf wreath with a flattened bottom. The tie was replaced with a box to hold the number. This box had the numbers polished with the field blackened. Again in this case all the numbered badges were identical, unlike their Army counterparts.

The Citation is unknown as is the form of container for the badge.

Silver Tank Battle Badge (L.024) (Tim Stannard Collection).

Silver Tank Battle Badge — 50 Class (L.026). Note that the eagle only appears black because the silver has dropped (J.R. Angolia Collection).

L.029 Black Tank Battle Badge

This badge was also introduced on 3 November 1944 to reward members of the Panzergrenadiers and took the form of an oval wreath of oak leaves with a tie at the bottom, surmounted by a flying Luftwaffe eagle in matt silver. The central motif was a tank running through the wreath. In this case, the wreath was blackened as was the tank. The reverse of the badge was flat with a vertical pin and was made of pot metal.

The Criteria for the award were:
1) Three engagements on three separate days by Panzergrenadier formations in front line positions.
2) Three engagements on three separate days by armoured reconnaissance units.
3) Three engagements on three separate days by medical personnel attached to Panzergrenadier formations.

The Citation for this award again is unknown to this author, as is the form of container, but it is assumed to be a paper packet.

L.030 Black Tank Battle Badge—25 Class
L.031 Black Tank Battle Badge—50 Class
L.032 Black Tank Battle Badge—75 Class
L.033 Black Tank Battle Badge—100 Class

On 10 November 1944 the higher grades of this badge were introduced to further reward the Luftwaffe Panzergrenadier units. The badge was slightly larger, again with an oak leaf wreath, but with a distinctive flatter bottom. The tie was replaced with a box to hold the number, while the high parts of the number were burnished bronze and the field was blackened. All these numbered badges were identical, unlike their Army counterparts. The wreath was blackened as was the tank, while the eagle was matt silver.

Again, the Citation is unknown as is the form of container.

L.034 Sea Battle Badge

To reward personnel employed in a naval capacity assisting the Luftwaffe, a badge was introduced by Herman Göring on 27 November 1944. It was primarily awarded for air-sea rescue, for which the Luftwaffe had made up a special force of air sailors, with a distinctive uniform and cap badge, but the personnel of other ships such as supply vessels in the service of the Luftwaffe were also eligible. All personnel who performed air-related duties were under the control of the Luftwaffe, as the navy did not have an air arm to its service. Reconnaissance aircraft on German naval vessels were manned by Luftwaffe personnel under the direct control of the Reichsmarschall, Herman Göring.

The design of the badge consisted of an oak leaf wreath with a tie at the bottom, and surmounting this wreath at the top was a Luftwaffe eagle. The central motif of the badge

Sea Battle Badge (L.034).

was a ship with rigging and smoke emitting from its funnel. The wreath was gilded, the eagle matt silver and the ship, rigging and smoke were blackened.

The Criteria for the award were:
1) For Luftwaffe surface craft and supply ships—
   a) If a naval award badge had been awarded for the same action, this badge could not be then awarded for the action.
   b) Service at sea, was made up as sea days calculated as ten hours at sea, comprising either sixty days at sea in the north or east sea, between 5° and 20° longitude, and south of the 60th degree of latitude, or in the Mediterranean, including the Black Sea and Aegean Sea, twenty days' ser-

vice was required.
2) For air-sea rescue launches—
   a) If a naval badge had been awarded for the same action, this badge could not be then awarded for the action.
   b) Twenty sea days with a maximum of one rescue attempt.
   c) Ten sea days with a successful rescue attempt.
   d) Twenty sea days made up of ten hours, as previously stated, but with trips of not less than three hours' duration to be included in those twenty sea days.

The badge was awarded with a Citation, but again the exact details are not known, nor is the type of container for the badge, but that is assumed to be a paper packet with the badge name printed on it.

L.035 Day Fighter Operational Flying Clasp—Bronze Class
L.036 Day Fighter Operational Flying Clasp—Silver Class
L.037 Day Fighter Operational Flying Clasp—Gold Class

As the air war progressed, it was felt that the Luftwaffe personnel should be rewarded for their flying activities and service in the air by a special badge. It was to take the form of a round wreath of laurel leaves with a Swastika at its base, and on each side of this wreath a sprig of oak leaves. The central motif, which was superimposed on the centre, was to be a device of the individual badge. This

device was made in silver or white metal, which was blackened and riveted on to the badge. The silver overpiece was the same design as the badge underneath, but in later war badges the silver overpiece is often omitted due to restrictions on the availability of scarce materials. This left just the rivet hole in the centre of the device.

This badge was introduced on 30

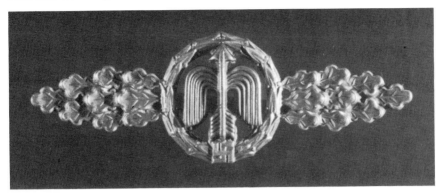

Day Fighter Operational Flying Clasp — Silver Class (L.036).

January 1941, being designed by Professor von Weech of Berlin, and consisted of a winged arrow pointing upwards. The reverse had a horizontal pin and usually the maker's mark. The pin was either flat or fluted and the quality was very good. The composition of the badge was from nickel silver through to pot metal. The overall colour of the badge represented its grade or class. Thus the bronze class was for twenty operations, silver for sixty and gold for 110 operations. As the war progressed it was decided to introduce a series of pendants to hang below the wreath. These took the form of a little star with a small sprig of laurel leaves projecting from each side. The date of instigation of this device, or Anhanger, was 26 June 1942. In this case the pendant represented 500

missions above the 110 of the original badge. As the war continued, it was obvious that this was confusing so on 29 April 1944, a simpler method of numbering was introduced. The pendants were modified to a panel in which the number of missions was struck, these numbers being in gold and ranging from 200 to 2,000. The field behind the numbers was blackened. The outside of the box had the same laurel sprigs on either side.

The badge was issued in a blue box with a cream base, with the badge type stencilled in gold on the lid. There was a cloth version for officers in bullion and presumably cotton thread for NCOs.

The Citation was a plain piece of white paper with a facsimile of the badge on its top. The printing was in black and the commanding officer's signature at its base, with the unit's stamp in the left-hand lower corner.

L.038 Day Fighter Operational Flying Clasp—Diamond Class

Little is known of this badge or the reason for its award. It took the form

of the standard badge, L.035, with the exception that it was produced in solid gold. The expectation is that it was produced by the firm of Klien and that the quality of the gold was .535 standard. The diamonds which surmounted and went round the wreath were rose-cut and mounted similarly to those that are found on the badge of Hans Rudel, L.060, and were set in platinum. In this case the badge did not have a hanger below the flight bar as was in the case of Rudel's example. The central device, it would seem logical, was produced, as was the badge L.060, as an individual item that was affixed to the body of the badge by a single rivet and was also produced in platinum. This central device was an arrow pointing upwards and the clasp was presented to Oberst Werner Mölders. A theory, but one which might explain the presentation, is that this clasp was awarded to Mölders by Göring when he had gained his Oak Leaves, Swords and Diamonds, D.021, to his Knights Cross of the Iron Cross (D.018), which he did on 16 July 1941. The present whereabouts of this clasp is not known.

L.039 Bomber Operational Flying Clasp—Bronze Class
L.040 Bomber Operational Flying Clasp—Silver Class
L.041 Bomber Operational Flying Clasp—Gold Class

Again on 30 January 1941 this badge was introduced to reward the crews

Bomber Operational Flying Clasp — Silver Class (L.040).

of heavy, medium and dive bombers. The design was identical to that of the former badge, but had a winged bomb pointing downwards. Again the bronze badge was for twenty, silver for sixty and gold for 110

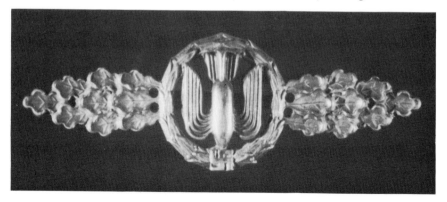

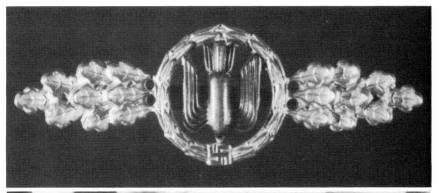

Top *Bomber Operational Flying Clasp —
Gold Class (L.041).*

Above *Stabsfeldwebel Ludwig Bellof (left)
on the award of the Knights Cross (D.018)
on 28 January 1945. He and his companion,
Leopold Hackl, both of 1./NJG3, wear the
Bomber Operational Flying Clasp (L.041)
with Anhanger.*

missions. The pendant device was
used, and this time it represented, in
the case of dive bomber units 400

missions, and heavy and medium
bombers, 300 missions. This obviously gave rise to some confusion as
the badge was identical for each type
of squadron, and the later numbering
method greatly simplified this series
of badges.

The badge was awarded in a blue
box with a cream base liner, with gold
lettering for the individual grade and
type on the lid.

The Citation was a plain piece of
paper with a facsimile of the badge

printed on the top, the printing was in black with the commanding officer's signature and unit at the bottom.

In the left-hand corner at the bottom was the unit's stamp.

L.042 Reconnaissance Operational Flying Clasp—Bronze Class
L.043 Reconnaissance Operational Flying Clasp—Silver Class
L.044 Reconnaissance Operational Flying Clasp—Gold Class

Again on 30 January 1941, this badge was introduced to reward the reconnaissance, air-sea rescue and meteorologists of the Luftwaffe and

took the form of a wide eyed eagle, which looked to the left. This badge I find most appealing and possibly one of the best examples of contemporary

Below *A variant design of the Reconnaissance Operational Flying Clasp — Bronze Class (L.042).*

Bottom *Reverse of the variant design of the Reconnaissance Operational Flying Clasp — Bronze Class (L.042).*

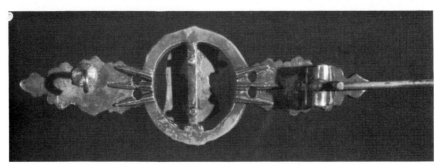

Top *Reconnaissance Operational Flying Clasp — Silver Class (L.043).*

Above *Reconnaissance Operational Flying Clasp — Gold Class with Anhanger (L.044).*

design, being very stylized. Again, the mission requirements were twenty for the bronze class, sixty for silver and 110 for gold. Confusion was applicable in the case of the star pendant, as it represented, in the case of air-sea rescue and meteorological squadrons, 300 missions, and in reconnaissance squadrons 250 missions. This confusion was replaced after 28 April 1944 by the method of numbered pendants.

The badge was awarded in a blue box with cream base liner, and gold lettering giving the type on the lid.

The Citation once more had the badge at its top and followed the same format as the other award documents.

L.045 Transport and Glider Operational Flying Clasp—Bronze Class
L.046 Transport and Glider Operational Flying Clasp—Silver Class
L.047 Transport and Glider Operational Flying Clasp—Gold Class

This badge was introduced on 19 November 1941 and comprised the wreath of laurels with a Luftwaffe eagle clutching a Swastika, flying to its left. As before, the mission prerequisites were bronze twenty, silver sixty and gold. 110 missions. The pendant hanger in this case represented 500 missions.

It was issued in a blue box with a cream base, and the type of the award stencilled in gold block letters on the lid.

The Citation had the badge at its top and followed the same format as the previous Citations.

Top right *Transport and Glider Operational Flying Clasp — Silver Class (L.046).*

L.048 Long Range Day Fighters Operational Flying Clasp—Bronze Class
L.049 Long Range Day Fighters Operational Flying Clasp—Silver Class
L.050 Long Range Day Fighters Operational Flying Clasp—Gold Class

This badge was introduced on 13 May 1942, to reward the long-range day fighter and air-to-ground support personnel. It took the form of a winged arrow pointing downwards. As before, the central motif was a wreath of laurels, with oak leaf sprigs from each side.

The missions were bronze twenty, silver sixty and gold 110. The star pendant in these cases represented 400 missions.

The box that it was issued in followed the same form as the previous ones, with the cream flocked base and gold stencilled letters on the lid.

The Citation again had a facsimile of the badge at its top and took the same format as the previous Citations.

Above right *Long Range Day Fighters Operational Flying Clasps: top, Silver Class (L.049); bottom, Gold Class with Anhanger (L.050)* (Tim Stannard Collection).

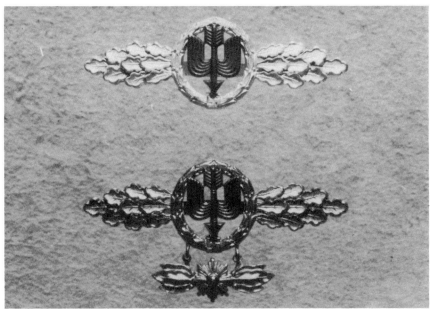

L.051 Long Range Night Fighters
Operational Flying Clasp—Bronze Class
L.052 Long Range Night Fighters
Operational Flying Clasp—Silver Class
L.053 Long Range Night Fighters
Operational Flying Clasp—Gold Class

With the increase in bomber activity by the RAF during the night, there was a need to reward the night fighter squadrons who intercepted and des-

Long Range Night Fighters Operational Flying Clasp — Gold Class with 1,300-mission Anhanger (L.053).

troyed the incoming bombers, so on 14 August 1942 a new flying clasp was introduced. This took the form of the previous one with a round wreath of laurel leaves, with Swastika at its base and sprigs of oak leaves on either side. This time it had an arrow pointing downwards, and the wreath was blackened in each grade to represent the darkness of the night.

Again the missions were bronze with black wreath twenty, silver with black wreath sixty and gold with black wreath 110 missions. In this case the star pendant represented 250 missions.

Again the badge was awarded in a blue box with a cream flocked base, the title being stencilled on the lid.

The Citation had a facsimile of the badge to include the black wreath at its top, the rest of the printing and signatures took the same format as before.

L.054 Short Range Night Fighter Operational Flying Clasp—Bronze Class
L.055 Short Range Night Fighter Operational Flying Clasp—Silver Class
L.056 Short Range Night Fighter Operational Flying Clasp—Gold Class

With the increase in air activity over occupied Europe, there was also a

need to reward the short-range night fighter squadrons, and again on 14

August 1942 a new clasp was introduced. It was identical to the former clasps, with a wreath of laurels with an oak leaf sprig on either side. In this case the wreath was also blackened in all grades, but with the Swastika polished to show the colour of the grade. The central device was a winged arrow pointing upwards. The missions were twenty for bronze, sixty for silver and 110 for gold, and the star pendant represented 250 missions.

The badge was awarded in a blue box with cream flock base.

The Citation had a facsimile of the badge at its head and the rest of the printing, signature and stamps as before.

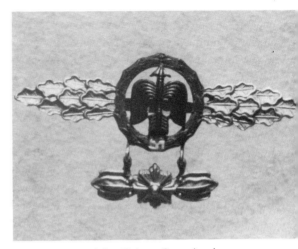

Short Range Night Fighter Operational Flying Clasp — Gold Class with Anhanger (L.056) (Tim Stannard Collection).

L.057 Air-to-Ground Support Operational Flying Clasp—Bronze Class
L.058 Air-to-Ground Support Operational Flying Clasp—Silver Class
L.059 Air-to-Ground Support Operational Flying Clasp—Gold Class

With the war in Russia taking a terrific toll on men and machinery, a new form of air war emerged, and this needed a special badge to reward the fliers who had so successfully damaged the Russian armour. So, on 20 April 1944, a new clasp was introduced for these 'Tank busters' which consisted, as in the former badges, of a laurel wreath with a Swastika at its base and an oak leaf sprig on either side. The central device of this badge was a pair of crossed swords similar to those on the Knights Cross with Oak Leaves

and Swords.

Again the missions required for the badge were bronze twenty, silver sixty and gold 110. As the change in the pendant and the introduction of the badge came within seventeen days, it is unlikely that you will encounter this badge with the star pendant which would have represented 400 missions, but with the pendant with just the numbers. Because of the lateness of the introduction of this badge, this is a rare award and much rarer with a pendant attached.

Top *Air-to-Ground Support Operational Flying Clasp — Silver Class (L.058).*

Above *Air-to-Ground Support Operational Flying Clasp — Gold Class with Anhanger (L.059).*

It was awarded in a blue box with a cream base, with the type stencilled on the lid in gold.

The Citation had a facsimile of the badge at its head, and the rest of the printing, signature and stamps in a corresponding manner.

L.060 Air-to-Ground Support Operational Flying Clasp—Diamond Class

In April 1944, Oberst Hans Rudel, the famous 'tank buster' received from Herman Göring a version of the badge in gold with diamonds for 2,000 missions accomplished. In correspondence with me he supplied me with photographs of all his awards and documents, and a full description of this badge. The body of the badge itself was constructed of 22 carat gold, as was the pendant. The pin on the reverse was of the flat blade type, and was plain and devoid of any maker's marks. The Swastika and crossed swords were made in platinum as was the figure 2,000 that made up the central device of the pendant hanger. Round the wreath were twenty rose-cut diamonds, the setting of these again was of platinum. The 2,000 number was filled with small chips of diamonds, and the numbers themselves were segmented or pierced, so that the light could be seen through them.

The box or case for this award is unknown, if any ever existed. Rudel stated in correspondence that Göring just placed the badge in his hand, and he has no recollection of any protective case.

The Citation again does not exist and if one was to have been awarded

at a later date, it did not find the recipient of the award, even if it was ever produced.

Below *Air-to-Ground Support Operational Flying Clasp — Diamond Class (L.060).*

Bottom *Hans Rudel photographed with Luftwaffe and Army officers in the east in February 1945. In addition to his Knights Cross with Golden Oak Leaves, Swords and Diamonds (D.022), Iron Cross First Class (D.016) and German Cross in Gold (D.025), he is also wearing his Pilots Badge (L.002), Combined Pilots and Observers Badge in Gold with Diamonds (L.004) and Air-to-Ground Support Operational Flying Clasp — Diamond Class (L.060) — with its 2,000-sortie Anhanger.*

Ribbon Awards

The ribbons shown on this page are the only ones awarded to accompany the decorations featured in this book.

Key
White
Black
Red
Yellow

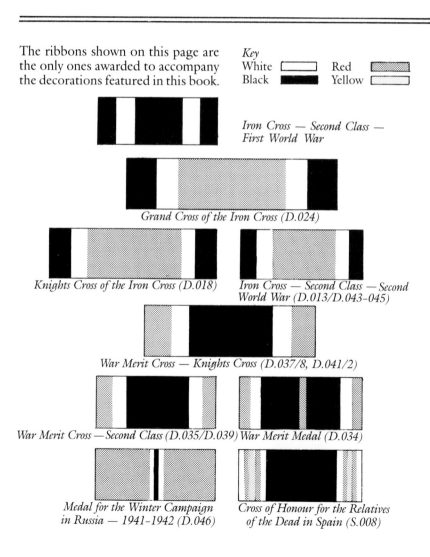

Iron Cross — Second Class — First World War

Grand Cross of the Iron Cross (D.024)

Knights Cross of the Iron Cross (D.018)

Iron Cross — Second Class — Second World War (D.013/D.043–045)

War Merit Cross — Knights Cross (D.037/8, D.041/2)

War Merit Cross — Second Class (D.035/D.039)

War Merit Medal (D.034)

Medal for the Winter Campaign in Russia — 1941-1942 (D.046)

Cross of Honour for the Relatives of the Dead in Spain (S.008)

Glossary

This final chapter it is hoped will explain some of the terminology used in the text of the book, to describe the method of production and manufacture and the subsequent markings that those medals and badges have applied to them in various ways. It has been split into two sections, the first covering those medals and the second to explain the abbreviations of the organisations which subsequently after their production used them to reward the relevant personnel. Certain terms in the names of manufacturers or their logos have not been included in the text but are included in the glossary so that when a political or diplomatic item is encountered in a collection, it will be easily recognisable from those which are included in the text. I hope that the experienced collector will bear with me for this deviation from what should be included, but I feel sure the novice and inexperienced collector will benefit from its explanation.

The method of marking medals and badges underwent a number of changes during the period of the Third Reich, and is quite a complex study in itself. But to introduce the collector to these marks is the essence of this brief discussion and further research is much needed in this very important field. With the aid of computers I hope to try and amass as much information on the subject as possible in the future.

The types of mark that can be encountered on medals and badges I have codified down for simplicity into seven types: 1) maker's name and address; 2) maker's logo; 3) RZM code; 4) mint mark; 5) serial number; 6) silver mark; and, 7) LDO number.

1) Maker's name and address

This was found on the best quality badges and could be either cast or struck into the design of the reverse of the badge. On some examples where the address has been actually stamped into the badge, it is found either on the pin or the body of the applied insignia. It is interesting to note that not all the badges of one manufacturer, at the same time of production, carried the name and address, indicating that they possibly wholesaled the item to a third party for finishing, or that they selected superior quality items only to bear their name. But any of these reasons are pure conjecture, and further research or information would be welcomed.

2) Maker's logo

This fell into the same category as that of the name which has been fully described above and was often used in conjunction with it, as this was used as the trade mark of that firm or organisation.

3) RZM code

This was the authority that authorized the production of the awards manufactured for the Party and permitted, on instruction from the Party through this controlling organization (which was situated at the Brown House in Munich and Party headquarters in Berlin), the relevant manufacturers to produce those awards. This code has been included in this section to explain its meaning, although it will not be found on the awards in the book. The Reichszeugmeisterei, or RZM for short, would award a number which was accompanied by a logo formed by the letters RZM which was contained in a circle with the M at the bottom M11/1 was issued to the company Steinhauer and Luck and could be awarded with an LDO number L/16. Depending on the type of award that the company was producing, the relevant form of coding would be applied.

4) Mint mark

This form of mark was found on the badges and medals produced in the state mints on any medals and again they are rarely found on medals covered by this volume, but have been included to help the coverage of the methods of marking.

5) Serial number

Serial numbers, or individual naming of medals, were used on very few awards in Germany as the award document was the important part of the medal and it was possible to purchase extra examples of nearly all awarded medals, with the exception of possibly the Knights Cross of the Iron Cross. These numbers are encountered on such examples as the Golden Party Badge, Blood Order and TeNo Honour Badge.

6) Silver marks

These give the percentage of silver per 1,000 parts of pure metal, that is to say .950 contains 950 parts of silver to 1,000 parts and these marks can be in any combination. As a guide the British standard of silver was set down in 1238 AD as 92.5 per cent pure which is represented by .925 and is also known as Sterling Silver.

7) LDO number

This was introduced in 1941 to try and control the production of medals and orders. During the early years local dignitaries were able to produce all kinds of awards which, in some instances, became elevated to official awards. Officially introduced awards, however, were strictly controlled from the Führer's Chancellery and rigidly upheld by the Leistungs Gemeinschaft Deutscher Ordenshersteller or, it was known by its abbreviations, LDO. They published information booklets about the profession to record the producers' award of new developments and production methods and can be considered very much a trade guild.

Licences were issued for the manufacture of these officially recognized orders, decorations and badges which was to be accompanied by a code designation, or as it was known, Herstellellungszeichen. From March 1941, the organization required producers to stamp their L number on their products. The Chancellery laid down the regulations and the LDO supervised their implementation as a self-regulating organization. This seems somewhat confused, considering the L designation changed nearly annually from its introduction. Some firms entered they system, being awarded and L number, and then, when they were either dropped or withdrew from the organization, subsequently to be reinstated, were given a different L number. For some unexplained reason, some manufacturers were awarded more than one L number.

All of these factors lead to the near impossible task, of putting a number to a manufacturer, but I have included a list provided by Steinhauer and Luck of Ludenscheid. The only known multiple numbers were awarded to C. E. Juncker of Berlin (2) and Godet, also of Berlin (21); the LDO number 12 can also be found on badges produced by both these firms in addition to those of Frank & Reif. Where gaps appear in the numerical sequence, the identity of the manufacturer is unknown. At the end of the list are seven known manufacturers whose LDO numbers are unknown, and it is possible that their names should fill some of the gaps in the numbering sequence. If any reader can supply information or photographs of these, the author would be grateful.

LDO No	Firm	Maker's mark	Location
1	Descjler & Sohn		Munchen
2	C. E. Juncker	CEJ	Berlin
3	Wilhelm Deumer		Ludenscheid
4	Steinhauer & Luck	S&L	Ludenscheid
5	Hermann Wernstein		Jena-Lobstedt
6	Fritz Zimmermann	FZS	Stuttgart
7	Paul Meybauer	PM	Berlin
8	Ferdinand Hoffstadter		Bonn a. Rhein
9	Leifergsmeinschaft Pforzheimer Schmuckhandwerker		Pforzheim
10	Foerster & Barth		Pforzhiem
11	Grossmann & Co		Wein
12	Frank & Reif		Stuttgart-Zuffenhausen
13	Gustave Brehmer	GB	Markneukirchen/Sa.
14	L. Chr. Lauer		Nurnberg-W
15	Friedrich Orth		Wien
16	Alois Rettenmaier		Schwabisch-Gmund
17			
18	Karl Wurster K.G.		Markenkirchen/Sa.
19	E. Ferd Weidmann		Frankfurt/Main
20	C. F. Zimmermann		Pforzheim
21	Gebr. Godet & Co.		Berlin
22	Boerger & Co.		Berlin
23	Arbeitsgemeinschaft fur Heresbedard in der Graveur–u. Ziseleurinnung		Berlin
24	Arbeitsgemeinschaft der Hanauer Plaketten-Hersteller		Hanau/M
25	Arbeitsgemeinschaft der Graveur-Gold- und Silber-schmeide-Innungen		Hanau/M
26	B. H. Mayer's Kunstpragaenstalt		Pforzheim
27	Anton Schenkl's Nachf.		Wien
28	Eugen Schmidthaussler		Pforzheim
29	Hauptmunzamt		Berlin
30	Hauptmunzamt		Wien
31	Hans Gnad		Wien
32	W. Hobachter		Wien
33	Friedrich Linden	FFL	Ludenscheid
34	Willy Annetsberger		Munchen
35	F. W. Assmann & Sohn	A	Ludenscheid
36	Bury & Leonhard		Hanau a. M.
37	Ad. Baumeister		Ludenscheid
38			
39	Rudolf Bergs		Gablonz. a.d.N.

LDO No	Firm	Maker's mark	Location
40	Berg & Nolte	B&NL	Ludenscheid
41	Gebr. Bender		Oberstein/Nahe
42	Beidermann & Co		Oberkassel b/Bonn
43	Julis Bauer Sohne		Zella Mehlis i/Thur
44	Jakob Bengel		Idar/Oberdonau
45	Franz Jungwirth		Wien
46	Hans Doppler		Wels/Oberdonau
47	Erhard & Sohne A.G.		Schwabisch Gmund
48	Richard Reix		Gablonz a.d.N.
49	Josef Feix Sohne	JFS	Gablonz a.d.N.
50	Karl Gschiermeister		Wien
51	Eduard Gorlach & Sohne		Gablonz/N.
52	Gottleib & Wagner		Idar/Oberstein
53	Glaser & Sohne		Dresden
54			
55	J. E. Hammer & Sohne		Dresden
56	Robert Hauschild		Pforzheim
57	Karl Hensler		Pforzheim
58	Artur Jokel & Co		Gablonz/N.
59	Louis Keller		Oberstein
60	Katz & Deyhle		Pforzheim
61	Rudolf A. Karneth & Sohne	RK	Gablonz a.N.
62	Kerbach & Oesterhelt		Dresden
63	Franz Klamt & Sohne		Gablonz a.N.
64	Gottl. Fr. Keck & Sohn		Pforzheim
65	Klein & Quenzer A.G.		Idar/Oberstein
66	Friedrich Keller		Oberstein
67	R. Kreisel		Gablonz a.N.
68	Alfred Knoblock		Gablonz a.N
69	Alois Klammer		Innsbruck
70	Lind & Meyrer		Oberstein a.d.N.
71	Rudolf Leukert		Gablonz a.N.
72	Franz Lipp		Pforzheim
73	Frank Monert		Gablonz a.N.
74	Carl Meurer Sohn		Oberstein/Nahe
75			
76	Ernst L. Muller		Pforzheim
77	Bayer. Hauptmunzamt		Munchen
78	Gustav Miksch		Gablonz/N
79			
80	G. H. Osang		Dressden
81	Overhoff & Cie		Ludenscheid
82	Augustin Prager		Gablonz a.N.

LDO No	Firm	Maker's mark	Location
83	Emil Peukert		Gablonz a.N.
84	Carl Posllath		Schrobenhausen
85	Julius Pietsch		Gablonz/N
86	Pulmann & Crone		Ludenscheid
87	Roman Palme		Gablonz a.N
88	Werner Redo		Saarlautern
89	Rudolf Richter	RRS	Schlag 244 b.Gablonz
90	Aug. F. Richter K.G.		Hamburg
91	Josef Rossler & Co		Gablonz a.d.N.
92	Josef Rucker & Sohn		Gablonz a.d.N.
93	Richard Simm & Sohn	RS&S	Gablonz a.d.N.
94			
95	Adolf Scholze		Grunwald a.d.N.
96			
97			
98	Rudolf Souval	RS	Wien
99	Schwertner & Cie		Graz-Eggenberg
100	Rudolf Wachtler & Lange		Mittweida i.Sa.
101	Rudolf Tham		Gablonz a.d.N.
102	Philipp Turks Ww		Wien
103	Aug. G. Tham		Gablonz a.d.N.
104	Hein Ulbricht's Ww		Kaufing b/Schwanenstadt
105	Heinrich Vogt		Pforzheim
106	Bruder Schneider A.G.	BSW	Wien
107	Carl Wild		Hamburg
108	Arno Wallpach		Salzburg
109	Walter & Henlein	WH	Gablonz a.d.N.
110	Otto Zappe		Gablonz a.d.N.
111	Ziemer & Sohne		Oberstein
112	Argentor Werke Rust & Hetzel		Wien
113	Hermann Aurich	HA	Dresden
114	Ludwig Bertsch		Karlsruhe
115			
116	Funke & Bruninghaus	F&BL	Ludenscheid
117	Hugo Lang		Wiesenthal a.N.
118	August Menzs & Sohn		Wiesenthal a.N.
119			
120	Franz Petzl		Wien
121			
122	J. J. Stahl		Strassburg
123	Beck, Hassinger & Co		Strassburg
124	Rudolf Schanes		Wien
125	Eugen Gauss		Pforzheim

LDO No	Firm	Maker's mark	Location
126	Eduard Hahn	EH	Oberstein/Nahe
127	Moritz Hausch A.G.		Pforzheim
128	S. Jablonski G.m.b.H.		Posen
129	Fritz Kohm		Pforzheim
130	Wilh. Schroder & Co		Ludenscheid
	Adolf Bock		Berlin
	Laura		Nurnberg & Berlin
	Wilhelm Ernst Peekhaus		Berlin
	Otto Placzek		Berlin
	Rath		Munchen
	Schwerin		Berlin
	Rudolf Stubiger		Wien

7a) Multiple LDO numbers

The list below comprises manufacturers who had multiple 'L' numbers. These 'L' numbers apparently indicate full licences and part licences to produce certain state awards, such as the Iron Cross and Eagle Order. However, more research is required, as has been previously stated, with the full list and these two subsequent lists are interesting in that they run from 10 to 26 and 50 to 66. The numerical relationship is identical in both groupings, but whether any intermediate listings are available is unsure and further information and research would be greatly welcomed. Both of these lists go some way towards supporting the theory I put forward that certain manufacturers produced parts and other manufacturers were engaged in the finishing of those medals, and it is possible that these listings are relevant to that process.

LDO No	Maker's mark	Address
L/10		Deschler & Sohn, Munchen 9, Wirthstrasse 9
L/11		Wilhelm Deumer, Ludenscheid, Postfach 161
L/12	CEJ	C. E. Juncker, Berlin S.W.68, Altejacobstrasse 13
L/13	PM	Paul Meybauer, Berlin S.W.68, Junkerstrasse 19
L/14	FO	Fredrich Orth, Wien, V1/6 56, Schmalzhofgasse 18
L/15		Otto Schickle-Pforzheim
L/16	S&L	Steinhauer & Luck, Ludenscheid
L/17		Herman Wernstein, Jena Lobstedt
L/18		B. H. Mayer's, Hofkunstprageanstalt, Pforzheim
L/19		Ferdinand Hoffstatter, Bonn/Rhein, Postfach 161
L/20		No maker known
L/21		Foerster & Barth, Pforzheim, Tunnelstrasse 71

LDO No	Maker's mark	Address
L/22	RS	Rudolf Souval, Wien, V11/62, Strasse der Julihamfer 23
L/23		Julius Maurer, Oberstein/Nahe
L/24	FZS	Fritz Zimmerman, Stuttgart-W, Silberburgstrasse 58a
L/25		A. E. Kochert, Wien 1, Neuer Markt 15
L/26		Klein & Quenzer, Oberstein/Nahe
L/50		Gebr. Godet & Co, Berlin W8, Jägerstrasse 19
L/51		E. Ferd. Wiedmann, Frankfurt-M 5–10, Schifferstrasse 52–54
L/52		C. F. Zimmermann, Pforzheim, Dr. Fritz-Todt-Strasse 55
L/53		Hymmen & Co, Ludenscheid, Karl Strasse
L/54		Schauerte & Hohfeld, Ludenscheid
L/55		Wachtler & Lange Rudolf, Mitwaida/Sa
L/56		Funcke & Bruninghaus
L/57		Boerger & Co, Berlin SO 16, Adalbertstrasse 42
L/58		Glaser & Sohn, Dresen-A, Borngasse 5
L/59		Alois Rettenmaier, Schwabisch-Gmund, Parlerstrasse 27
L/60	GB	Gustav Brehmer, Markneukirchen/SR
L/61	FLL	Friedrich Linden, Ludenscheid
L/62		Werner Redo, Saarlautern
L/63		G. H. Osang, Dresden A-1, Neue Gasse 30
L/64	A	F. A. Assmann & Sohne, Ludenscheid
L/65		Dr. Franke & Co, KG, Ludenscheid
L/66		A. D. Schwerdt, Stuttgart-S, Splittlerstrasse 36

8) 'BeVo'

This is the name given to the process of weaving insignia by the Jacquard method and commonnly referred to in the 'collecting world' as BeVo, although not all the insignia that are known by this collector's title were in fact produced by the BeVo-Wuppertal firm. The term 'BeVo' comes from the trade name found on much of the woven insignia of all the political and military organizations.

The 'Be' stands for Beteiligung, which when translated into English becomes 'partnership' and 'Vo' stands for Vorsteher. The amalgamation of the firms of Lucas Vorsteher of Lenneper Strasse 50 and Ewelda Vorsteher of Krenz Strasse 72, both from Wuppertal-Bermen, and thus the logo of the new firm was produced, 'BeVo-Wuppertal'.

9) Monkey metal

This is the term used to explain the alloy in which the late war badges were produced. It has a high proportion of zinc in its makeup and it also deteriorates over the years; this deterioration facilitates the absorption of the gilding that in many cases has been applied to it. It also has a low melting point which makes repairs to badges constructed in this manner particularly difficult. The metal, when of this age, also exudes a very faint acrid smell which is a good indicator of originality.

10) Pot metal

This is a similar alloy to monkey metal but the quality is better as the use of sub-standard additives to the mixture is less.

11) White metal

This is also known as a blanket term to encompass cupro-nickel and gives the impression of silver. It can also be considered as German silver, which has a nickel content of twelve per cent. It can be artificially aged and forms a good patina as found on silver coins, and it is resistant to wear. It also takes up the design from a die very well but requires great pressure from the minting engine. This metal produces the finest quality of badges, rivalling only the appearance of that of genuine silver.

12) Rose-cut

This is the name used in conjunction with diamond cutting and produces a hemispherical diamond with curved parts in triangular facets. This was particularly popular on the continent from 1900 through to 1940 when the diamond industry was decimated in Holland by the escape of the diamond cutters and merchants to England. Because the diamond industry was mainly a Jewish institution, the SS had the final word with those that remained. The main centre and the style gives rise to the name Rotterdam Rose-Cut. After 1945, the design of cuts changed, in part due to the British influence exerted upon the Dutch cutters from their counterparts in Hatton Garden, London, the British diamond centre.

13) Double struck

This is when the die is reinforced from the reverse, giving the impression of the obverse not in as much detail, and in some cases just forming lines in the obverse. It produces a very distinct obverse design.

Organizations mentioned in the book

DLV—Deutsche Luftsport-Verband—This was the formation of the clandestine Luftwaffe and, translated into English, means the German Airsports Club. It was the body that taught all flying-minded Germans and those who had flying training kept them in touch with modern aeronautical developments. This organization was subsequently disbanded and re-formed into the NSFK as Hitler and his Party machine took greater control over all forms of German life.

HISMA—This was the organization that Hitler put together to transport General Franco's troops from north Africa to Spain, subsequently becoming the transport command of the Condor Legion.

NSDAP—National Sozialistische Deutsche Arbeiter Partei—This party was formed in 1919 and Hitler gravitated to it, becoming its Führer. It was to become the organ of power and control of Germany and was also known as the Nazi Party.

NSFK—National Sozialistische Fliege Korps-This organization was formed from the Deutsche Luftsport-Verband and was transformed into a politically regimented subsidiary unit of the NSDAP. It came into being on 7 April 1937. The organization was led by the general of aviators, Friedrich Christiansen. Membership was voluntary and exclusive. Members in the organization could belong to no other party organization, that is to say the SS, SA or NSKK.

ODR—Ordegemeinschaft der Ritterkreuztrager—Old comrades association of the Knights Cross of the Iron Cross. This organization is not easily comparable to anything in either Great Britain or the United States of America, in the fact that it is nearly akin, in many accepted senses, to that which is found in British Free Masonry. That is to say, it is not a dead organization as it accepts into its body erudite collectors and researchers and looks after the widows of those former winners, organizing their welfare as well as those of current living members. It also helps in research. It is headed by a president, who at the present time is the able personage of Generalmajor, a. D. Horst Niemack. I was accorded the honour of being made an official sammler—in English an accredited collector/researcher—affiliated to the ODR in 1982, an honour which I hold very highly.

OKL—Oberkommando der Luftwaffe—The High Command of the German Air Force. This was the equivalent to the OKH and was responsible for the conduct of military operations of the Luftwaffe.

OKM—Oberkommando der Kriegsmarine—The High Command of the German Navy. This was also the equivalent to the OKH and was responsible for the conduct of military operations of the Navy.

OKH—Oberkommando des Heeres —The Army High Command. The successor to the Imperial and then the

Reichswehr General Staff. After 1941 the OKH was primarily responsible for the conduct of military operations on the eastern front.

OKW—Oberkommando der Wehrmacht— Armed Forces High Command. Created by Adolf Hitler in 1938 as a counterbalance to the old line, predominantly Prussian staff officers of OKH, the OKW included representatives of the Navy and the Luftwaffe and was responsible for military operations in the west, in north Africa, and throughout the Mediterranean region. General, later Feldmarschall, Wilhelm Keitel was OKW Chief-of-Staff from 1938–1945.

SS—Schutzstaffel—Guard detachments. Originally one of the several Nazi para-military organizations, after 1934 Heinrich Himmler's SS 'state within a state' became the principal instrument of political repression and systematic terror in the Third Reich.

Waffen-SS—The armed SS—These were the Party's élite front line combat troops and were devised by Himmler, aided by Gotlob Berger, and were completely separate from the men of the regular Army. Originally their ranks were only open to Germans of proven Aryan descent, but as the war deteriorated, divisions were raised from all over occupied Europe, to include France, the Low Countries, Norway, Denmark and the Baltic countries and even a small contingent from Great Britain.

Conclusion

At the beginning of this book I posed the question, 'what is available?' and replied 'everything — and in its respective cloth form. However, the problem is 'where?!' This difficulty confronted me when I began collecting and, as I have already indicated, learning the ropes can be an expensive and painful business. I have thus added in conclusion the names of some dealers whom I have found to be particularly helpful and who give a money-back guarantee that all they sell is genuine. I must stress that this recommendation is based upon my own personal experience and is totally unsolicited by any of the people listed below. Their willingness to share their knowledge with collectors who deal with them is most gratifying.

If any would-be collector has difficulty in getting started, either on a theme as I have suggested, or from 'cold', please feel that you can contact me for advice. Again quoting my own words, 'make as much contact with other collectors and take every opportunity to interchange information and look at rare and interesting pieces', for handling an original piece speaks a thousand words.

United Kingdom

Colin Brown,
18 Longcroft Park,
Beverley,
N. Humberside

Adrian Forman,
13 Shepherd Market,
London W1

Forman of Piccadilly Ltd,
92 Piccadilly,
London W1

M&T Militaria,
The Bank,
Bank Lane,
Victoria Road,
Carlisle, CA1 2UA

The Old Brigade,
10A Harborough Road,
Kingsthorpe,
Northampton

Spink & Son,
5, 6 & 7 King Street,
St James,
London, SW1Y 6QF

United States of America

The Cracked Pot,
PO Box 114,
Buffalo,
NY 14211

Germany

Peter Groch,
Geruinusstrasse 16,
D-1000 Berlin 12

For repairs to the metal structure or enamel of medals, the most expert person in the field I have encountered, and whom I have no hesitation in recommending whole-heartedly, is:

Keith Thompson,
52 Drybread Road,
Whittlesey,
Nr Peterborough,
Cambs.

Indexes

Index of personalities

The list of personalities in this section is to be used as an index and method of cross reference for further research, thus the important medals, awards, Party and SS numbers that the recipient was awarded or received, and which are referred to in the text, have been highlighted beside the page number by the addition of the reference number. That reference number enables you to pick out from the medal index the date of introduction of that medal and its full title and grade. The date next to the recipient's entry should fulfil most enquiries as to the date when a person received a particular award. Further information will be most welcome to increase the statistical background of this section. Where a medal has not been discussed in the book, its reference number has been included, wherever possible, plus the symbol * to indicate that it has not been referred to in this work but will be covered in a future volume of the series. This will make reference to the medals in those volumes easier and hopefully allow more autobiographical information to be included without duplication. The nationality, when not German, of the personality has also been indicated as has his fate, which has been abreviated by the use of the table below. Numbers in *italics* are page numbers.

EA   = Executed by the Allies
KIA = Killed in action
D   = Died of natural causes
S   = Suicide
A   = Accidental death
ER   = Executed by the Reich
*   = Medals covered in a future volume.

Alpers, Friedrich, SS-Obergruppenführer, *frontispiece*. 25 March 1901–3 September 1944. KIA. Staat Secretariat to the Reich Forestmeister. General Forestmeister and General Jägermeister. C-in-C Stadtwach und Landwach. Staff Reichführer-SS. MdL Brunswick. Party No 132812; SS No 6427; Iron Cross — Second Class (D.013); Iron Cross — First Class (D.016); 14 October 1942 Knights Cross (D.018); 20 April 1942 German Cross in Gold (D.025); Observers Bade (L.007); Reconnaissance Operational Flying Clasp — Silver Class (L.043); Golden Party Badge (Honour Award) (P.008)*; 6 November 1936 SA Brunswick 1931 Rally Badge — First Pattern (P.040)*; German Horsemans Badge — Gold (E.003)*; SS Honour Ring; SS Honour Sword; Göring Presentation Hunting Association Dagger.

Antonescue, Ion, Marshal (Romanian), *98, 197.* 2 Febuary 1882 — 1 June 1946.EA. Combined Pilots and Observers Badge in Gold with Diamonds (L.004); Crimean Shield — Gold Class (AS.005); Meritorious Order of the German Eagle Grand Cross in Gold 1939 (SI.043)*.

Von Arent, Benno, SS-Oberführer, *100, 110* 19 June 1898 — . Party Number 1105236; SS Number 36320; Iron Cross — Second Class 1939 Bar — First Type (D.0014); War Merit Cross—Second Class—Bronze without Swords (D.035).

Assmann, Heinz, Kapitän zur See, *40.* Wound Badge '20 July 1944' — Black Class — First Type (D.004).

Bach-Zelewski, Eric von Dem, SS-Obergruppenführer, *105, 179.* 1 March 1899-. Party Number 489101; SS Number 9831; Knights Cross (D.018); German Cross in Gold (D.025); Iron Cross — First Class 1939 Bar (D.017); War merit Cross—First Class—Silver with Swords (D.040); Golden Party Badge (P.010)*.

Balbo, Italo, Air Marshal (Italian), *197.* 5 June 1896 — 38 June 1940.KIA. Combined Pilots and Observers Badge in Gold with Diamonds (L.004).

Balck, Herman, General der Panzertruppe, *63.* 7 December 1893 — . 3 June 1940 Knights Cross (D.018); 20 December 1942 Oak Leaves (D.019); 4 March 1943 Oak Leaves & Swords (D.020); 31 August 1944 Oak Leaves, Swords & Diamonds (D.021).

Balthasar, Wilhelm, Oberleutnant, *26.* 2 February 1914-4 July 1941. KIA. 14 June 1940 Knights Cross (D.018); 3 July 1941 Oak Leaves (D.019); June 1939 Spanish Cross in Gold with Diamonds (S.006).

Baumbach, Werner, Hauptmann, *197.* 27 December 1916-20 October 1953.A. 8 May 1940 Knights Cross (D.018); 14 July 1941 Oak Leaves (D.019); 16 August 1942 Oak Leaves & Swords (D.020); August 1940 Combined Pilots and Observers Badge in Gold with Diamonds (L.004).

Baur, *197* Combined Pilots and Observers Badge in Gold with Diamonds (L.004).

Becker, Hellmuth, SS-Brigadeführer und Generalmajor der Waffen-SS, *89.* 12 August 1902 - . Party Number 1592593; SS Number 113174; Knights Cross (D.018); Oak Leaves (D.019).

Von Below, Nicolaus, Oberst, *40,197.* Combined Pilots and Observers Badge in Gold with Diamonds (L.004); Wound Badge '20 July 1944'—Black Class — First Type (D.004).

Berger (Civilian), *40.* 20 July 1944. KIA Wound Badge '20 July 1944'—Gold Class — First Type (D.006).

Berger, Gottlob, SS-Obergruppenführer, *156, 157.* 16 July 1896 - . Party Number 426875; SS Number 275991; War Merit Cross—Knights Cross—Silver with Swords (D.041); German Cross in Silver (D.030); Iron Cross—First Class 1939 Bar (D.017);

War Merit Cross—First Class—Silver with Swords (D.040).

Bertram, Otto, Oberleutnant, *26.* 30 April 1916 - . June 1939 Spanish Cross in Gold with Diamonds (S.0067; 28 October 1940 Knights Cross (D.018).

Beuche, Friedrich, *30.* KIA Spain 1936-1939. Cross of Honour for the Relatives of the Dead in Spain (S.008).

Von Blomberg, Werner, Feldmarschal, *197.* 2 September 1870-14 March 1946. D. Combined Pilots and Observers Badge in Gold with Diamonds (L.004).

Boche, Unteroffizier, *31.* Tank Badge of the Condor Legion — First Type (S.009); June 1939 Spanish Cross with Swords — Silver (S.002).

Bodden, Wilhelm, *26, 30.* KIA Spain 1936 - 1939. 6 June 1939 Spanish Cross in Gold with Diamonds (S.006); Cross of Honour for the Relatives of the Dead in Spain (S.008).

Boehme, General, *108.*

Bodenschatz, Karl, General der Flieger, *40, 197.* 11 December 1890 - . Combined Pilots and Observers Badge in Gold with Diamonds (L.004); Wound Badge '20 July 1944'—Gold Class — First type (D.006); 11 December 1940 Golden Party Badge (P.008)*.

Borgman, G., Oberleutnant, *40.* Wound Badge '20 July 1944'—Silver Class — First Type (D.005).

Bonisch, Ulrich, *30.* KIA Spain 1936-1939. Cross of Honour for the Relatives of the Dead in Spain (S.008).

Bonte, Commodore, *126.*

Brandi, Albrecht, Fregattenkapitän, *63, 122.* 20 June 1914-6 January 1966. D. 21 June 1943 Knights Cross (D.018); 11 April 1943 Oak Leaves (D.019); 9 May 1944 Oak Leaves & Swords (D.020); 24 November 1944 Oak Leaves, Swords & Diamonds (D.021); U-boat War Badge with Diamonds (N.004).

Brant, Heinz, Oberst, *40, 41.* 20 July 1944 KIA. Wound Badge '20 July 1944'—Gold Class — First Type (D.006).

Von Brauchitsch, Bernd, Oberst, *197.* Combined Pilots and Observers Badge in Gold with Diamonds (L.004).

Von Brauchitsch, Walter, Generaloberst, *31, 58, 90, 161, 163, 168.* 4 October 1881–18 October 1948. D. 27 October 1939 Knights Cross (D.018); 15/16 March 1939 Golden Party Badge (P.012)*.

Graf Brockdorff-Ahlefeldt, Walter, General der Infanterie, *100.* 13 July 1887–9 May 1943. D. 15 July 1941 Knights Cross (D.018); 27 June 1942 Oak Leaves (D.019).

Buchs, *41.* Wound Badge '20 July 1944'— Black Class — First Type (D.004).

Buhle, Walter, General der Infanterie, *40.* Wound Badge '20 July 1944'—Gold Class — First Type (D.006).

Von Bulow, Otto, Korvettenkapitän, *122.* 16 Octover 1911 - . 20 October 1942 Knights Cross (D.018); 26 April 1943 Oak Leaves (D.019); U-boat War Badge with Diamonds (N.004).

Bleichrodt, Heinrich, Korvettenkapitän, *122.* 21 October 1909 - . 24 October 1940 Knights Cross (D.018); 23 September 1942 Oak Leaves (D.019); U-boat War Badge with Diamonds (N.004).

Canaris, Wilhelm, Admiral, *154.* 1 January 1887–9 April 1945. ER.

Chapman, Eddy. (triple spy) (British), *48.* Iron Cross — Second Class (D.013).

Christiansen, Friedrich, Generalmajor Luftwaffe and Korpsführer der NSFK, *197.* 12 December 1879 - . Autumn 1940 Combined Pilots and Observers Badge in Gold with Diamonds (L.004); 11 December 1917 Pour le Mérite*.

Christiansen, George, Korvettenkapitän, *133.* 21 October 1914 - . 8 May 1941 Knights Cross (D.018); 13 November 1943 Oak Leaves (D.019); E-boat War Badge with Diamonds (N.015).

Cooper, Thomas Hellor, Sergeant (British), *39.* 29 August 1919 - . Wound Badge 1939 — Black Class (D.001).

Degrelle, Leon, SS-Sturmbannführer (Belgian), *55.* 15 June 1906 - . 2 March 1942 Iron Cross — Second Class (D.013); 18 May 1942 Iron Cross — First Class (D.016); 20 February 1944 Knights Cross (D.018); 27 August 1944 Oak Leaves (D.019); 30 August 1942

Infantry Assault Badge — Silver Class (A.002).

Deriesch, Willi, *30.* KIA Spain 1936–1939. Cross of Honour for the Relatives of the Dead in Spain (S.008).

Dietrich, Joseph, SS-Oberstgruppenführer und Generaloberst der Waffen-SS, *62, 88, 89, 197.* 28 May 1892–21 April 1966. D. Party Number 89015; SS Number 1177; Iron Cross — First Class 1939 Bar (D.017); 4 July 1940 Knights Cross (D.018); 31 December 1941 Oak Leaves (D.019); 16 March 1943 Oak Leaves & Swords (D.020); 6 August 1944 Oak Leaves, Swords & Diamonds (D.021); 1943 Combined Pilots and Observers Badge in Gold with Diamonds (L.004); Blood Order — First Pattern No 10 (P.020)*; Golden Party Badge — Type C (P.003)*; Iron Cross Second Class WW1*; Iron Cross First Class WW1*; Cross of Honour 1914 — 1918 for Combatants (V.013)*; First World War Commemorative Tank Battle Badge (V.017)*.

Dirlewanger, Dr Oskar, Oberführer der SS, *105.* 26 September 1895 - . Party Number 1098716; SS Number 357267; Knights Cross (D.018); Iron Cross — First Class 1939 Bar (D.017).

Dönitz, Karl, Grandadmiral, *83, 116, 118, 121, 123, 124, 125, 133, 146, 197.* 16 September 1891–24 December 1980. D. 21 April 1940 Knights Cross (D.018); 6 April 1943 Oak Leaves (D.019); U-boat War Badge with Diamonds for Dönitz (N.003); 1943 combined Pilots and Observers Badge in Gold with Diamonds (L.004); German Order (P.024)*; U-boat War Badge WW1 (V.018) 1 February 1918–23 May 1945*.

Eberhard, Kraft, Oberleutnant, *26.* June 1939 Spanish Cross in Gold with Diamonds (S.006).

Echart, Albert, *30.* KIA Spain 1936–1939. Cross of Honour for the Relatives of the Dead in Spain (S.008).

Eicke, Theodore, SS-Obergruppenführer und General der Waffen-SS, *156, 157.* 17 Octover 1892–26 February 1943. KIA. Party Number 114901; SS Number 2921; 26 December 1941 Knights Cross (D.018); 20 April 1942 oak Leaves (D.019).

Eigener, Ernst, 109, 110.

Emmermann, Carl, Korvettenkapitän, *123.* 6 March 1915 - . 27 November 1942 Knights Cross (D.018); 4 July 1943 Oak Leaves (D.019); U-boat War Badge with Diamonds (N.004).

Endrass, Engelbert, Kapitänleutnant, *123.* 2 March 1911-21 December 1941. KIA. 5 September 1940 Knights Cross (D.018); 10 July 1941 Oak Leaves (D.019); U-boat War Badge with Diamonds (N.004).

Ensseln, Wilhelm, Oberleutnant, *26.* June 1939 Spanish Cross in Gold with Diamonds (S.006).

Euler, August, *185.* 1 February 1910 Pilots Badge WW1 (27 January 1913-31 January 1921)*.

Fegelein, Herman, SS-Gruppenführer, *40.* 30 October 1906-29 April 1945. ER. Party Number 1200158; SS Number 66680; Iron Cross Second Class (D.013); Iron Cross First Class (D.016); 2 March 1942 Knights Cross (D.018); 22 December 1942 Oak Leaves (D.019); 30 July 1944 Oak Leaves & Swords (D.020); Wound Badge 1939 — Black Class (D.001); Wound Badge 1939 — Silver Class (D.002); Wound Badge '20 July 1944' — Silver Class — First Type (D.005); German Cross in Gold (D.025); War Merit Cross — Second Class — Bronze with Swords (D.039); German Horsemans Badge — Gold (E.003)*.

Fehihaber, Paul, Leutnant, *26.* June 1939 Spanish Cross in Gold with Diamonds (S.006).

Fehrenberg, Marinebaurat, *106.*

Feldt, Klaus, Korvettenkapitän, *133.* 14 April 1912 - . 25 April 1941 Knights Cross (D.018); 1 January 1944 Oak Leaves (D.019); E-boat War Badge with Diamonds (N.015).

Fischer, Werner, *30.* KIA Spain 1939. Cross of Honour for the Relatives of the Dead in Spain (S.008).

Fraff, *197.* Combined Pilots and Observers Badge in Gold with Diamonds (L.004).

Franco, Francisco Bahamonde, General (Spanish), *21, 22, 197.* 1892-1975. D. Combined Pilots and Observers Badge in Gold with Diamonds (L.004); Meritorious Order of the German Eagle Grand Cross in Gold 1939 (SI.043)*.

Frisius, Frederich, Konteradmiral, *112, 113.*

Frhr von Fritsch, Werner, Generaloberst, *160.* 4 August 1880-22 September 1939. KIA.

Von Gablens, *197.* Combined Pilots and Observers Badge in Gold with Diamonds (L.004).

Galland, Adolf, Generalleutnant, *21, 26, 62, 197.* 19 March 1912 - . 15 September 1939 Iron Cross — Second Class (D.013); 20 May 1940 Iron Cross - First Class (D.016); 1 August 1940 Knights Cross (D.018); 25 September 1940 Oak Leaves (D.019); 21 June 1941 Oak Leaves & Swords (D.020); 28 January 1942 Oak Leaves, Swords & Diamonds (D.021); 7 June 1939 Spanish Cross in Gold with Diamonds (S.006); 20 August 1940 Combined Pilots and Observers Badge in Gold with Diamonds (L.004); 7 June 1939 Medalla de La Campana*; 7 June 1939 Medalla Militar*.

Gille, Herbert Otto, SS-Obergruppenführer und General der Waffen-SS, *62.* 8 March 1897-27 December 1966. D. Party Number 537337; SS Number 39854; 8 October 1942 Knights Cross (D.018); 1 November 1943 Oak Leaves (D.019); 20 February 1944 Oak Leaves & Swords (D.020); 19 April 1944 Oak Leaves, Swords & Diamonds (D.021);

Goebbels, Dr Josef, Reich Propaganda Minister and Gauleiter for Berlin, *38, 52, 157.* 28 October 1897-1 May 1945. S.

Golob, Gordon, Major, *62, 197.* 16 June 1912 - . 18 September 1941 Knights Cross (D.018); 26 October 1941 Oak Leaves (D.019); 23 June 1942 Oak leaves & Swords (D.020); 30 August 1942 Oak Leaves, Swords & Diamonds (D.021); Combined Pilots and Observers Badge in Gold with Diamonds (L.004).

Göring, Hermann, Reichsmarschall, *17, 18, 22, 63, 69, 79, 84, 116, 123, 187, 191, 194, 197, 208, 213, 216, 224, 225.* 12 January 1893-15 October 1946. S. Iron Cross — First Class 1939 Bar (D.017); Knights Cross (D.018); 19 July 1940 Grand Cross of the Iron Cross (D.024); Combined Pilots and Observers Badge in Gold with Diamonds (L.004); Blood Order — First Type (P.020)*; Danzig Cross First Class*; Olympic Games Decoration — First Class (CD.001)*; Decoration of the Red Cross — First Class 1934 (RC.003)*; Decoration of the Red Cross — Grand Cross Special Grade 1934 (RC.005)*; German Academy for Aeronautical Research Chain of Office (SI.018)*; 2 June 1918 Pour Le Merite*; Iron Cross Second ClassWW1 *; Iron Cross First Class WW1*; Royal Prussian House of Hohenzollern Knight's Cross with Swords*; Karl Friedrich of Baden Military Service Cross Knight's Cross*; Knight's Cross of the Zahringer Lion with Oak Leaves & Swords*; Pilots Badge (27 January 1913–31 January 1921)*; Observers Badge (227 January 1914–31 January 1921)*; Wound Badge WW1*; Ernestine House Order*.

Graft, Hermann, Oberst, *62*. 24 October 1912 - . 24 January 1942 Knights Cross (D.018); 17 May 1942 Oak Leaves (D.019); 19 May 1942 Oak Leaves & Swords (D.020); 16 September 1942 Oak Leaves, Swords & Diamonds (D.021).

Graf, Werner, Sanitäts Unteroffizer, *31*. 10 May 1940 Tank Badge of the Condor Legion — First Type (S.009).

Ritter von Greim, Robert, Generalfeldmarschall, Luftwaffe, *187, 197*. 22 June 1892–24 May 1945. S. 24 June 1940 Knights Cross (D.018); 2 April 1943 Oak Leaves (D.019); 28 August 1944 Oak Leaves & Swords (D.020); 17 April 1945 Combined Pilots and Observers Badge in Gold with Diamonds (L.004); 8 October 1918 Pour Le Mérite*.

Guggenberger, Friedrich, Kapitänleutnant, *123*. 6 March 1915 - . 10 December 1941 Knights Cross (D.018); 8 January 1943 Oak Leaves (D.019); U-boat War Badge with Diamonds (N.004).

Gunsche, Otto, SS-Hauptsturmführer, *40*. Wound Badge '20 July 1944'—Black Class — First Type (D.004).

Gysae, Robert, Korvettenkapitän, *123*. 4 January 1911 - . 31 December 1941 Knights Cross (D.018); 31 May 1943 Oak Leaves (D.019); U-boat War Badge with Diamonds (N.004).

Hagan, *41* Wound Badge '20 July 1944'— Black Class — First Type (D.004).

Hardegen, Reinhard, Korvettenkapitän, *123*. 18 March 1913 - . 23 January 1942 Knights Cross (D.018); 23 April 1942 Oak Leaves (D.019); U-baoat War Badge with Diamonds (N.004).

Harder, Harro, Hauptmann, *26*. June 1939 Spanish Cross in Gold with Diamonds (S.006).

Harlinghausen, Martin, Major, *26, 197*. 17 January 1902 - . 4 May 1940 Knights Cross (D.018); 30 January 1941 Oak Leaves (D.019); December 1940 Combined Pilots and Observers Badge in Gold with Diamonds (L.004); June 1939 Spanish Cross in Gold with Diamonds (S.006).

Harrer, Obersturmführer, *157*.

Hartmann, Eric, Major, *62, 197*. 19 April 1922 - . 29 October 1943 Knights Cross (D.018); 2 March 1944 Oak Leaves (D.019); 4 July 1944 Oak Leaves & Swords (D.020); 25 August 1944 Oak Leaves, Swords & Diamonds (D.021); August 1944 Combined Pilots and Observers Badge in Gold with Diamonds (L.004).

Hartmann, Werner, Kapitän zur See, *123*. Knights Cross (D.018); Oak Leaves (D.019); U-boat War Badge with Diamonds (N.004).

Henke, Werner, Korvettenkapitän *123*. 13 May 1908 - . 17 December 1942 Knights Cross (D.018); 4 July 1943 Oak Leaves (D.019); U-boat War Badge with Diamonds (N.004).

Henneke, Admiral, *106*.

Henrici, Oskar, Leutnant, *26*. Spanish Cross in Gold with Diamonds (S.006).

Heusinger, Adolf, Generalleutnant, *40*. 1897 - . Wound Badge '20 July 1944'—Silver Class — First Type (D.005).

Hewell, Walter, (civilian) Honorary SS.Brigadeführer, *41*. 25 March 1904–2 May 1945. KIA Party Number 3280789; SS Number 283985; Wound Badge '20 July 1944'—Black Class — First Type (D.004); Blood Order — First Pattern No 90 (P.020)*; Stosstruppe Adolf Hitler.

Hierl, Konstantine, Reichsaarbeitsführer, *81*. 1875 - . War Merit Cross — First Class — Silver with Swords (D.040); 24 February 1945 German Order with Oak Leaves and Swords (P.024)*.

Himmler, Heinrich, Reichsführer–SS u Chef der Deutschen Polizei, *116, 155, 156, 157, 158, 179, 197*. 7 October 1900–23 May 1945. S.

Party Number 14303; SS Number 168; July 1942 Combined Pilots and Observers Badge in Gold with Diamonds (L.004); Blood Order — First Pattern No 3 (P.020)*; Golden Party Badge (P.001)*; SS Long Service Cross Twelve Years Service (LS.008)*; NSDAP Long Service Medal — Fifteen Years (P.030)*. NSDAP Long Service Medal — Ten Years (P.029)*; Commemorative Medal of 13 March 1938 — Second Type — Silver (OC.002)*; Commemorative Medal of 1 October 1938 (OC.004)*; Prague Castle Bar (OC.005)*; Commemorative Medal for the Return of the Memel Region — Bronze (OC.006)*; German Defence Medal (CD.027)*.

Hitler, Adolf, Führer, *10, 17, 18, 19, 21, 22, 24, 25, 30, 35, 38, 40, 41, 43, 47, 51, 55, 56, 58, 63, 75, 76, 77, 79, 81, 82, 84, 89, 93, 94, 109, 110, 112, 114, 115, 116, 118, 124, 133, 143, 153, 154, 155, 158, 172, 179, 186, 187.* 20 April 1889-30 April 1945. S. Party No 1; Golden Party Badge No 1 (P.001)*; Blood order — First Pattern No 0 (P.020)*; Iron Cross — Second Class WW1*; Iron Cross — First Class. WW1*; Wound Badge — First World War — Black Class (V.019)*.

Hoepner, Erich, General, *156.* 14 September 1882-8 August 1944. ER.

Horthy, Miklos, Admiral (Hungarian), *197.* 18 June 1868-9 February 1957. D. Combined Pilots and Observers Badge in Gold with Diamonds (L.004); Meritorious Order of the German Eagle Grand Cross in Gold 1939 (SI.043)*.

Graf Hoyos, Max, Oberleutnant, *26.* June 1939 Spanish Cross in Gold with Diamonds (S.006).

Hube, Hans, Generaloberst, *62.* 29 October 1890-21 April 1944. A. 1 August 1941 Knights Cross (D.018); 16 January 1942 Oak Leaves (D.019); 21 December 1942 Oak Leaves & Swords (D.020); 20 April 1944 Oak Leaves, Swords & Diamonds (D.021).

Jeschonnek, Hans, Generaloberst, *197.* 9 April 1899-18 August 1943. S. Combined Pilots and observers Badge in Gold with Diamonds (L.004).

Jodl, Alfred, Generaloberst, *40, 154.* 10 May 1890-16 October 1946. EA. Wound Badge

'20 July 1944'—Black Class — First Type (D.004).

Von John, Oberleutnant, *41.* Wound Badge '20 July 1944'—Black Class — First Type (D.004).

Joyce, William (Lord Haw Haw. and Wilhelm Froehlich) (broadcaster) (British), *41.* 1906 - 1946. EA. War Merit Cross—Second Class—Bronze without Swords (D.035); War Merit Cross—First Class—Silver without Swords (D.036).

Kaminski, Bronislav, Brigadeführer der SS (Russian), *105.* September 1944. ER.

Kammhuber, Josef, Generalmajor, *197.* 19 August 1896- . Combined Pilots and Observers Badge in Gold with Diamonds (L.004); 9 July 1941 Knights Cross (D.018).

Kastner, *197.* Combined Pilots and Observers Badge in Gold with Diamonds (L.004).

Keitel, Wilhelm, Generalfeldmarschall, *40, 154.* 22 September 1882-16 October 1946. EA. Knights Cross (D018); Iron Cross — Second Class 1939 Bar (D.014); Iron Cross — First Class 1939 Bar (D.017); Wound Badge '20 July 1944'—Black Class — First Type (D.004).

Keller Alfred, Generaloberst, *197.* 19 September 1882-11 February 1974. D. 24 June 1940 Knights Cross (D.018); Combined Pilots and Observers Badge in Gold with Diamonds (L.004); 4 December 1917 Pour Le Mérite*.

Kemnade, Friedrich, Korvettenkapitän, *133.* 12 December 1911 - . 23 July 1942 Knights Cross (D.018); 23 May 1943 Oak Leaves (D.019); E-boat War Badge with Diamonds (N.015).

Kern, Erich, *157.*

Von Kessel, Hans Detlef, Oberleutnant, *26.* June 1939 Spanish Cross in Gold with Diamonds (S.006).

Kesselring, Albert, Generalfeldmarschall, *62, 197.* 20 November 1885-15 July 1960. D. 30 September 1939 Knights Cross (D.018); 25 February 1942 Oak Leaves (D.019); 18 July 1942 Oak Leaves & Swords (D.020); 19 July 1944 Oak Leaves, Swords & Diamonds (D.021); Combined Pilots and Observers

Badge in Gold with Diamonds (L.004).

Von Kleist, Ewald, Generalfeldmarschall, *100.* 8 August 1881–October 1954. D. 15 May 1940 Knights Cross (D.018); 17 February 1942 Oak Leaves (D.019); 30 March 1944 Oak Leaves & Swords (D.020).

Klug, Bernd, Korvettenkapitän, *133.* 12 December 1914 - . 12 March 1941 Knights Cross (D.018); 1 January 1944 Oak Leaves (D.019); E-boat War Badge with Diamonds (N.015).

Korten, Gunter, General der Flieger, *40, 41, 197.* 22 July 1944. KIA. 1940 Combined Pilots and Observers Badge in Gold with Diamonds (L.004); Wound Badge '20 July 1944'—Gold Class — First Type (D.006).

Krancke, Admiral, *112.*

Kraus, Ernst, SS-Unterscharführer, *85.*

Kretschmer, Otto, Fregattenkapitän, *122.* 1 May 1912 - . 4 August 1940 Knights Cross (D.018); 4 November 1940 Oak Leaves (D.019); 26 December 1941 Oak Leaves & Swords (D.020); U-boat War Badge with Diamonds (N.004).

Kreutz, Karl, SS-Standartenführer, *89.* 20 September 1909 - . Party number 656236; SS Number 50559; Knights Cross (D.018).

Kruder, Ernst-Felix, Kapitän zur See, *135.* 6 December 1897-8 May 1941. KIA. 22 December 1940 Knights Cross (D.018); 15 November 1941 Oak leaves (D.019); Auxiliary Cruisers War badge with Diamonds (N.018).

Kuhbandner, Eric, SS-Obersturmführer, *179, 180.* 21 October 1921 - . SS Number 421069 (V) Infantry Assault Badge - Bronze Class (A.003); October 1941 Wound Badge 1939 — Black Class (D.001); Iron Cross — Second Class (D.013); 17 March 1944 Iron Cross — First Class (D.016); 15 February 1945 Anti-Partisan War Badge — Gold Class (A.031); Golden Hitler Youth Honour Badge (P. 065)*.

Kumm, Otto, SS-Brigadeführer und Generalmajor der Waffen-SS, *89.* 1 October 1909 - . Party Number 421230; SS Number 18727; 16 February 1942 Knights Cross (D.018); 6 April 1943 Oak Leaves (D.019); 17 March 1945 Oak Leaves & Swords (D.020).

Lang, Hans Günther Kapitänleutnant, *123.* Knights Cross (D.018); 1943 Oak Leaves (D.019); U-boat War Badge with Diamonds (N.004).

Lassen, Georg, Korvettenkapitän, *123.* 12 May 1915 - . 10 August 1942 Knights Cross (D.018); 7 March 1943 1943 Oak Leaves (D.019); U-boat War Badge with Diamonds (N.004).

Lehman-Wilenbrock, Heinrich, Fregattenkapitän, *123.* 11 December 1911 - . 26 February 1941 Knights Cross (D.018); 31 December 1941 1943 Oak Leaves (D.019).

Lent, Helmut, Oberleutnant, *62, 197.* 13 June 1918-5 October 1944. A. 21 September 1939 iron Cross — second class (D.013); 11 May 1940 Iron Cross — First Class (D.016); 30 January 1941 Narvik Shield — Silver (AS.001); 30 August 1941 Knights Cross (D.018); 6 June 1942 Oak Leaves (D.019); 2 August 1943 Oak Leaves & Swords (D.020); 31 July 1944 Oak Leaves, Swords & Diamonds (D.021); Combined Pilots and Observers Badge in Gold with Diamonds (L.004). Four Year Long Service Medal (LS.001)*; Commemorative Medal 1 October 1938 (OC.004)*; Prague Castle Bar (OC.005)*.

Leroy, Jacques, SS-Untersturmführer, *55, 56.* 10 October 1925 - . 20 April 1945 Knights Cross (D.018).

Liebe, Heinrich, Fregattenkapitän, *123.* 29 January 1908 - . 14 August 1940 Knights Cross (D.018); 10 June 1941 1943 Oak Leaves (D.019); U-boat War Badge with Diamonds (N.004).

Loerzer, Bruno, Generaloberst, *197.* 22 January 1891 - . Knights Cross (D.018); Iron Cross — Second Class 1939 Bar — First Type (D.014); Combined Pilots and Observers Badge in Gold with Diamonds (L.004); 12 February 1918 Pour Le Mérite*.

Lohr, Alexander, Generaloberst (Austrian), *197.* 20 May 1885-27 February 1946.EA. Knights Cross (D.018); Oak Leaves (D.019); Combined Pilots and Observers Badge in Gold with Diamonds (L.004); Kreta Commemorative Cuff Title (C.001).

Luth, Wolfgang, Kapitän zur See, *62, 122, 124.* 15 October 1913-14 May 1945. A. 24

October 1940 Knights Cross (D.018); 13 November 1942 Oak Leaves (D.019); 15 April 1943 Oak Leaves & Swords (D.020); 9 August 1943 Oak Leaves, Swords & Diamonds (D.021); U-boat war Badge with Diamonds (N.004); Spanish Cross without Swords — Silver (S.005).

Lutzow, Gunther, Hauptmann, *21, 26.* 4 September 1912-24 April 1945. KIA. 18 September 1940 Knights Cross (D.018): 20 July 1941 Oak leaves (D.019); 11 October 1941 Oak Leaves & Swords (D.020); Spanish Cross in Gold with Diamonds (S.006).

Mahlmann, Albert, Obergefreiter, *211.* 19 December 1944 Close Combat Clasp – Bronze Class (L.021).

von Mannerheim, Carl Gustav Emil Barron, Marshal (Finnish), *197.* 4 June 1867-27 January 1951.D. Knights Cross (D.018); 1942 Combined Pilots and Observers Badge in Gold with Diamonds (L.004); Meritorious Order of the German Eagle Grand Cross in Gold 1939 (SI.043)*.

von Manstein, Erich, Feldmarschall, *98* 24 November 1887-10 June 1973. D. 19 July 1940 Knights Cross (D.018); 14 March 1943 oak Leaves (D.019); 30 March 1944 Oak Leaves & Swords (D.020); Crimean Shield — Gold Class (AS.005).

von Manteuffel, Hasso Eccard, General der Panzertruppe, *63.* 14 January 1897-24 September 1978. D. 27 November 1941 Knights Cross (D.018); 1943 Oak Leaves (D.019); 22 February 1944 Oak Leaves & Swords (D.020); 18 February 1945 Oak Leaves, Swords & Diamonds (D.021).

Marseilles, Hans Joachim, Hauptmann, *62,197.* 13 December 1919-30 September 1942. KIA. 22 February 1942 Knights Cross (D.018); 6 June 1942 Oak leaves (D.019); 18 June 1942 Oak Leaves & Swords (D.020); 2 September 1942 Oak Leaves, Swords & Diamonds (D.021); Combined Pilots and Observers Badge in Gold with Diamonds (L.004).

Mauss, Dr Karl, Generalleutnant, *63.* 17 May 1898-9 February 1959. D. 26 February 1941 Knights Cross (D.018); 24 November 1943 1943 Oak Leaves (D.019); 23 October 1944 Oak Leaves & Swords (D.020); 15 April 1945 Oak Leaves, Swords & Diamonds (D.021).

Mehnert, Karl, Oberleutnant, *26.* June 1939 Spanish Cross in Gold with Diamonds (S.006).

Frhr von Mirbach, Kapitänleutnant, *132.* Knights Cross (D.018); Oak Leaves (D.019); E-boat War Badge with Diamonds (N.015).

Merten, Karl Friedrich, Kapitän Zur See, *123.* 15 August 1905 - . 13 June 1942 Knights Cross (D.018); 16 November 1942 1943 Oak leaves (D.019); U-boat War Badge with Diamonds (N.004); June 1939 Spanish Cross without Swords — Silver (S.005).

Milch, Erhard, Feldmarschall, Luftwaffe, *197.* 30 March 1892-25 January 1972. D. Knights Cross (D.018); 11 November 1935 Combined Pilots and Observers Badge in Gold with Diamonds (L.004).

Model, Walter, Generalfeldmarschall, *63.* 24 January 1891-21 April 1945. S. 9 July 1941 Knights Cross (D.018); 17 February 1942 Oak Leaves (D.019); 2 April 1943 Oak Leaves & Swords (D.020); 17 August 1944 Oak Leaves, Swords & Diamonds (D.021).

Mohr, Johann, Korvettenkapitän, *123.* 12 June 1916-3 April 1943. KIA. 27 March 1942 Knights Cross (D.018); 13 January 1943 Oak Leaves (D.019); U-boat War Badge with Diamonds (N.004).

Mölders, Werner, Oberst, *21, 26, 62, 197, 216.* 18 March 1913-22 November 1941. D. 29 May 1940 Knights Cross (D.018); 21 September 1940 Oak Leaves (D.019); 22 June 1941 Oak Leaves & Swords (D.020); 16 July Oak Leaves, Swords & Diamonds (D.021); Day Fighter Operational Flying Clasp — Diamond Class (L.038); Spanish Cross in Gold with Diamonds (S.006); August 1940 Combined Pilots and Observers Badge in Gold with Diamonds (L.004).

Frhr von Moreau, Rudolf, Hauptmann, *26.* June 1939 Spanish Cross in Gold with Diamonds (S.006).

Müller, Georg, Leutnant, *39, 47, 51, 85.* 30 January 1905 - . D. Party Number 46581; SS Number 4700; 9 July Iron Cross — Second Class (D.013); 13 June 1942 Iron Cross — First Class (D.016); 10 December 1941 Infantry Assault Badge — Silver Class (A.002); 15 February 1942 Wound Badge 1939 — Black Class (D.001); 23 November 1942 Wound

Badge 1939 — Silver Class (D.002); 5 September 1942 Medal for the Winter Campaign in Russia — 1941-1942 (D.046); 20 April 1945 War Merit Cross — Second Class — Bronze with Swords (D.039); 12 December 1933 Golden Party Badge (P.001)*; 1 August 1935 Gau Essen — Gold (P.048)*; SA Brunswick 1931 Rally Badge — First Pattern (P.040)*; Nurnberg Party Day Badge of 1929 (P.036)*; SA Sports Badge — First Type in Bronze (SP.020)*.

Mussolini, Benito (I Duce) (Italian), *18, 197.* 29 July 1883 - 28 April 1945. EA. April 1937 Combined Pilots and Observers Badge (L.003); Combined Pilots and Observers Badge in Gold with Diamonds (L.004); Meritorious Order of the German Eagle Grand Cross in Gold 1939 (SI.043)*; Decoration of the Red Cross — Grand Cross Special Grade 1934 (RC.005)*.

Mutzelburg, Rolf, Kapitänleutnant, *123.* 23 June 1913 - 11 September 1942. KIA. 17 November 1941 Knights Cross (D.018); 15 July 1942 1943 Oak Leaves (D.019); U-boat War Badge with Diamonds (N.004).

Naurasil, Freidrich, (Croatian), *197.* Combined Pilots and Observers Badge in Gold with Diamonds (L.004).

Neudorfter, Wolfgang, Hauptmann, *26.* June 1939 Spanish Cross in Gold with Diamonds (S.006).

Nowotny, Walter, Major, *62, 197.* 7 December 1920–8 November 1944. KIA. 4 September 1942 Knights Cross (D.018); 4 September 1943 Oak Leaves (D.019); 22 September 1943 Oak Leaves & Swords (D.020); 19 October 1943 Oak leaves, Swords & Diamonds (D.021); Combined Pilots and Observers Badge in Gold with Diamonds (L.004).

Nubeker, Otfried (badge designer), *150.*

Oesau, Walter, Oberleutanant, *26, 34.* 28 June 1913 - 11 May 1944. KIA. 20 August 1940 Knights Cross (D.018); 6 February 1941 Oak Leaves (D.019); 15 July 1941 Oak Leaves & Swords (D.020); Spanish Cross in Gold with Diamonds (S.006); Spanish Wound Badge — Bronze Class (S.014).

Olendorff, Hugo, *143.* 1 July 1941 Blockade Runners Badge (N.022).

Olesh, Fredrich, SS-Oberscharführer (Romanian), *110.* Wound Badge 1939 — Black Class (D.001); Iron Cross — Second Class (D.013); Balkan Shield (AS.014).

Parani (Italian), *197.* Combined Pilots and Observers Badge in Gold with Diamonds (L.004).

Von Paulus, Friedrich, Feldmarschall, *110.* 23 September 1890 - 1 February 1957. D. 26 August 1942 Knights Cross (D.018); 15 January 1943 Oak Leaves (D.019).

Peltz, Friedrich, Oberst, *197.* Combined Pilots and Observers Badge in Gold with Diamonds (L.004).

Peterson, Rudolf, Korvettenkapitän, *130, 132.* Knights Cross (D.018); Oak Leaves (D.019); E-boat War Badge with Diamonds (N.015).

Pflugbeil, *197.* Combined Pilots and Observers Badge in Gold with Diamonds (L.004).

Phleps, Arthur, SS-Gruppenführer und Generalleutnant der Waffen-SS (Romanian), *110.* 1890 - . 4 July 1943 Knights Cross (D.018); 24 November 1944 Oak Leaves (D.019).

Possl, Walter, Hauptmann (Austrian), *71, 165.* 16 September 1909–25 September 1944. KIA. 14 August 1939 Iron Cross Second Class (D.013); 13 July 1941 Iron Cross First Class (D.016); 20 April 1943 Knights Cross (D.018); 16 October 1941 Silver Tank Battle Badge (A.004); 27 March 1944 Silver Tank Battle Badge 25 Class (A.005); (15 September 1942 Entered on the Roll of Honour); Roll of Honour Clasp — Army (D.043); 18 October 1942 German Cross in Gold (D.025); Austrian Silver Service Cross*.

Prien, Gunther, Korvettenkapitän, *123.* 16 January 1908 - 7 March 1941. KIA. 18 October 1939 Knights Cross (D.018); 20 October 1940 Oak Leaves (D.019); U-boat War Badge with Diamonds (N.004).

Von Puttkamer, Jeskoi, Konteradmiral, *40.* Wound Badge '20 July 1944' — Black Class — First Type (D.004).

Raeder, Erich, Grandadmiral, *115, 116, 121, 125, 128, 133, 135, 136, 144.* 24 April 1876 - 6 November 1960. D. Iron Cross — First Class

1939 Bar (D.017); Knights Cross (D.018); Golden Party Badge (Honour Award) (P.008)*.

Ramcke, Bernard Herman, General der Fall-schirmtruppe, *63, 197.* 24 January 1889-4 July 1968. D. 21 August 1941 Knights Cross (D.018); 13 November 1942 Oak Leaves (D.019); 19 September 1944 Oak Leaves & Swords (D.020); 20 September 1944 Oak Leaves, Swords & Diamonds (D. 021); Combined Pilots and Observers Badge in Gold with Diamonds (L.004).

von Reichenau, Walther, Generalfeldmar-schall, *58.* 8 October 1884-17 October 1942. D. Knights Cross (D.018).

Reitsch, Hanna, Flugkapitän, *197, 198.* 5 September 1979. D. 28 March 1941 Iron Cross — Second Class (D.013); 5 November 1942 Iron Cross — First Class (D.016); March 1941 Combined Pilots and Observers Badge in Gold with Diamonds — Female Class (L.006).

Ribbentrop, Joachim, Foreign Minister, Honorary SS-General, *18.* Party Number 1·199927; SS Number 63083; 30 April 1893-16 October 11946. EA. Golden Party Badge (P.010)*.

von Richthofen, Wolfram, Generalmajor, *21, 26, 197.* 10 October 1895-12 July 1945. D. 17 May 1940 Knights Cross (D.018); 17 July 1941 Oak Leaves (D.019); Combined Pilots and Observers Badge in with Diamonds (L.004); Spanish Cross in Gold with Diamonds (S.006).

Rogge, Bernard, Vize–Admiral, *116, 135, 136.* 4 November 1899-28 June 1982. D. 7 December 1940 Knights Cross (D.018); 31 December 1941 Oak Leaves (D.019); January 1942 Auxiliary Cruisers War Badge with Diamonds (N.018).

Rohm, Ernst, Kapitän, *155.* 1887-6 July 1934. ER.

Rommel, Erwin, Generalfeldmarschall, *62, 197.* 15 November 1891-14 October 1944. S (ER). 26 May 1940 Knights Cross (D.018); 20 March 1941 Oak Leaves (D.019); 20 January 1942 Oak Leaves & Swords (D.020); 11 March 1943 Oak Leaves, Swords & Diamonds (D.021); Iron Cross — First Class 1939 Bar (D.017); Silver Tank Battle Badge

(A.004); Combined Pilots and Observers Badge in Gold with Diamonds (L.004); 7 January 1918 Pour Le Mérite*.

Ruckeschell, Hellmuth, Kapitän zur See, *136.* 23 March 1890-24 September 1948. D. 31 October 1940 Knights Cross (D.018); 22 December 1942 Oak Leaves (D.019); Auxiliary Cruisers War Badge with Diamonds (?) (N.018).

Rudel, Hans Ulrich, Oberst, *10, 62, 63, 197, 216, 224, 225.* 2 July 1916-18 December 1982. D. 6 January 1942 Knights Cross (D.018); 14 April 1943 Oak Leaves (D.019), 25 November 1943 Oak Leaves & Swords (D.020); 29 March 1944 Oak Leaves, Swords & Diamonds (D.021); 1 January 1945 Golden Oak leaves, Swords & Diamonds (D.022); November 1939 Iron Cross — Second Class (D.013); July 1941 Iron Cross — First Class (D.016); July 1941 Bomber Operational Flying Clasp — Bronze Class (L.039); September 1941 Honour Goblet*; December 1941 German Cross in Gold (D.025); March 1944 Combined Pilots and Observers Badge in Gold with Diamonds (L.004); April 1944 Air-to-Ground Support Operational Flying Clasp — Diamond Class (L.060); 15 January 1945 Hungarrian Golden Medal for Bravery*.

von Rundstedt, Gerd, Generalfedlmarschal, *58.* 12 December 1875 — 24 February 1953. D. 30 September 1939 Knights Cross (D.018); 1 July 1944 Oak Leaves (D.019); 18 February 1945 Oak Leaves & Swords (D.020).

Runze, Heinz, Leutnant, *26.* June 1939 Spanish Cross in Gold with Diamonds (S.006).

von Saucken, Dietrich, General der Panzer-truppe, *63.* 16 May 1892 - . 6 January 1942 Knights Cross (D.018); 22 August 1943 Oak Leaves (D.019); 20 February 1944 Oak Leaves & Swords (D.020); 9 May 1945 Oak Leaves, Swords & Diamonds (D.021).

Schellmann, Wolfgang, Hauptmann, *26.* June 1939 Spanish Cross in Gold with Diamonds (S.006).

Scherer, Theodore, Generalmajor, *97.* 1888 - . 22 February 1942 Knights Cross (D.018); 5 May 1942 Oak Leaves (D.019).

Schepke, Joachim, Kapitänleutnant, *123.* 8 March 1912-17 March 1941. KIA 24 September 1940 Knights Cross (D.018); 1

December 1940 Oak Leaves (D.019); U-boat War Badge with Diamonds (N.004).

Scherff, Walter, Generalmajor, *40, 41.* Wound Badge '20 July 1944' — Gold Class — First Type (D.006).

von Schimanski, Hauptmann, *41.* Sound Badge '20 July 1944' — Black Class — First Type (D.004).

Schlichting, Joachim, Hauptmann, *26.* June 1939 Spanish Cross in Gold with Diamonds (S.006).

Schmuckle, Willi, Leutnant, *93.* 24 October 1921 - . March 1945 Knights Cross (D.018).

Schmundt, Rudolf, Generalleutnant, *40, 41.* 22 July 1944. KIA. Wound Badge '20 July 1944' — Gold Class — First Type (D.006); 7 October 1944 German Order Posthumous (P.023)*.

Schnaufer, Heinz Wolfgang, Major *63.* 16 February 1922–15 July 1950. D. 31 December 1943 Knights Cross (D.018); 24 June 1944 Oak Leaves (D.019); 30 July 1944 Oak Leoaves & Swords (D.020); 16 October 1944 Oak Leaves, Swords & Diamonds (D.021).

Schnee, Adalbert, Korvettenkapitän, *123, 124,* U-boat War Badge with Diamonds (N.004).

Schneider Kostalski, Ferdinand, Oberstleutnant (Austrian), *55, 56.* 20 July 1908–1 September 1944. KIA. 25 September 1939 Iron Cross Second Class (D.013); 3 June 1940 Iron Cross First Class (D.016); 9 July 1941 Knights Cross (D.018); 20 May 1940 Silver Tank Battle Badge (A.004); 5 October 1942 Crimea Shield (AS.004); Wound Badge 1939 — Black Class (D.001).

Scholtz, Klaus, Kapitän zur See, *123.* 22 March 1908 - . 26 December 1941 Knights Cross (D.018); 10 September 1942 Oak Leaves (D.019); U-boat War Badge with Diamonds (N.004).

Schorner, Ferdinand, Generalfeldmarschall, *63, 94.* 12 May 1892 - 2 July 1973. D. 20 April 1941 Knights Cross (D.018); 17 February 1944 Oak Leaves (D.019); 28 August 1944 Oak Leaves & Swords (D.020); 1 January 1945 Oak Leaves, Swords & Diamonds (D.021).

Schrynen, Remy, SS-Unterscharführer (ABelgian) *35.* 24 December 1921 - . Iron Cross — Second Class (D.013); Iron Cross — First Class (D.016); 21 September 1944 Knights Cross (D.018); Infantry Assault Badge — Silver Class (A.002); Wound Badge 1939 — Gold Class (D.003); Tollenaere Commemorative Badge (BF.003)*; VNV Golden Party Badge, Five Years Service — Bronze (BF.005)*.

Schulz, Adalbert, Generalmajor, *62.* 20 December 1903–28 January 1944. KIA. 29 September 1940 Knights Cross (D.018); 31 December 1941 Oak Leaves (D.019); 6 August 1943 Oak Leaves & Swords (D.020); 14 December 1943 Oak leaves, Swords & Diamonds (D.021).

Schutze, Herbert, Korvettenkapitän, *123.* 24 July 1909 - . 1 March 1940 Knights Cross (D.018); 12 June 1941 Oak Leaves (D.019); U-boat War Badge with Diamonds (N.004).

Schutze, Victor, Kapitän zur See, *123.* 16 February 1906–23 September 1950. D. 11 December 1940 Knights Cross (D.018); 14 July 1941 Knight Cross (D.018); U-boat War Badge with Diamonds (N.004).

Seiler, Reinhard, Oberleutnant, *26.* 30 August 1909 - . 20 December 1941 Knights Cross (D.018); 2 March 1944 Oak Leaves (D.019); June 1939 Spanish Cross in Gold with Diamonds (S.006).

Simon, Max, SS-Gruppenführer, *71.* 6 January 1899–1 February 1961. D. Party number 1359576; SS Number 83086; Knights Cross (D.018); Oak Leaves (D.019); Iron Cross — First Class (D.016); Iron Cross — Second Class 1939 Bar — First Type (D.014); 9 October 1944 German Cross in Gold (D.025); Wound Badge 1939 — Black Class (D.001); 13 July 1942 Medal for the Winter Campaign in Russia (D.046); 31 December 1943 Demjansk Shield (AS.006); 24 October 1939 Danzig Cross — First Class (CD.001)*;19 December 1941 Italian Order of the Crown Officers Cross*.

Skorzeny, Otto, SS-Sturmbannführer, *197.* 12 June 1908–8 July 1975. D. Party Number 1083671; SS Number 295979; Knights Cross (D.018); Oak Leaves (D.019); Combined Pilots and Observers Badge in Gold with Diamonds (L.004).

Sperrle, Hugo, General der Flieger *21, 26, 197.* 7 February 1885-2 April 1953. D. Knights Cross (D.018); June 1939 Spanish Cross in Gold with Diamonds (S.006); 19 November 1937 Combined Pilots and Observers Badge in Gold with Diamonds (L.004).

Starcke, Bernhard, Oberleutnant, *26.* June 1939 Spanish Cross in Gold with Diamonds (S.006).

von Stauffenberg, Graf Claus Schenk, Oberst, *40.* 15 November 1907–20 July 1944. ER.

Von Stauffenberg, Grafin (Frau), *197, 198.* Combined Pilots and Observers Badge in Gold with Diamonds (L.004).

Graf Strachwitz, Hyazinth, Generalleutnant, *62.* 30 July 1893 – . 25 August 1941 Knights Cross (D.018); 13 November 1942 Oak Leaves (D.019); 28 March 1943 Oak Leaves & Swords (D.020); 15 April 1944 Oak Leaves, Swords & Diamonds (D.021).

Stopf, General, *78.* Knights Cross (D.018); War Merit Cross — Knights Cross — Silver with Swords (D.041).

Stadler, Sylvester, SS-Brigadeführer und Generalmajor der Waffen-SS, *89.* 30 December 1910 – . SS Number 139495; 6 April 1943 Knights Cross (D.018); 16 September 1943 Oak Leaves (D.019); 6 May 1945 Oak Leaves & Swords (D.020).

Student, Kurt, Generaloberst der Luftwaffe, *197.* 12 May 1890 – 1 July 1978. D. 12 May 1940 Knights Cross (D.018); 27 September 1943 Oak Leaves (D.019); 2 September 1940 Combined Pilots and Observers Badge in Gold with Diamonds (L.004); Wound Badge 1939 - Silver Class (D.002); Iron Cross — First Class 1939 Bar (D.017); Kreta Commemorative Cuff Title (C.001).

Stumpff, Hans-Jurgen, Generaloberst, *197.* 15 June 1889–9 March 1968. D. Combined Pilots and Observers Badge in Gold with Diamonds (L.004).

Suhren, Reinhard, Fregattenkapitän, *122.* 16 April 1916 - . 3 November 1940 Knights Cross (D.018); 31 December 1941 Oak Leaves (D.019); 1 September 1942 Oak Leaves & Swords (D.020); U-boat War Badge with Diamonds (N.004).

Teuteberg, Otto, SS-Schutze, *157.* 5 June 1945. EA.

von Thoma, Wilhelm, Oberst, *22, 30, 31, 32.* 31 December 1941 Knights Cross (D.018); Tank Badge of the Condor Legion — Gold Type (S.010).

Thomsen Rolf, Kapitänleutnant, *123.* Knights Cross (D.018); Oak leaves (D.019); U-boat War Badge with Diamonds (N.004).

Tolsdorf, Theodor, Generalmajor, *63.* 3 November 1909–1979. D. 4 December 1941 Knights Cross Knights Cross (D.018); 15 September 1943 Oak Leaves (D.018); 18 July 1944 Oak Leaves & Swords (D.020); 18 March 1945 Oak Leaves, Swords & Diamonds (D.021).

Toniges, Werner, Kapitänleutnant, *132.* 7 January 1910 – . 25 February 1941 Knights Cross (D.018); 13 November 1942 Oak Leaves (D.019); E-boat War Badge with Diamonds (N.015).

Topp, Eroic, Fregattenkapitän, *122.* 2 July 1914 - . 20 June 1941 Knights Cross (D.018); 11 April 1942 Oak Leaves (D.019); 17 August 1942 Oak Leaves & Swords (D.020); U-boat War Badge with Diamonds (N.004).

Trettner, *197.* Combined Pilots and Observers Badge in Gold with Diamonds (L.004).

Udet, Ernst, Generaloberst, *197.* 26 April 1896–17 November 1941. S. Knights Cross (D.018); Combined Pilots and Observers Badge in Gold with Diamonds (L.004); 9 April 1918 Pour le Mérite*.

Valle, General (Italian), *197.* Combined Pilots and Observers Badge in Gold with Diamonds (L.004); The Golden Badge of The Academy for Aeronautical Research Large (SI.019)*; Meritorious Order of The German Eagle Grand Cross 1939 (SI.047)*; Meritorious Order of The German Eagle Grand Cross 1939 with Swords (SI.049)*.

Verling, Erik, *171.* General Assault Badge — Bronze Class (A.021).

Volkmann, Helmut, General der Flieger, *21, 26.* June 1939 Spanish Cross in Gold with Diamonds (S.006).

Voss, Hans Erich, Konteradmiral, *40.* Wound Badge '20 July 1944' — Black Class — First

Type (D.004); Wound Badge '20 July 1944' – Silver Class — First Type (D.005) (subsequent wound).

Vogt, Rudolf, Oberfeldwebel, *31.* Tank Badge of the Condor Legion — First Type (S.009); Spanish Cross with Swords — Silver (S.002); Silver Tank Battle Badge (A.004); Iron Cross — Second Class (D.013).

Warlimont, Walter, General Der Artillerie, *40.* Wound Badge '20 July 1944' — Black Class — First Type (D.004).

Wastian, Roger, SS-Hauptsturmführer, *55.* 30 October 1921 – .

Von Weech, Professor, *215.*

Weizenegger, Oberleutnant, *41.* Wound

Badge '20 July 1944' — Black Class — First Type (D.004).

Wever, General den Luftwaffe, *196, 197.* 3 June 1936. A. 11 November 1935 Combined Pilots and Observers Badge in Gold with Diamonds (L.004).

Von Witzleben, Erwin, Feldmarschall, *153.* 4 December 1881 – 8 August 1944. ER.

Wolff, Karl Heinz, Major, *26.* June 1939 Spanish Cross in Gold with Diamonds (S.006).

Wuppermann, Siegried, Oberleutnant zur See, *133.* 15 December 1916 – . 3 August 1941 Knights Cross (D.018); 14 April 1943 Oak Leaves (D.019); E-boat War Badge with Diamonds (N.015).

Index of medals

In each entry the name of the award is given first, followed by its reference number in brackets, date of introduction where known, and page number(s) in *italics*.

'Afrika' Commemorative Cuff Title [C.002], 15.1.1943, *90*

Aircrew Badge [L.001], ?.2.1934, *190*

Air-to-Ground Support Operational Flying Clasp, — Bronze Class [L.057], 12.4.1944, *223.*

Air-to-Ground Support Operational Flying Clasp — Diamond Class [L.060], 29.4.1944, *224*

Air-to-Ground Support Operational Flying Clasp — Gold Class [L.059], 12.4.1944, *223*

Air-to-Ground Support Operational Flying Clasp — Silver Class [L.058], 12.4.1944, *223*

Air Gunners and Flight Engineers Badge [L.009], 22.6.1942, *202*

Anti-Aircraft War Badge [L.015], 10.1.1941, *207*

Anti-Partisan War Badge — Bronze Class — First Type [A.029], 30.1.1944, *179*

Anti-Partisan War Badge — Bronze Class — Second Type [A.032], 30.1.1944, *181*

Anti-Partisan War Badge in Gold with Diamonds [A.035], ?.?.?, *181*

Anti-Partisan War Badge — Gold Class — First Type [A.031], 30.1.1944, *179*

Anti-Partisan War Badge — Gold Class — Second Type [A.034], 30.1.1944, *181*

Anti-Partisan War Badge — Silver Class — First Type [A.030], 30.1.1944, *179*

Anti-Partisan War Badge — Silver Class — Second Type [A.033], 30.1.1944, *181*

Army Balloon Observers Badge — Bronze Class [A.026], 8.7.1944, *178*

Army Balloon Observers Badge — Gold Class [A.028], 8.7.1944, *178*

Army Balloon Observers Badge – Silver Class [A.027], 8.7.1944, *178*

Army Flak Badge [A.022], 18.7.1941, *171*

Army Parachutists Badge [A.001], 15.6.1937, *159*

Auxiliary Cruisers War Badge with Diamonds [N.018], ?.?.?, *135*

Auxiliary Cruisers War Badge — First Type [N.016], 24.4.1941, *133*

Auxiliary Cruisers War Badge – Second Type [N.017], 24.4.1941, *134*

Badge for Shooting Down Low Flying Aircraft, — Gold Class [A.039], 12.2.1945, *182*

Badge for Shooting Down Low Flying Aircraft, — Silver Class [A.038], 12.1.1945, *182*

Balkan Shield [AS.014], 7.3.1945, *110*

Black Tank Battle Badge [L.029], 3.11.1944, *212*

Black Tank Battle Badge — 25 Class [L.030], 10.11.1944, *213*

Black Tank Battle Badge — 50 Class [L.031], 10.11.1944, *213*

Black Tank Battle Badge — 75 Class [L.032], 10.11.1944, *213*

Blank Tank Battle Badge — 100 Class [L.033], 10.11.1944, *213*

Blockade Runners Badge [N.022], 1.4.1941, *143*

Blockade Runners Badge — Civilian Wear [N.023], 1.4.1941, *143*

Bomber Operational Flying Clasp — Bronze Class [L.039], 30.1.1941, *216*

Bomber Operational Flying Clasp — Gold Class [L.041], 30.1.1941, *216*

Bomber Operational Flying Clasp — Silver Class [L.040], 30.1.1941, *216*

Bronze Tank Battle Badge [A.010], 20.12.1939, *167*

Bronze Tank Battle Badge — 25 Class [A.011], 22.6.1943, *167*

Bronze Tank Battle Badge — 50 Class [A.012], 22.6.1943, *167*

Bronze Tank Battle Badge — 75 Class [A.013], 22.6.1943, *168*

Bronze Tank Battle Badge — 200 Class [A.015], ?.?.?, *168*

Cholm Shield [AS.003], 1.7.1942, *97*

Close Combat Bar — Bronze Class [A.023], 25.11.1942, *172*

Close Combat Bar — Gold Class [A.025], 25.11.1942, *172*

Close Combat Bar — Silver Class [A.024], 25.11.1942, *172*

Close Combat Clasp — Bronze Class [L.021], 3.11.1944, *210*

Close Combat Clasp — Gold Class [L.023], 3.11.1944, *210*

Close Combat Clasp — Silver Class [L.022], 3.11.1944, *210*

Coastal Artillery War Badge — First Type [N.024.6.1941, *144*

Coastal Artillery War Badge — Second Type [N.025], 24.6.1941, *145*

Combat Badge of the Small Battle Units — Bar, Bronze Class [N.031], 13.11.1944, *150*

Combat Badge of the Small Battle Units — Bar, Gold Class [N.033], 13.11.1944, *150*

Combat Badge of the Small Battle Units — Bar, Silver Class [N.032], 13.11.1944, *150*

Combat Badge of the Small Battle Units — First Class [N.030], 13.11.1944, *149*

Combat Badge of the Small Battle Units — Fourth Class [N.027], 13.11.1944, *149*

Combat Badge of the Small Battle Units —

Fourth Class [N.027], 13.11.1944, *149*

Combat Badge of the Small Battle Units — Second Class [N.029], 13.11.1944, *149*

Combat Badge of the Small Battle Units — Third Class [N.028], 13.11.1944, *149*

Combined Pilots and Observers Badge [L.003], 26.3.1936, *194*

Combined Pilots and Observers Badge in Gold with Diamonds [L.004], 11.11.1935, *194*

Combined Pilots and Observers Badge in Gold with Diamonds [Dress Copy] [L.005], 11.11.1935, *197*

Combined Pilots and Observers Badge, in Gold with Diamonds [Female Class] [L.006], 11.11.1935, *198*

Crimea Shield [AS.004], 25.7.1942, *98*

Crimea Shield — Gold Class [As.005], ?.?.?, *98*

Cross of Honour for the Relatives of the Dead in Spain [S.008], 14.4.1939, *29*

Cuff Title 'Spain 1936–1939' [S.012], ?.?.?, *32*

Cuff Title 'Spain 1936–1939' (Gothic Script) [S.013], ?.?.?, *33*

Day Fighter Operational Flying Clasp — Bronze Class [L.035], 30.1.1941, *214*

Day Fighter Operational Flying Clasp — Diamond Class [L.038], ?.?.?, *215*

Day Fighter Operational Flying Clasp — Gold Class [L.037], 30.1.1941, *214*

Day Fighter Operational Flying Clasp — Silver Class [L.036], 30.1.1941, *214*

Demjansk Shield [AS.006], 25.4.1943, *99*

Destroyers War Badge with Diamonds [N.009], ?.?.?, *127*

Destroyers War Badge — First Type [N.007], 4.6.1940, *125*

Destroyers War Badge — Second Type [N.008], 4.6.1940, *126*

Dunkirk Shield [AS.016], ?.?.?, *112*

E-Boat War Badge with Diamonds [N.015], ?.?.?, *132*

E-Boat War Badge with Diamonds — Variation [NV.015], ?.?.?, *133*

E-Boat War Badge — First Type [N.012], 30.5.1941, *130*

E-Boat War Badge — Second Type [N.013], 30.5.1941, *130*

E-Boat War Badge — Third Type [N.014], 30.5.1941, *131*

Flyers Commemorative Badge [L.013], 26.3.1936, *206*

Führer Commendation Certificate [D.047], ?.?.?, *86*

General Assault Badge [A.016], 1.6.1940, *168*

General Assault Badge — Variation [AV.016],

?.?.?, *168*

General Assault Badge — Bronze Class [A.021], ?.?.?, *171*

General Assault Badge — 25 Class [A.017], 22.6.1943, *169*

General Assault Badge — 50 Class [A.018], 22.6.1943, *169*

General Assault Badge — 75 Class [A.019], 22.6.1943, *170*

General Assault Badge — 100 Class [A.020], 22.6.1943, *170*

German Cross in Gold [D.025], 28.9.1941, *70*

German Cross in Gold — Cloth Version — Airforce Blue [D.027], 28.9.1941, *73*

German Cross in Gold — Cloth Version — Field Grey [D.029], 28.9.41, *73*

German Cross in Gold — Cloth Version — Navy Blue [D.028], 28.9.1941, *73*

German Cross in Gold with Diamonds [d.026], ?.?.?, *72*

German Cross in Silver [D.030], 28.9.1941, *73*

German Cross in Silver — Cloth Version — Airforce Blue [D.031], 28.9.1941, *74*

German Cross in Silver — Cloth Version — Field Grey [D.032], 28.9.41, *74*

German Cross in Silver — Cloth Version — Navy Blue [D.033], 28.9.1941, *74*

Glider Pilots Badge — First Type [L.011], 16.12.1940, *204*

Glider Pilots Badge — Second Type [L.012], 16.12.1940, *204*

Grand Cross of the Iron Cross [D.024], 1.9.1939, *69*

Ground Combat Badge [L.o16], 31.3.1942, *208*

Ground Combat Badge — 25 Class [L.017], 10.11.1944, *209*

Ground Combat Badge — 50 Class [L.018], 10.11.1944, *209*

Ground Combat Badge — 75 Class [L.019], 10.11.1944, *209*

Ground Combat Badge — 100 Class [L.020], 10.11.1944, *209*

High Seas Fleet War Badge with Diamonds [N.021], ?.?.?, *142*

High Seas Fleet War Badge — First Type [N.019], 30.4.1941, *136*

High Seas Fleet War Badge — Second Type [N.020], 30.4.1941, *141*

Infantry Assault Badge — Bronze Class [A.003], 20.12.1939, *160*

Infantry Assault Badge — Silver Class [A.002], 20.12.1939, *160*

Infantry Assault Badge — Silver Class —

Variation [AV.002], ?.?.?, *160*

Iron Cross — First Class [D.016], 1.9.1939, *60*

Iron Cross — First Class 1939 Bar [D.017], 1.9.39, *51*

Iron Cross — First Class 1939 Bar — Combination Variation [DV.017], 1.9.1939, *52*

Iron Cross — Second Class [D.013], 1.9.1939, *45*

Iron Cross — Second Class 1939 Bar — First Type [D.014], 1.9.1939, *48*

Iron Cross — Second Class 1939 Bar — Second Type [D.015], 1.9.1939, *49*

Knights Cross of the Iron Cross [D.018], 1.9.1939, *52*

Knights Cross of the Iron Cross with Golden Oak leaves, Swords and Diamonds [D.022], 29.12.1944, *63*

Knights Cross of the Iron Cross with Oak Leaves [D.019], 3.6.1940, *58*

Knights Cross of the Iron Cross with Oak Leaves and Swords [D.020], 28.9.1944, *69*

Knights Cross of the Iron Cross with Oak Leaves, Swords and Diamonds [D.021], 28.9.1941, *61*

'Kreta' Commemorative Cuff Title [C.001], 16.10.1942, *89*

Kuban Shield [AS.007], 20.9.1943, *100*

'Kurland' Commemorative Cuff Title [C.004], ?.?.1945, *94*

Lapland Shield [AS.011], ?.2.1945, *108*

Long Range Day Fighter Operational Flying Clasp, — Bronze Class [L.048], 13.5.1944, *220*

Long Range Day Fighter Operational Flying Clasp — Gold Class [L.050], 13.5.1942, *220*

Long Range Day Fighter Operational Flying Clasp — Silver Class [L.049], 13.5.1942, *220*

Long Range Night Fighter Operational Flying Clasp, — Bronze Class [L.051], 14.8.1942, *221*

Long Range Night Fighter Operational Flying Clasp — Gold Class [L.053], 14.8.1942, *221*

Long Range Night Fighter Operational Flying Clasp — Silver Class [L.052], 14.8.1942, *221*

Lorient Shield — First Type [AS.009], ?.12.1944, *106*

Lorient Shield — First Type — Variant [ASV.009], ?.12.1944, *107*

Lorient Shield — Second Type [AS.010], ?.12.1944, *107*

Medal for the Winter Campaign in Russia 1941–1942 [D.046], 26.5.1942, *84*

Memel Shield [AS.015], ?.?.?, *111*

'Metz 1944' Commemorative Cuff Title [C.003], 24.10.1944, *93*

Mine Sweepers, Sub Chasers and and Escort Vessels War Badge — First Type [N.010], 31.8.1940, *12*

Mine Sweepers, Sub Chasers and Escort Vessels War Badge — Second Type [N.011], 31.8.1940, *12*

Narvik Shield — Gold Class [AS.002], 19.8.1940, *96*

Narvik Shield — Silver Class [AS.001], 19.8.1940, *96*

Naval Combat Clasp [N.026], 19.11.1944, *146*

Observers Badge [L.007], 26.3.1936, *196*

Parachutists Badge [L.014], 5.11.1936, *206*

Pilots Badge [L.0002], 26.3.1936, *191*

Pilots Badge — Variation [LV.002], ?.?.?, *193*

Radio Operator and Air Gunners Badge [L.008], 26.3.1936, *201*

Reconnaissance Operational Flying Clasp — Bronze Class [L.042], 30.1.1941, *218*

Reconnaissance Operational Flying Clasp — Gold Class [L.044], 30.1.1941, *218*

Reconnaissance Operational Flying Clasp — Silver Class [L.043], 30.1.1941, *218*

Roll of Honour Clasp — Army [D.043], 30.1.1944, *82*

Roll of Honour Clasp — Luftwaffe [D.045], 5.7.1944, *84*

Roll of Honour Clasp — Navy [D.044], 13.5.1944, *83*

Sea Battle Badge [L.034], 27.11.1944, *213*

Short Range Night Fighter Operational Flying Clasp, — Bronze Class [L.054], 14.8.1942, *222*

Short Range night Fighter Operational Flying Clasp — Gold Class [L.056], 14.8.1942, *222*

Short Range Night Fighter Operational Flying Clasp — Silver Class [L.055], 14.8.1942, *222*

Silver Tank Battle Badge — Army [A.004], 20.12.1939, *163*; Luftwaffe [L.024], 3.11.1944, *211*

Silver Tank Battle Badge — 25 Class — Army [A.005], 22.6.1943, *164*; Luftwaffe [L.025], 10.11.1944, *211*

Silver Tank Battle Badge — 50 Class — Army [A.006], 22.6.1943, *164*; Luftwaffe [l.026], 10.11.1944, *211*

Silver Tank Battle Badge — 75 Class — Army [A.007], 22.6.1943, *164*; Luftwaffe [L.027], 10.11.1944, *211*

Silver Tank Battle Badge — 100 Class — Army [A.008], 22.6.1943, *164*; Luftwaffe [L.028], 10.111.1944, *211*

Silver Tank Battle Badge — 200 Class [A.009], ?.?.?, *166*

Snipers Badge — First Class [A.040], 20.8.1944, *183*

Snipers Badge — Second Class [A.041], 20.8.1944, *183*

Snipers Badge — Third Class [A.042], 20.8.1944, *183*

Spanish Cross in Gold with Diamonds [S.006], 14.4.1939, *25*

Spanish Cross in Gold with Diamonds — Dress Copy [S.007], 14,4.1939, *28*

Spanish Cross with Swords — Bronze [S.001], 14.4.1939, *23*

Spanish Cross with Swords — Gold [S.003], 14.4.1939, *23*

Spanish Cross with Swords — Silver [S.002], 14.4.1939, *23*

Spanish Cross without Swords — Bronze [S.004], 14.4.1939, *24*

Spanish Cross without Swords — Silver [S.005], 14.4.1939, *24*

Spanish Wound Badge — Bronze Class [S.014], 22.5.1939, *34*

Spanish Wound Badge — Gold Class [S.016], 22.5.1939, *34*

Spanish Wound Badge — Silver Class [S.015], 22.5.1939, *34*

Special Badge for Singlehanded Destruction of a Tank — Gold Class [A.037], 18.12.1943, *181*

Special Badge for Singlehanded Destruction of a Tank — Silver Class [A.036], 9.3.1941, *181*

Stalingrad Shield — First Type [AS.012], ?.?.?, *109*

Stalingrad Shield — Second Type [AS.013], ?.?.?, *110*

Star of the Grand Cross [D.023], ?.?.?, *64*

Tank Badge of the Condor Legion — First Type [S.009], ?.?. 1936, *30*

Tank Badge of the Condor Legion — Gold Type [S.011], ?.4.1939, *32*

Tank Badge of the Condor Legion — Second Type [S.010], ?.?.1939, *31*

Transport and Glider Operational Flying Clasp; — Bronze Class [L.045], 19.11.1941, *220*

Transport and Glider Operational Flying

Clasp, — Gold Class [L.047], 19.11.1941, *220*

Transport and Glider Operational Flying Clasp, — Silver Class [L.046], 19.11.1941, *220*

U-boat Combat Clasp — Bronze Class [N.005], 15.5.1944, *124*

U-boat Combat Clasp — Silver Class [N.006], 24.11.1944, *124*

U-boat War Badge with Diamonds [N.004], ?.?.?., *122*

U-boat War Badge with Diamonds for Dönitz [N.003], ?.?.?, *120*

U-boat War Badge — First Type [N.001], 13.10.1939, *118*

U-boat War Badge — First Type — Variation [NV.001], 13.10.1939, *119*

U-boat War Badge — Second Type [N.002], 13.10.1939, *120*

Unqualified Air Gunners and Flight Engineers Badge [L.010], 25.4.1944, *203*

War merit Cross — First Class — Silver with Swords [D.040], 18.9.1939, *80*

War Merit Cross — First Class — Silver without Swords [D.036], 18.9.1939, *77*

War merit Cross — Knights Cross — Gold with Swords [D.042], 8.7.1944, *82*

War Merit Cross — Knights Cross — Gold with Swords [D.042], 8.7.1944, *82*

War Merit Cross — Knights Cross — Gold without Swordfs [D.038], 8.7.1944, *79*

War Merit Cross — Knights Cross — Silver with Swords [D.041], 19.8.1940, *81*

War Merit Cross — Knights Cross — Silver without Swords [D.037], 19.8.1940, *78*

War Merit Cross — Second Class — Bronze with Swords [D.039], 18.9.1939, *79*

War Merit Cross — Second Class — Bronze without Swords [D.035], 18.9.1939, *75*

War Merit Medal [D.034], 19.8.1940, *74*

Warsaw Shield [AS.008], 10.12.1940, *105*

Wound Badge 1939 — Black Class [D.001], 1.9.1939, *38*

Wound Badge 1939 — Gold Class [D.003], 1.9.1939, *38*

Wound Badge 1939 — Silver Class [D.002], 1.9.1939, *38*

Wound Badge '20 July 1944' — Black Class — First Type [D.004], 20.8.1944, *40*

Wound Badge '20 July 1944' — Gold Class — First Type [D.006], 20.8.1944, *40*

Wound Badge '20 July 1944' — Silver Class — First Type [D.005], 20.8.1944, *40*

Wound Badge '20 July 1944' — Black Class — Second Type [D.007], 20.8.1944, *43*

Wound Badge '20 July 1944' — Gold Class — Second Type [D.009], 20.8.1944, *43*

Wound Badge '20 July 1944' — Silver Class — Second Type [D.008], 20.8.1944, *43*

Wound Badge '20 July 1944' — Black Class — Third Type [D.010], 20.8.1944, *45*

Wound Badge '20 July 1944' — Gold Class — Third Type [D.021], 20.8.1944, *45*

Wound Badge '20 July 1944' — Silver Class — Third Type [D.011], 20.8.1944, *45*

Index to subsidiary medals

Afrika Cuff Title, *91*

Afrika Korps Cuff Title, *90*

Anhanger, *215*

Ascertainment, *55*

Austrian — Type P, *71, 72, 74*

Blood Order, *18*

Breast Star of the Eagle Order, *64*

Coberg Badge, *12*

Eagle Order Medal—Bronze, *75*

Eagle Order Medal—Silver, *75*

Engineers Assault Badge, *168*

Gau Berlin—Gold, *12*

Gau Berlin—Silver, *12*

German Order — Order of the Dead, *14*

German Red Cross Cross of Merit 1937-1939, *24*

German Red Cross Frauenkreuz 1937-1939, *24*

Gibraltar Cuff Title, *87*

Goblet of Honour, *92*

Golden Flags, *76*

Golden Party Badge, *18*

Grand Cross of the Iron Cross, 1813, *69*

Grand Cross of the Iron Cross, 1870, *69*

Grand Cross of the Iron Cross, 1914, *69*

Headquarters Cuff Title, *88*

Iron Cross, First World War, *48, 49, 50, 75*

Military Pilots Badge, *185*

Order of the Dead — German Order, *14*

Order of the Red Eagle, *46*

Pour le Mérite, *12, 17, 46, 78*

Prinzen, *50*

Salver of Honour, *92*

Stosstruppe Adolf Hitler 1923 Cuff title, *87*

Wound Badge, First World War, *18*

Wristwatch (Presentation), *110*

Index of places

Afghanistan, *114*
Africa, *21, 90, 91, 115*
America, *69*
Atlantic, *116, 121*
Austria, *18, 36, 64, 87, 114, 115, 196*
Austro-Hungarian Empire, *21, 114*
Axis countries, *157*
Balkan region, *110, 114*
Baltic, *114*
Belgium, *153, 156*
Berlin, *31, 43, 45, 69*
Berlin's Lustgarten, *22*
Britain, *110, 114, 115, 156, 171*
British India, *114*
Braunschweig, *158*
Bucharest, *98*
Chanea, *90*
Cholm, *97*
Courland (Kurland), *94*
Crete, *98*
Czechoslovakia, *18*
Demjansk, *99*
Denmark, *114, 157*
Dresden, *178*
Duisberg, *157*
Dunkirk, *112, 113*
East Africa, *115*
Finnish-Russian Border, *85*
Flossenburg Concentration Camp, *154*
Fort Gambelleta, *93*
France, *45, 87, 115, 120, 141, 145, 153, 156,*
    157, 187
German States, *114, 153*
Germany, *19, 22, 32, 35, 43, 93, 115, 116, 143,*
    154, 158, 182, 185
Gibraltar, *24, 87*
Greece, *114*
Hamburg, *22, 114*
Holland, *156*
Ibiza, *24*
Iraklion, *90*
Jutland, *115*
Kalinin, *97*
Kingdom of Hannover, *87*
Krymskaja, *100*
Kuldiga, *94*
La Rochelle, *112*
Lagunen, *100*

Landsberg prison, *155*
Latvia, *94*
Laurient, *112*
Lisbon, *31*
Lipezk Airfield, *186*
Low Countries, *69, 157, 187*
Lovat, River, *97*
Luneberg, *113, 157*
Malemes, *90*
Metz, *93*
Meuse, River, *156*
Mitau, *94*
Morkeberg, *147*
Moscow, *58, 114*
Munich, *18, 72, 74*
Narvik, *126*
Nieuport, *112*
North Sea, *116*
Norway, *96, 157*
Noword, *100*
Nurenberg, *154, 163*
Ostend, *112*
Ostland, *85*
Poland, *19, 153*
Prussia, *45, 46, 87, 114, 153*
Rastenburg, *40*
Retminnon, *90*
Rhineland, *187*
Romania, *98*
Russia, *18, 84, 97, 114, 115, 170, 178, 186, 210,*
    223
Scapa Flow, *115*
Schleissheim, *187*
Silesia, *153*
Spanish Morocco, *25, 29*
Spain, *18, 19, 21, 22, 25, 29, 87, 187*
Ssijsk, *100*
St Nazaire, *112*
Stalingrad, *109, 110*
Turkey, *114*
USA, *134*
Ukraine, *85*
Vienna, *89, 197*
Warsaw, *105*
Western Europe, *134*
Wolf's Lair — Hitler's Eastern Headquarters,
    40